Bible
Speaks
today

T0341749

the message of

WISDOM

Series editors:
Alec Motyer (OT)
John Stott (NT)
Derek Tidball (Bible Themes)

'This book is powerful, pastoral and trustworthy, and makes wisdom accessible to contemporary believers. Dan Estes explains the text in a clear and balanced way, and only introduces other scholarly views to clarify what the passage actually means. He has one foot firmly planted in the world of Old Testament wisdom, but the other one is just as firmly grounded in the contemporary world. He rightly sees that wisdom is not simply confined to a few books, but it flows into other parts of the Old Testament ("like a recurrent motif woven throughout a symphony"), and into the teaching of Jesus and the apostles. Estes teaches wisdom wisely, and this book will make you want to preach a series on wisdom.'
Lindsay Wilson, Senior Lecturer in Old Testament, Ridley College, Melbourne, Australia

the message of

WISDOM

Learning and living
the way of the Lord

Daniel J. Estes

INTER-VARSITY PRESS
36 Causton Street, London SW1P 4ST, England
Email: ivp@ivpbooks.com
Website: www.ivpbooks.com

First published 2020

British Library Cataloguing-in-Publication Data
A catalogue record for this book is available from the British Library.

ISBN: 978–1–78359–982–0
eBook ISBN: 978–1–78359–983–7

Set in 9.5/13pt Karmina
Typeset in Great Britain by CRB Associates, Potterhanworth, Lincolnshire

*Inter-Varsity Press publishes Christian books that are true to the Bible
and that communicate the gospel, develop discipleship and strengthen the church
for its mission in the world.*

*IVP originated within the Inter-Varsity Fellowship, now the Universities and Colleges
Christian Fellowship, a student movement connecting Christian Unions in universities
and colleges throughout Great Britain, and a member movement of the International
Fellowship of Evangelical Students. Website: www.uccf.org.uk. That historic association
is maintained, and all senior IVP staff and committee members subscribe
to the UCCF Basis of Faith.*

Dedicated to
Christiana Estes Trecker,
with my deep love

Contents

Part 4: The complexity of wisdom

Part 5: The culmination of wisdom

Bible Speaks today

GENERAL PREFACE

The Bible Speaks Today describes three series of expositions, based on the books of the Old and New Testaments, and on Bible themes that run through the whole of Scripture. Each series is characterized by a threefold ideal:

- to expound the biblical text with accuracy
- to relate it to contemporary life, and
- to be readable.

These books are, therefore, not 'commentaries', for the commentary seeks rather to elucidate the text than to apply it, and tends to be a work rather of reference than of literature. Nor, on the other hand, do they contain the kinds of 'sermons' that attempt to be contemporary and readable without taking Scripture seriously enough. The contributors to The Bible Speaks Today series are all united in their convictions that God still speaks through what he has spoken, and that nothing is more necessary for the life, health and growth of Christians than that they should hear what the Spirit is saying to them through his ancient – yet ever modern – Word.

ALEC MOTYER
JOHN STOTT
DEREK TIDBALL
Series editors

Author's preface

In over forty years of ministry in both church and university settings, I have often preached and taught from the wisdom texts of the Bible. The books of Proverbs, Job and Ecclesiastes, as well as many other passages of Scripture that contain similar themes, have instructed me in how to live a godly life, and they have provided wise guidance for my students as they seek to live for the Lord. It is a privilege now to be able to share the biblical message of wisdom with a wider audience in this volume in The Bible Speaks Today series.

I am grateful to Derek Tidball for inviting me to write this book and for serving as my editor, and to Philip Duce, who once again has been so helpful in guiding one of my books to publication. My adult Bible fellowship at Linworth Baptist Church and my students at Cedarville University have been very encouraging to me as they responded eagerly to earlier versions of these expositions. I am deeply thankful for my wife, Carol, for the blessing she has been as we have walked together for over forty-four years on the Lord's good path for us. Her love, grace and wisdom have truly given me joy on our journey.

I am pleased to dedicate this work to my daughter, Christiana, whose good heart, keen mind and generous spirit make her so special to all who know her, and especially to me.

DANIEL J. ESTES

Abbreviations

AB	Anchor Bible
ANE	Ancient Near East(ern)
AOTC	Apollos Old Testament Commentary
AYB	Anchor Yale Bible
BAG	W. Bauer (trans. and ed.), W. R. Arndt and F. W. Gingrich, *A Greek–English Lexicon of the New Testament and Other Early Christian Literature* (Chicago: University of Chicago Press, 1957).
BBC	J. H. Walton, V. H. Matthews and M. W. Chavalas (eds.), *The IVP Bible Background Commentary: Old Testament* (Downers Grove: IVP Academic, 2000).
BCOTWP	Baker Commentary on the Old Testament Wisdom and Psalms
BECNT	Baker Exegetical Commentary on the New Testament
BST	The Bible Speaks Today
DBI	L. Ryken, J. C. Wilhoit and T. Longman (eds.), *Dictionary of Biblical Imagery* (Downers Grove: IVP Academic, 1998).
DSB	Daily Study Bible
EBC	*Expositor's Bible Commentary*
GKC	E. Kautzsch (ed.), *Gesenius's Hebrew Grammar*, trans. A. E. Cowley (Oxford: Clarendon, 1910).
HS	*Hebrew Studies*
Int	*Interpretation*
IRT	Issues in Religion and Theology
IVPNTC	IVP New Testament Commentary
JESOT	*Journal for the Evangelical Study of the Old Testament*

JSNTSup	Journal for the Study of the New Testament Supplement Series
LXX	Septuagint
NAC	New American Commentary
NASB	New American Standard Bible
NCBC	New Century Bible Commentary
NDBT	T. D. Alexander, B. S. Rosner, D. A. Carson and G. Goldsworthy (eds.), *New Dictionary of Biblical Theology* (Downers Grove: InterVarsity Press, 2000).
NICNT	New International Commentary on the New Testament
NICOT	New International Commentary on the Old Testament
NIDOTTE	W. A. VanGemeren (ed.), *New International Dictionary of Old Testament Theology and Exegesis*, 5 vols. (Grand Rapids: Zondervan, 1997).
NIGTC	New International Greek Testament Commentary
NIV	New International Version, Anglicized
NIVAC	New International Version Application Commentary
NSBT	New Studies in Biblical Theology
NT	New Testament
OT	Old Testament
OTL	Old Testament Library
TDNTA	G. Bromiley (ed.), *Theological Dictionary of the New Testament, Abridged* (Grand Rapids: Eerdmans, 1985).
TDOT	G. J. Botterweck, H. Ringgren and H.-J. Fabry (eds.), *Theological Dictionary of the Old Testament*, 16 vols. (Grand Rapids: Eerdmans, 1974–2018).
THNTC	Two Horizons New Testament Commentary
TNTC	Tyndale New Testament Commentaries
TOTC	Tyndale Old Testament Commentaries
TWOT	R. L. Harris (ed.), *Theological Wordbook of the Old Testament*, 2 vols. (Chicago: Moody, 1980).
TynBul	*Tyndale Bulletin*
v(v).	verse(s)
WBC	Word Biblical Commentary
ZECNT	Zondervan Exegetical Commentary on the New Testament
ZTK	*Zeitschrift für Theologie und Kirche*

Select bibliography

Aitken, K. T., *Proverbs*, DSB (Philadelphia: Westminster, 1976).

Alden, R. L., *Proverbs* (Grand Rapids: Baker, 1983).

Allen, L. C., *Jeremiah: A Commentary*, OTL (Louisville: Westminster John Knox, 2008).

——, *Psalms 101 – 150*, WBC 21, rev. edn (Nashville: Thomas Nelson, 2002).

Alter, R., *The Book of Psalms* (New York: W. W. Norton, 2007).

Arnold, C. E., *Ephesians*, ZECNT 10 (Grand Rapids: Zondervan, 2010).

Bartholomew, C. G., and R. P. O'Dowd, *Old Testament Wisdom Literature: A Theological Introduction* (Downers Grove: IVP Academic, 2011).

Beal, L. M. Wray, *1 & 2 Kings*, AOTC 9 (Downers Grove: InterVarsity Press, 2014).

Bellah, R. N., *Habits of the Heart: Individualism and Commitment in American Life* (Berkeley: University of California Press, 2008).

Blocher, H., 'The Fear of the Lord as the "Principle" of Wisdom', *TynBul* 28 (1977), pp. 3–28.

Block, D. I., *Deuteronomy*, NIVAC (Grand Rapids: Zondervan, 2012).

Blomberg, C. L., *1 Corinthians*, NIVAC (Grand Rapids: Zondervan, 1994).

Blomberg, C. L., and M. J. Kamell, *James*, ZECNT (Grand Rapids: Zondervan, 2008).

Bollhagen, J., *Ecclesiastes*, Concordia (St. Louis: Concordia, 2011).

Boström, L., 'Retribution and Wisdom Literature', in D. G. Firth and L. Wilson (eds.), *Interpreting Old Testament Wisdom Literature* (Downers Grove: IVP Academic, 2017), pp. 134–154.

Brown, R., *The Message of Deuteronomy*, BST (Downers Grove: InterVarsity Press, 1993).

Brown, W. P., *Wisdom's Wonder: Character, Creation, and Crisis in the Biblical Wisdom Literature* (Grand Rapids: Eerdmans, 2014).

Brueggemann, W., *1 & 2 Kings* (Macon: Smyth & Helwys, 2000).

——, *A Commentary on Jeremiah: Exile and Homecoming* (Grand Rapids: Eerdmans, 1998).

Carson, D. A., 'Matthew', *EBC*, vol. 8, rev. edn (Grand Rapids: Zondervan, 2010), pp. 23–670.

Carson, D. A. (ed.), *NIV Biblical Theology Study Bible* (Grand Rapids: Zondervan, 2018).

——, *NIV Zondervan Study Bible* (Grand Rapids: Zondervan, 2015).

Clements, R. E., *Jeremiah*, Interpretation (Atlanta: John Knox, 1988).

Clifford, R. J., *Proverbs*, OTL (Louisville: Westminster John Knox, 1999).

Cox, D., *Proverbs with an Introduction to Sapiential Books*, Old Testament Message 17 (Wilmington: Michael Glazier, 1982).

Craigie, P. C., *Deuteronomy*, NICOT (Grand Rapids: Eerdmans, 1976).

Craigie, P. C., P. H. Kelley and J. F. Drinkard, *Jeremiah 1 – 25*, WBC 26 (Dallas: Word, 1991).

Day, P. L., *An Adversary in Heaven: śāṭān in the Hebrew Bible*, Harvard Semitic Monographs 43 (Atlanta: Scholars, 1988).

DeVries, S. J., *1 Kings*, WBC 12 (Nashville: Thomas Nelson, 2003).

Ebert, D. J., *Wisdom Christology: How Jesus Becomes God's Wisdom for Us*, Explorations in Biblical Theology (Phillipsburg: P&R, 2011).

Estes, D. J., *Handbook on the Wisdom Books and Psalms* (Grand Rapids: Baker Academic, 2005).

——, *Hear, My Son*, NSBT 4 (Downers Grove: InterVarsity Press, 1997).

——, *Job*, Teach the Text (Grand Rapids: Baker, 2013).

——, 'Job 28 in Its Literary Context', *JESOT* 2 (2013), pp. 151–164.

——, 'Proverbial Lessons: Leadership in the Proverbs', in B. K. Forrest and C. Roden (eds.), *Biblical Leadership: Theology for the Everyday Leader* (Grand Rapids: Kregel Academic, 2017), pp. 163–171.

——, *Psalms 73 – 150*, NAC 13 (Nashville: B&H, 2019).

Fee, G., *The First Epistle to the Corinthians*, NICNT, rev. edn (Grand Rapids: Eerdmans, 2014).

Fox, M. V., *Proverbs 1 – 9*, AYB 18A (New Haven: Yale University Press, 2000).

——, *Proverbs 10 – 31*, AYB 18B (New Haven: Yale University Press, 2009).

France, R. T., *The Gospel according to Matthew*, TNTC (Downers Grove: InterVarsity Press, 1988).

Fretheim, T. E., *First and Second Kings*, Westminster Bible Companion (Louisville: Westminster John Knox, 1999).

——, *Jeremiah* (Macon: Smyth & Helwys, 2002).

Garland, D. E., *1 Corinthians*, BECNT (Grand Rapids: Baker Academic, 2003).

Garrett, D. A., *Proverbs, Ecclesiastes, Song of Songs*, NAC 14 (Nashville: Broadman, 1993).

Goldingay, J., *Psalms, Volume 3: Psalms 90 – 150*, BCOTWP (Grand Rapids: Baker Academic, 2008).

Hagner, D. A., *Matthew 1 – 13*, WBC 33A (Dallas: Word, 1993).

Harrison, R. K., *Jeremiah and Lamentations*, TOTC 19 (Downers Grove: InterVarsity Press, 1973).

Hays, R. B., *First Corinthians*, Interpretation (Louisville: John Knox, 1997).

Hengel, M., *Studies in Early Christianity* (London: T&T Clark, 2004).

Hoehner, H. W., *Ephesians: An Exegetical Commentary* (Grand Rapids: Baker Academic, 2002).

Holladay, W. L., *Jeremiah 1*, Hermeneia (Philadelphia: Fortress, 1986).

House, P. R., *1, 2 Kings*, NAC 8 (Nashville: Broadman & Holman, 1995).

Hubbard, D. A., *Proverbs*, The Communicator's Commentary 15A (Dallas: Word, 1989).

Huey, F. B., *Jeremiah, Lamentations*, NAC 16 (Nashville: Broadman, 1993).

Kaiser, W. C., *Ecclesiastes: Total Life*, Everyman's Bible Commentary (Chicago: Moody, 1979).

——, *The Messiah in the Old Testament*, Studies in Old Testament Biblical Theology (Grand Rapids: Zondervan, 1995).

Keener, C. S., *Matthew*, IVPNTC 1 (Downers Grove: InterVarsity Press, 1997).

Kidner, D., *Proverbs: An Introduction and Commentary*, TOTC 17 (Nottingham: Inter-Varsity Press, 2008 [1964]).

Kitchen, J. A., *Proverbs*, Mentor Commentary (Fearn, Ross-shire: Christian Focus, 2006).

Koch, K., 'Gibt es ein Vergeltungsdogma im Alten Testament?', *ZTK* 52 (1955), pp. 1–42. English trans.: 'Is There a Doctrine of Retribution in the Old Testament?', in J. L. Crenshaw (ed.), *Theodicy in the Old Testament*, IRT 4 (Philadelphia: Fortress, 1983), pp. 57–87.

Konkel, A. H., *1 & 2 Kings*, NIVAC (Grand Rapids: Zondervan, 2006).

Lalleman, H., *Jeremiah and Lamentations*, TOTC 21 (Downers Grove: InterVarsity Press, 2013).

Lampe, P., 'Theological Wisdom and the "Word about the Cross": The Rhetorical Scheme in 1 Corinthians 1 – 4', *Int* 44 (1990), pp. 117–131.

Leupold, H. C., *Expositions of Ecclesiastes* (Grand Rapids: Baker, 1952).

Limburg, J., *Psalms*, Westminster Bible Companion (Louisville: Westminster John Knox, 2000).

Lincoln, A. T., *Ephesians*, WBC 42 (Dallas: Word, 1990).

Litfin, A. D., *Paul's Theology of Preaching: The Apostle's Challenge to the Art of Persuasion in Ancient Corinth* (Downers Grove: IVP Academic, 2015).

Lloyd-Jones, D. M., *Studies in the Sermon on the Mount* (Grand Rapids: Eerdmans, 1971).

Longman, T., *The Book of Ecclesiastes*, NICOT (Grand Rapids: Eerdmans, 1998).

——, *The Fear of the Lord Is Wisdom: A Theological Introduction to Wisdom in Israel* (Grand Rapids: Baker Academic, 2017).

——, *Proverbs*, BCOTWP (Grand Rapids: Baker Academic, 2006).

Lucas, E. C., 'The Book of Proverbs: Some Current Issues', in D. G. Firth and L. Wilson (eds.), *Interpreting Old Testament Wisdom Literature* (Downers Grove: IVP Academic, 2017), pp. 37–59.

McCartney, D. G., *James*, BECNT (Grand Rapids: Baker Academic, 2009).

McConville, J. G., *Deuteronomy*, AOTC 5 (Downers Grove: InterVarsity Press, 2002).

McKane, W., *Proverbs*, OTL (Philadelphia: Westminster, 1970).

McKnight, S., *The Letter of James*, NICNT (Grand Rapids: Eerdmans, 2011).

Marr, S., *Proverbs for Business: Daily Wisdom for the Workplace* (Grand Rapids: Revell, 2006).

Martin, R. P., *James*, WBC 48 (Waco: Word, 1988).

Mays, J. L., *Psalms*, Interpretation (Louisville: John Knox, 1994).

Merrill, E. H., *Deuteronomy*, NAC 4 (Nashville: Broadman & Holman, 1994).

Meye Thompson, M., *Colossians and Philemon*, THNTC (Grand Rapids: Eerdmans, 2005).

Miller, P. D., *Deuteronomy*, Interpretation (Louisville: John Knox, 1990).

——, *Sin and Judgment in the Prophets: A Stylistic and Theological Analysis* (Chico: Scholars, 1982).

Moo, D. J., *The Letter of James*, Pillar (Grand Rapids: Eerdmans, 2000).

——, *The Letters to the Colossians and to Philemon*, Pillar (Grand Rapids: Eerdmans, 2008).

Morris, L., *The Gospel according to Matthew*, Pillar (Grand Rapids: Eerdmans, 1992).

Murphy, R. E., *Proverbs*, WBC 22 (Nashville: Thomas Nelson, 1998).

——, *The Tree of Life: An Exploration of Biblical Wisdom Literature*, 3rd edn (Grand Rapids: Eerdmans, 2002).

Nelson, R., *First and Second Kings*, Interpretation (Louisville: John Knox, 1987).

Nyberg, D., *The Varnished Truth: Truth Telling and Deceiving in Ordinary Life* (Chicago: University of Chicago Press, 1993).

O'Brien, P. T., *Ephesians*, Pillar (Grand Rapids: Eerdmans, 1999).

Pao, D. W., *Colossians and Philemon*, ZECNT (Grand Rapids: Zondervan, 2012).

Plaut, W. G., *Book of Proverbs*, The Jewish Commentary for Bible Readers (New York: Union of American Hebrew Congregations, 1961).

Provan, I. W., *1 & 2 Kings*, Understanding the Bible Commentary Series (Grand Rapids: Baker Books, 1995).

Rad, G. von, *Deuteronomy*, trans. D. Barton, OTL (Philadelphia: Westminster, 1966).

Riesner, R., 'Jesus as Preacher and Teacher', in H. Wansbrough (ed.), *Jesus and the Oral Gospel Tradition*, JSNTSup 64 (Sheffield: Sheffield Academic Press, 1991), pp. 185–210.

Ross, A. P., 'Proverbs', *EBC*, vol. 5 (Grand Rapids: Zondervan, 1991), pp. 881–1134.

Seow, C.-L., *Ecclesiastes*, AB 18C (New York: Doubleday, 1997).

Snodgrass, K., *Ephesians*, NIVAC (Grand Rapids: Zondervan, 1996).

Tasker, R. V. G., *The Gospel according to St Matthew*, TNTC 1 (Grand Rapids: Eerdmans, 1961).

Taylor, M., *1 Corinthians*, NAC 28 (Nashville: B&H, 2014).

Thielman, F., *Ephesians*, BECNT (Grand Rapids: Baker Academic, 2010).

Thiselton, A. C., *The First Epistle to the Corinthians: A Commentary on the Greek Text*, NIGTC (Grand Rapids: Eerdmans, 2000).

Thompson, J. A., *The Book of Jeremiah*, NICOT (Grand Rapids: Eerdmans, 1980).

——, *Deuteronomy*, TOTC 5 (Downers Grove: InterVarsity Press, 1974).

Turner, D. L., *Matthew*, BECNT (Grand Rapids: Baker Academic, 2008).

Van Leeuwen, R. C., 'Wealth and Poverty: System and Contradiction in Proverbs', *HS* 33 (1992), pp. 25–36.

Vaughan, C., 'Colossians', *EBC*, vol. 11 (Grand Rapids: Zondervan, 1978), pp. 161–226.

Walsh, J. T., *1 Kings*, Berit Olam: Studies in Hebrew Narrative & Poetry (Collegeville: Liturgical Press, 1996).

Waltke, B. K., *The Book of Proverbs Chapters 1–15*, NICOT (Grand Rapids: Eerdmans, 2004).

——, *The Book of Proverbs Chapters 15–31*, NICOT (Grand Rapids: Eerdmans, 2005).

Watson, N., *The First Epistle to the Corinthians*, Epworth, 2nd edn (London: Epworth, 2005).

Weiser, A., *The Psalms*, trans. H. Hartwell, OTL (Philadelphia: Westminster, 1962).

Whybray, R. N., *Proverbs*, NCBC (Grand Rapids: Eerdmans, 1994).

Wilkins, M. J., *Matthew*, NIVAC (Grand Rapids: Zondervan, 2004).

Wiseman, D. J., *1 & 2 Kings*, TOTC 9 (Downers Grove: InterVarsity Press, 1993).

Witherington, B., *The Letters to Philemon, the Colossians, and the Ephesians: A Socio-Rhetorical Commentary on the Captivity Epistles* (Grand Rapids: Eerdmans, 2007).

Wright, C. J. H., *Deuteronomy*, Understanding the Bible Commentary Series (Grand Rapids: Baker, 2012).

——, *The Message of Jeremiah*, BST (Downers Grove: InterVarsity Press, 2014).

Zornberg, A. G., *Malbim on Mishley: The Commentary of Rabbi Meir Leibush Malbim on the Book of Proverbs* (Jerusalem: Feldheim, 1982).

Zuck, R. B., *Job*, Everyman's Bible Commentary (Chicago: Moody, 1978).

Introduction

When I was just ten years old, I set out with my father on a week-long road trip. As we began our journey, I had only a general notion of where we were going and what we would be doing, but there were many unanticipated adventures along the way that I can still remember decades later. How much I learned on that trip, and how I enjoyed that special time with my dad!

In many respects, what I experienced as a young boy is what I hope will be the experience of those who read this book on 'the message of wisdom'. You likely have a general sense of what wisdom is, and perhaps you have heard sermons and lessons taken from some of the wisdom texts in the Bible. However, there is so much that the Bible says about this theme that merits further investigation. I certainly do not know all that the Bible teaches about wisdom, but I would like to share some of what I have been able to learn as I have studied it for a number of years. The more I have read, preached and taught on biblical wisdom, the more I have come to understand what the Lord desires for his people as they learn to live wisely as he intends them to live.

The three Old Testament books of Proverbs, Job and Ecclesiastes are often referred to as the wisdom books of the Bible. Numerous excellent commentaries have been written expounding each of these books, and there are also a number of fine volumes that expound what they as a group of wisdom texts teach.[1] Biblical wisdom, however, is not limited to these three books, but actually is a theme that pervades much of the Bible. The

---

[1] Two excellent recent introductions to the Old Testament wisdom literature are C. G. Bartholomew and R. P. O'Dowd, *Old Testament Wisdom Literature: A Theological Introduction* (Downers Grove: IVP Academic, 2011); and T. Longman, *The Fear of the Lord Is Wisdom: A Theological Introduction to Wisdom in Israel* (Grand Rapids: Baker Academic, 2017).

present work on the message of wisdom endeavours to trace this important theme, beginning in the book of Proverbs. It then expands into other parts of the Old Testament that speak of wisdom, including passages from the law, from history, from prophecy and from the Psalms. It discusses how wisdom in Proverbs connects with Job and Ecclesiastes, and then it extends into the New Testament to view how wisdom is presented in the life and person of Jesus, and in several of the epistles. This broad discussion is an exercise in biblical theology, which views the themes of the Bible in a synthetic fashion, and it complements the analytical approach that is typically featured in commentaries on specific books of the Bible.

One of the distinctive convictions of The Bible Speaks Today series is that God speaks today through the Bible he inspired. In keeping with that proper emphasis, in this volume I have not so much spoken *about* wisdom as presented key passages of Scripture as they elucidate wisdom. My goal is to guide readers so that they can understand what God teaches about wisdom through his Word. At times, I will provide information to assist them in understanding the texts, but mainly I want the Scriptures to speak for themselves, because, as Paul says to Timothy, it is the Scriptures 'which are able to make you wise for salvation through faith in Christ Jesus' (2 Tim. 3:15).

My initial ideas for this book can be found in a two-page note that I composed for the *NIV Zondervan Study Bible*.[2] In the present book, I have taken that earlier sketch, developed it in detail and added colour to the picture. In the first part, we investigate the concept of wisdom as it is presented in the book of Proverbs, with expositions on passages from Proverbs 1, 2, 8 and 9 teaching what wisdom is and how it calls out to human beings to follow its path. In the second part, we delve into how wisdom is presented in various contexts in the Old Testament, as we look at passages from the law (Deut. 30), history (1 Kgs 3 – 4), prophecy (Jer. 8 – 9) and Psalm 112. The third part takes us back to the book of Proverbs, as we take a topical approach to learn how wisdom affects our conduct in our work, our speech, our decisions and our righteous living. There is complexity in the biblical message of wisdom, as we see in part 4 as the prominent theme of retribution in Proverbs is balanced and qualified

---

[2] D. A. Carson (ed.), *NIV Zondervan Study Bible* (Grand Rapids: Zondervan, 2015), pp. 2674–2675. This article was recently reprinted in D. A. Carson (ed.), *NIV Biblical Theology Study Bible* (Grand Rapids: Zondervan, 2018), pp. 2362–2363.

in the books of Job and Ecclesiastes. In the final part, we examine the culmination of wisdom in the New Testament, where we learn that Jesus is the master teacher of wisdom and the source of all wisdom, and we are challenged to live by God's wisdom rather than falling into folly.

Throughout the Bible, we are constantly challenged to *learn* God's wisdom, to *live* God's wisdom and to *love* God's wisdom. My prayer is that these studies about the message of wisdom will have that effect as the Bible speaks today to us.

Part 1
The concept of wisdom

Proverbs 1:1–7

1. An invitation to wisdom

Just as an overture previews the music in an opera, and a broadcaster sets the scene for a televised sports event, so the book of Proverbs begins with a prologue that introduces its content for us as we read it. By this means, the initial paragraph provides us with an invitation to wisdom. In this opening section in Proverbs 1:1–7, the sage states the title for the book, discloses its purpose and articulates a succinct motto for biblical wisdom. Like a movie trailer, this paragraph orients us to read and to respond to the wisdom sayings in the collection to follow. This invitation prepares us for the vital truth that the book of Proverbs will teach us about wisdom.

1. Title (1:1)

The title in verse 1 describes the book as *The proverbs of Solomon son of David, king of Israel*. Every language has proverbial sayings, maxims and adages that express general truths in concise and memorable language, and these are passed down from generation to generation, often orally, and sometimes in written form as well. For example, proverbs in English include 'Haste makes waste' and 'A stitch in time saves nine'. The book of Proverbs preserves a number of statements like that from ancient Israel. The Hebrew term for *proverb* (*māšāl*) refers to a pithy statement that communicates truth about life by means of comparison.[1] This is the kind of teaching that we can expect to read in the book of Proverbs, and that

---

[1] A. P. Ross, 'Proverbs', *EBC*, vol. 5 (Grand Rapids: Zondervan, 1991), p. 904.

makes this collection distinct from most of the other books of the Bible, which feature other kinds of literature, such as narratives, laws, songs, prophecies and letters.

In the historical narrative in 1 Kings 3:7–12, the Lord endowed the young king Solomon with extraordinary wisdom and understanding. As a result, Solomon spoke three thousand proverbs on a wide range of topics (1 Kgs 4:29–34), a portion of which are collected in this book. Solomon's reputation for wisdom spread within Israel and throughout the Ancient Near Eastern world, so that even the Queen of Sheba travelled a great distance to Jerusalem to confirm the reports that she had received about him (1 Kgs 10:1–10). One scholar observes,

> The wisdom of Solomon constitutes a major feature of his biblical identity . . . His reputation for wisdom spread throughout Israel and the ANE, with the result that he became much sought after. Solomon's wisdom is said to have exceeded that of all of the people of the east, including Egypt. He composed 3,000 proverbs, 1,005 songs, and investigated natural science: trees, animals, birds, reptiles, and fish. Much of biblical Wisdom literature is associated with Solomon.[2]

Wisdom texts in other Ancient Near Eastern cultures such as Egypt and Mesopotamia typically were addressed to a specific person. By contrast, the title of Proverbs does not define a particular recipient. Rather, this book and its sayings have a broader purpose, because they are intended to shape the character of God's people in general, for the sayings in this book 'pertain to the interests of all people'.[3] For that reason, as we read Proverbs in the twenty-first century we have a keen sense that it is God's word written to us, and that its wisdom is crucial for our lives today. This is not just ancient wisdom to learn, but it is timeless wisdom to learn and *to live.*

2. Purpose (1:2–6)

After the title is stated in verse 1, first the purpose of the book is defined as three general outcomes in verses 2–3, and then specific details about

---

[2] G. H. Wilson, *NIDOTTE* 4:1234.

[3] B. K. Waltke, *The Book of Proverbs Chapters 1–15*, NICOT (Grand Rapids: Eerdmans, 2004), p. 174.

these outcomes are given in verses 4–6. The first outcome is *for gaining wisdom and instruction* (2a). The term *wisdom* is the Hebrew ḥokmâ, a frequent and important word in Proverbs. When it is used in general contexts, ḥokmâ refers to a variety of practical and artistic skills (Exod. 31:6; Ps. 107:27). When it is used in an ethical sense, it has the nuance of skill in living, and in Proverbs it most often refers specifically to skill in living according to the Lord's moral order.[4] In Proverbs ḥokmâ is 'the ability to make wise choices and live successfully according to the moral standards of the covenant community. The one who lives skillfully produces things of lasting value to God and to the community.'[5] *Instruction* is the Hebrew word mûsār, which indicates teaching by exhortation and warning, and it has nuances ranging from a positive example to stern punishment.[6] This is the kind of moral instruction that Proverbs seeks to instil in its readers, including us today.

The second outcome in verse 2b is *for understanding words of insight.* The verb bîn ('understand') speaks of the ability to discern between alternatives and to choose in accordance with the true essence of the issue. This discernment was evident in Solomon's skill in adjudicating the dispute between the two mothers in 1 Kings 3:16–28, as he was able to choose accurately which woman's claim to believe. It is implied that this collection of proverbs will provide its readers with genuine insight for life, so that they will be able to make good decisions. In the complex world in which we live today, where a few clicks on a computer or a smartphone deluge us with a torrent of information, the book of Proverbs is a crucial resource God has given to us, so that we can learn to choose wisely from among the many competing alternatives before us.

The third outcome in verse 3 is *for receiving instruction in prudent behaviour.* This general category is then specified as *doing what is right and just and fair.* What is *right* (ṣedeq) refers to what conforms to the Lord's righteous standard, what is *just* (mišpāṭ) indicates the proper way to behave, and what is *fair* (mēšārîm) speaks of honesty and fairness – for example, in political rule (cf. 1 Chr. 29:17). Wisdom in Proverbs, then, is much more than acquiring a lot of knowledge and instruction, but rather it is the ability to assess situations wisely, to make good decisions and to

---

[4] For a fine discussion of the words used for wisdom in Proverbs, see M. V. Fox, *Proverbs 1 – 9*, AYB 18A (New Haven: Yale University Press, 2000), pp. 29–38.

[5] Ross, 'Proverbs', p. 905.

[6] E. H. Merrill, *NIDOTTE* 2:480–481.

act responsibly,[7] all crucial life skills. In other Old Testament passages, these behaviours imitate the Lord's own attributes and values, and as Proverbs 2:9 indicates, they are the fruit of one's commitment to pursue divine wisdom.

Speaking more specifically in verse 4, the recipients are designated as *those who are simple* (*pĕtāʾîm*). These are impressionable youths who have not yet become firmly set in a course of life, and who can be influenced in the direction of either wisdom or folly (cf. Prov. 1:10–19). The language and illustrations used especially in Proverbs 1 – 9 indicate that youths on the cusp of adulthood are specifically in view, so this portion of God's Word has particular relevance to teens and young adults. The purpose of Proverbs is to give to the youth *prudence* (*ʿormâ*), that is, shrewdness to avoid pitfalls,[8] as well as *discretion* (*mĕzimmâ*), resourcefulness for life. This discretion 'imparts the ability to walk the path of life in a constructive way and to avoid the lures of the evil path (Prov. 2:11)'.[9] Although the primary intended audience of Proverbs is young adults, and many of the examples relate most specifically to young men, the instructions and principles in Proverbs are easily applied to all ages and genders. For that reason, this collection speaks with clarity and conviction into the lives of all of us who read it today.

The desired response to the wisdom sayings in Proverbs is a ready acceptance of instruction, reflecting a wholehearted desire for learning and wise guidance (5). The book of Proverbs endeavours to transform simple, mouldable youths who are easily influenced towards folly into adults whose lives are firmly committed to wisdom. Like Frodo Baggins, Luke Skywalker and Harry Potter, who all were guided by their mentors, those who are wise look beyond themselves to listen to those who can teach them wisdom (9:9). The term *listen* here as in verse 8 implies to listen attentively. This is more than just hearing something said, because it is an active response that fervently desires to learn and to change, and not just a passive awareness without effecting life change. Youths must recognize that there is a wealth of wisdom that can be handed down to them if they

---

[7] R. N. Whybray, *Proverbs*, NCBC (Grand Rapids: Eerdmans, 1994), p. 32, notes that the verbal form *haśkēl*, translated here 'prudent behaviour', 'carries the implication of an intelligent assessment of situations which can lead to practical decisions', and he suggests that an appropriate gloss is 'insight'.

[8] The term *ʿormâ* is used positively in Proverbs (cf. 8:5, 12; 19:25), but in other Old Testament books it can have a negative sense, as in Gen. 3:1, when it speaks of the craftiness of the serpent who tempted Adam and Eve.

[9] T. Longman, *Proverbs*, BCOTWP (Grand Rapids: Baker Academic, 2006), p. 97.

are receptive. There is indeed a cost to becoming wise, but learners who choose to purchase wisdom (the verb *qānâ*, rendered here as 'get', is a commercial term, as in 4:5, 7) will receive *guidance*, or skill in navigating the complexities of life.[10] This kind of skill is not intuitive, but it must be learned, and that is why it is essential for the wise to listen and for the discerning to get guidance from those who can teach them well. As an old Arabian proverb states, 'He who knows not and knows that he knows not, is a student; teach him.'

Wisdom skilfully uses language as it teaches effectively, and its sayings are carefully crafted to have the optimal penetrating effect, because the sage 'is the master of compressed, polished, epigrammatic utterance; he gathers his thoughts into memorable forms of expression'.[11] Ecclesiastes 12:9–11 opens a window into how a teacher of wisdom carefully crafted his sayings in order to express the truth incisively:

> Not only was the Teacher wise, but also he imparted knowledge to the people. He pondered and searched out and set in order many proverbs. The Teacher searched to find just the right words, and what he wrote was upright and true.
> The words of the wise are like goads, their collected sayings like firmly embedded nails – given by one shepherd.

Verse 6 includes several overlapping terms describing the language of wisdom. The general term *proverb* (*māšāl*) repeats the title of the book in verse 1, where it refers to memorable sayings that teach about life by comparisons. More specifically, the collection includes *parables* (*mělîṣâ*), which are enigmatic sayings using satire, sarcasm or innuendo to make their points incisively;[12] *sayings . . . of the wise*, which may well refer to written wisdom collections;[13] and *riddles* (*ḥîdâ*), which are difficult sayings that require interpretation (cf. Num. 12:8; 1 Kgs 10:1). There was intentional strategy involved in the sage's use of riddles, as one commentator explains:

---

[10] W. McKane, *Proverbs*, OTL (Philadelphia: Westminster, 1970), p. 266, elucidates the sense of *guidance*, the Hebrew term *taḥbulôt*: 'It is then a term for a kind of nautical expertise, the ability to steer a course through the trackless sea; and it lends itself readily to becoming a metaphor for the negotiating skills which discern the beginning and the end of a problem and perform each operation in the right place at the right time.'

[11] Ibid., p. 267.

[12] T. Powell, *NIDOTTE* 2:799.

[13] Longman, *Proverbs*, p. 100.

The outstanding feature of an enigma is its immediate obscurity. Its surface meaning is strange and irrational and obviously (or almost obviously) not the author's direct intention. Enigmas require decipherment to make any sense of them, not just to enrich their meaning. Words and images must be read as tokens of entities and events in another domain. An enigma deliberately blocks immediate understanding by ambiguities and obscurities before allowing the audience to push through to a deeper understanding.[14]

If the youth is to be helped towards wisdom, he must understand the proverbial language used by the teacher. In Proverbs the learner meets a style of teaching 'that provokes his thought, getting under his skin by thrusts of wit, paradox, common sense and teasing symbolism, in preference to the preacher's tactic of frontal assault'.[15]

3. Motto (1:7)

After detailing the major purposes of the book of Proverbs in verses 2–6, the sage concludes his invitation to wisdom by stating in concise form in verse 7 the central teaching of this collection when he says,

> *The fear of the LORD is the beginning of knowledge,*
>   *but fools despise wisdom and instruction.*

The *fear of the LORD* is not so much terror and dread of the Lord as reverence for the Lord that is expressed in the totality of a person's choices and actions. This humble stance before God

radiates out from our adoration and devotion to our everyday conduct that sees each moment as the Lord's time, each relationship as the Lord's opportunity, each duty as the Lord's command, and each blessing as the Lord's gift. It is a new way of looking at life and seeing what it is meant to be when viewed from God's perspective.[16]

---

[14] Fox, *Proverbs 1 – 9*, p. 65.

[15] D. Kidner, *Proverbs: An Introduction and Commentary*, TOTC 17 (Nottingham: Inter-Varsity Press, 2008 [1964]), p. 56.

[16] D. A. Hubbard, *Proverbs*, The Communicator's Commentary 15A (Dallas: Word, 1989), p. 48.

Reverence for the Lord is the beginning of knowledge (and of wisdom in 9:10), not in the sense that one begins with it and later abandons it for something else, but rather that it is the fundamental principle of wisdom, because 'What the alphabet is to reading, notes to reading music, and numerals to mathematics, the fear of the LORD is to attaining the revealed knowledge of the book.'[17] Advancing in God's school of wisdom requires more than intellectual prowess, accumulation of knowledge and expert ability. It demands an attitude of humility before the Lord that pervades the entire scope of one's education. Only those who revere the Lord will become wise, skilful in living as the Lord measures it.

By contrast, foolish people despise what the fear of the Lord and wisdom can teach them. The term used here for *fools* ('*ĕwîl*) refers to those who refuse to accept teaching and instruction, and consequently are unable to distinguish between right and wrong. Their folly is not fundamentally an intellectual deficiency, but instead it is their inability or unwillingness to conform their lives to the Lord's moral order. Their refusal to revere the Lord sets them on a path that leads away from wisdom and towards folly.

4. The concept of wisdom

Old Testament wisdom reflects the same world view that is evidenced throughout all of the Bible. According to Old Testament wisdom, Yahweh ('the LORD' in English translations) is the creator of the entire universe, not just a localized tribal deity as in other Ancient Near Eastern cultures. Because the Lord actively governs his world, it is not driven about by erratic and accidental forces, such as blind chance or impersonal fate. The Lord is intelligent, so there is recognizable design and a measure of predictability in his world, and therefore a rational framework of cause and effect. The Lord is also righteous and holy, so there is a moral structure that undergirds his world. Because the Lord rules over all of his world, the ethical standards that he mandates apply to all human beings – not just to those who believe in him, but also to those who disregard him.[18]

---

[17] Waltke, *Proverbs Chapters 1–15*, p. 181.

[18] For a fuller discussion of the world view of wisdom, see D. J. Estes, *Hear, My Son*, NSBT 4 (Downers Grove: InterVarsity Press, 1997), pp. 19–39.

Proverbs 3:19 states,

> By wisdom the LORD laid the earth's foundations,
>> by understanding he set the heavens in place.

This statement suggests that written into the very nature of the world is divine order, because

> Whatever the seeming randomness of life before us, wisdom assures us that there is still an order created by God for the very dilemma we face . . . In other words, wisdom affirms that God has established both an overall, dynamic world order and that this order provides for every moment and every person.[19]

This order is demonstrated by the causal relationships between acts and consequences that human beings can observe, for example, in the industry of the ant (Prov. 6:6–8). Wisdom often draws parallels from how the physical world works to how human beings should behave (6:9–11), as it derives lessons for wise living.[20]

The most prominent image in the book of Proverbs is represented by the term *derek*, which in its over seventy uses in Proverbs speaks of the path, way or journey of life. Actually, Proverbs contrasts two antithetical ways that human beings can take, as it echoes similar language by Moses in Deuteronomy 30:15–20 (see chapter 5) and by the psalmist in Psalm 1. In the New Testament, Jesus in Matthew 7:13–14 distinguishes between the broad road that leads to destruction and the narrow road that leads to life, using the familiar language of the Old Testament to make his point as he teaches in the Sermon on the Mount (see chapter 16).

On the one hand, there is the path of wisdom, which is skill in living according to the Lord's way, and this is contrasted to the path of folly, which either neglects or consciously chooses not to live according to the way of the Lord. According to Proverbs 12:15, fools presume to know what

---

[19] C. G. Bartholomew and R. P. O'Dowd, *Old Testament Wisdom Literature: A Theological Introduction* (Downers Grove: IVP Academic, 2011), p. 28.

[20] W. P. Brown, *Wisdom's Wonder: Character, Creation, and Crisis in the Bible's Wisdom Literature* (Grand Rapids: Eerdmans, 2014), p. 7, observes, 'Because God fashioned creation through wisdom, creation in turn reflects God's wisdom. The cosmos is deemed comprehensibly didactic. Creation's regularity allows for discerning observable patterns in which human actions have predictable consequences, and knowing these consequences leads to an informed life.'

is right, but those who are wise listen to the kind of counsel provided in this book so that they can learn the way that pleases the Lord. Wisdom is evidenced by righteous behaviour, actions, attitudes and values that correspond to the Lord's order. Folly, by contrast, is marked by wicked behaviour, actions, attitudes and values that deviate from the Lord's standard. The contrasting patterns of behaviour generated by wisdom and folly are pictured in Proverbs 4:18–19, which says,

> The path of the righteous is like the morning sun,
>> shining ever brighter till the full light of day.
> But the way of the wicked is like deep darkness;
>> they do not know what makes them stumble.

Both of these paths lead to destinations, and Proverbs is clear about where the contrasting paths of wisdom and folly end. The end in view includes the final destination, but the main focus of Proverbs is the quality of life that results from taking the path of wisdom or the path of folly. In Proverbs 8:35–36, wisdom is personified as saying,

> For those who find me find life
>> and receive favour from the Lord.
> But those who fail to find me harm themselves;
>> all who hate me love death.

This is in keeping with Moses' exhortation to the Israelites of his generation, 'I have set before you life and death, blessings and curses. Now choose life.'[21] The decision between the path of wisdom and the path of folly, then, is consequential, because it will lead either to life in all of its dimensions or to death in its various aspects. How crucial it is that young adults, as well as people of all ages, choose wisdom and life.

Wisdom in the book of Proverbs and throughout the Bible seeks to guide human beings, and especially the young, in the direction of the good life, not as contemporary culture measures it, but as the Lord defines it. It challenges them to make wise choices, manifesting understanding that is able to make discerning decisions when faced with competing alternatives. In Proverbs 9:6, wisdom is portrayed as a woman who calls out to the youth,

---

[21] Deut. 30:19.

> Leave your simple ways and you will live;
>> walk in the way of insight.

The sage also challenges his readers to make wise commitments, as he urges them,

> . . . get wisdom.
>> Though it cost all you have, get understanding.[22]

The book of Proverbs calls all who read it, including us today in the twenty-first century, to adopt a radical reorientation of life in which the pursuit of the Lord's wisdom becomes our prime value. Wisdom is far more than just a cosmetic makeover that alters the external appearance of a person. Rather, wisdom works from the inside out to transform the entire person in the heart, which in Hebrew thought encompasses the intellect, the emotions and the will. In this spirit, the psalmist in Psalm 86:11 articulates a commitment that should be the pattern for our commitment as well:

> Teach me your way, Lord,
>> that I may rely on your faithfulness;
> give me an undivided heart,
>> that I may fear your name.

The ultimate goal of wisdom is the formation of responsible moral character, or what later came to be known as virtue, because 'Wisdom is configuration of soul; it is *moral character*. And fostering moral character, it is no overstatement, is at all times the greatest goal of education.'[23] It is to the development of godly moral character that the sage invites us in the book of Proverbs.

5. Concluding comment

Every day we receive many invitations, some of them rather trivial and others of weighty significance. Every invitation that comes to us calls us to decide whether to accept it or not, and that decision sets into motion a

---

[22] Prov. 4:7.
[23] Fox, *Proverbs 1 – 9*, p. 620.

set of consequences. If we accept an invitation to dinner, we may experience an evening of enriching conversation. If we say yes to an invitation to a sports event, we could witness a thrilling game. If we receive a proposal of marriage, it can lead to decades of growing in love.

In contrast, succumbing to the temptation to cheat in an examination can lead to a pattern of deceitfulness that results in bigger and bigger betrayals of trust. Yielding to the enticements of lust or laziness can produce a pattern of sin and sloth. Following one's own heart rather than listening to God's Word can direct a person into a lifestyle that is truly heartbreaking.

The question is not whether we will receive invitations in life, but what we will do with the invitations we will inevitably be given. The invitation in the opening verses of the book of Proverbs challenges us to take God's wisdom seriously, because it will lead us to life. If we do not heed the teaching of this collection, we are in effect choosing a future that will be profoundly disappointing.

As a university professor for over thirty-five years, my greatest joy has come from investing in many students who have made intentional commitments to the Lord's path of wisdom. When they come back to campus to visit or when I happen to cross paths with them in various other places, I rejoice to see that they have indeed found the good life that the Lord's path of wisdom provides. They have chosen to listen to the Lord and to follow his way, and that choice has led them into the abundant life God desires for his people.

However, there is another, tragic side to the story, because my greatest heartbreak has come from some of my students who have chosen the path of folly. Even though they heard the same lectures, received the same warnings and observed the same examples, they failed to make an intentional commitment to live in the fear of the Lord. Because of that poor decision, they have tasted the bitter end to which folly leads. I am profoundly saddened when I see that, because what they have experienced is so much less than what the Lord desires for them. Their foolish choices have led to disastrous consequences in their lives.

The book of Proverbs teaches us that we all must choose which path to follow in life, the path of wisdom or the path of folly, and the path we choose will make all the difference. Because choices create character, what we choose today determines who we will become tomorrow. In choosing the path to follow, for good or for bad, we are also choosing the future we will find. In Proverbs, we are invited and urged to choose the path of wisdom that leads to life. This decision is a personal choice, so no-one else can make it for us. Wisdom issues its invitation to us, but we must choose whether to accept it or to decline it, and so much hangs in the balance in the choice we make.

Proverbs 2:1–11

2. Searching for wisdom

We all have times when we need to locate something that is valuable to us. It may be that the car keys have gone missing, or a tool is not in the box where it belongs when we need to use it, or a favourite book has disappeared when we want to read it again. When we misplace something we greatly want or need, we search diligently until we find it. A superficial glance around will not suffice, and a half-hearted effort is not good enough. We look and search and make every effort until we find what is important to us. In Proverbs 2:1–11, the sage urges his son, or student, to search for wisdom, and he assures him that as he seeks for God's wisdom he will find it and all that it has to offer for life. For God's wisdom, finders are seekers. However, we will only seek wisdom if we truly value it, so the book of Proverbs endeavours to cultivate in us a heart that so treasures God's wisdom that we will search diligently for it.

1. Searching for wisdom (2:1–4)

Wisdom does not come easily and naturally to us, but we must value and seek it intentionally. With the familiar expression *My son*, an address found about ten times in Proverbs 1 – 9, the sage seeks to inspire his biological son, or perhaps his intellectual student, to be a good learner of wisdom, and in particular he calls him to *accept* his words (1). This desired acceptance is the same joyful spirit that the psalmist reflects in Psalm 119:97:

Oh, how I love your law!
I meditate on it all day long.[1]

He reinforces this challenge by urging the son to *store up*[2] or treasure (cf. Prov. 10:14) his commands. Learning in the school of wisdom requires that the student has a responsive attitude, and this means taking a humble stance that is eager to be taught.

Every parent and teacher can attest to the difference that attitude makes when it comes to learning. Children and students who are unresponsive and proud resist instruction and direction. They do not value the counsel they are given, and they push back against those who endeavour to guide them. Their resistance makes teaching painful for both the teacher and the student, and it causes the relationship between a parent and a child to become strained. By contrast, children and students who are eager to learn value what they are taught, and they respond positively to those who endeavour to invest in their lives. Their responsiveness makes teaching them a pleasure, and it enhances how a parent and a child relate to one another. What is true in these human contexts applies equally to God's school of wisdom. To learn well, learners must accept joyfully the words of their wise teachers.

The father is teaching wisdom, but the son must listen carefully to it by *turning* his *ear to wisdom* (2). The image of turning the ear pictures an eager attentiveness to what is heard or seen rather than giving the teacher a blank stare or muttering a sullen 'Whatever'. Also, the sage urges the son to *apply* his *heart to understanding*. Many people today urge us to follow our hearts; however, Jeremiah 17:9 warns, 'The heart is deceitful above all things and beyond cure', so rather than following our heart, our heart has to be reoriented intentionally towards understanding (cf. Prov. 2:10; Ps. 90:12). The heart (*lēb*) in Old Testament thought speaks of the entire person, because

> The heart is the locus and organ of thought and the faculty of understanding (e.g., Prov 2:2; 3:1; 16:1; 18:15; and very often). It is also the

---

[1] Cf. also Ps. 1:2.

[2] W. G. Plaut, *Book of Proverbs*, The Jewish Commentary for Bible Readers (New York: Union of American Hebrew Congregations, 1961), p. 43, expounds on the implication of the verb *spn*: 'Most teachings cannot be immediately utilized, which is the chief reason both for the impatience people feel with education and for the frustration of educators. Much time will often pass before education's effects are felt. For essentially, moral teachings are to influence attitudes which then become the key to future actions.'

organ of psychological experiences that we currently classify as emotions (e.g., trust, 3:5; yearning, 7:25; 13:12; sorrow and happiness, 14:13; 15:13; pride, 16:5). But the intellectual exercise of the mind is not really detached from the emotional, and the modern dichotomy is artificial.[3]

This holistic sense of the heart means that every part of our life must be involved in learning the Lord's wise way, including our mind, our emotions and our will. It is not enough to give a partial effort to understanding, but it requires a total commitment of our entire life, including what we think, how we feel and why we make the choices we do. All of these are involved when we apply our heart to understanding, for as one scholar rightly observes,

> Wisdom is a closed door to a closed mind. And that, says the sage, is why there are so many fools around. They are so self-conceited that they think they know it all and have no need to learn from anyone.[4]

By contrast, wise learners realize how much they need to listen and to learn.

In God's school of wisdom a two-way communication is maintained between the teacher and the learner. In Proverbs 1:20; 8:1; and 9:3, wisdom calls out to the people, but here in verse 3 the son is urged to respond to the father's teaching by calling out to wisdom. The invitation by wisdom through the father needs to be accepted and responded to by the son. By calling out for insight, the son implies that he values what insight has to provide for him, and it is also his admission that he lacks and needs understanding, and that implies that he has the humble attitude that is essential for learning. The son wants to learn what he does not yet know, so he directs his attention to what he can learn as God teaches him through the sage. Rather than resisting his teacher, the son welcomes the opportunity to learn and to grow in understanding. His positive response reveals that he values the instruction he is receiving.

Verse 4 concludes the conditions (*if*) in verses 1–4 and prepares for the consequences (*then*) beginning in verse 5. The son must *look* diligently for wisdom, not just give it a passing, casual glance. He needs to value understanding as a priceless treasure,[5] because, as Proverbs 3:13–15 exclaims,

---

[3] M. V. Fox, *Proverbs 1 – 9*, AYB 18A (New Haven: Yale University Press, 2000), p. 109.

[4] K. T. Aitken, *Proverbs*, DSB (Philadelphia: Westminster, 1976), p. 27.

[5] A. E. Hill, *NIDOTTE* 2:377, observes that *maṭmôn* refers to a buried, hidden treasure that requires effort to be found.

> Blessed are those who find wisdom,
>> those who gain understanding,
> for she is more profitable than silver
>> and yields better returns than gold.
> She is more precious than rubies;
>> nothing you desire can compare with her.

Wisdom is here described in attractive terms, as inviting and desirable to the learner, but it will take focused intention and diligent effort for him to find wisdom and understanding. It will not just fall into his lap. To get wisdom and its attendant benefits, the learner must seek it carefully and search for it as the treasure it is. Only by seeking will wisdom be found.

2. Finding wisdom (2:5–11)

The conjunction *then* that begins both verse 5 and verse 9 introduces the consequences that come to the one who searches for wisdom (cf. 1–4). This indicates that the consequences of verses 5–11 cannot be attained until the conditions in verses 1–4 have been met. Searching for wisdom leads to the fear of the Lord in verse 5. Proverbs 9:10 states that the fear of the Lord, that is, reverence for the Lord manifested in obedience to his commands, is the essence of wisdom, and therefore it is the goal of the search for wisdom. In understanding the fear of the Lord, the son will find the knowledge of God. This is not just knowledge *about* God, but a personal knowledge *of* God that causes one to follow his way. It can be compared to the difference between a detective who has thoroughly investigated a criminal and so knows all about him, and a husband who over decades of marriage has come to know and to love his wife intimately. In God's school of wisdom we do indeed learn theology, so that we know about what God is like, but we also come to know God personally as we walk with him through the ups and downs and the twists and turns of life. The *knowledge of God*, then, speaks of fellowship with God and loyalty to him.[6] The search for wisdom is definitely worth the assiduous effort, because it yields a great treasure indeed, the treasure of truly knowing

---

[6] B. K. Waltke, *The Book of Proverbs Chapters 1–15*, NICOT (Grand Rapids: Eerdmans, 2004), p. 223, notes well, 'In short, "knowledge of God" refers to personal intimacy with him through obedience to his word (cf. 1 Sam. 3:7): the notions of cognitive response to his revelation and existential intimacy and obedience are inseparable.'

the Lord. That knowledge of God does not come easily or quickly, and it may take us on a painful path beset with adversity, but it is worth it all. In Philippians 3:7–8, Paul reflects on this calculation in his own life as he says,

> But whatever were gains to me I now consider loss for the sake of Christ. What is more, I consider everything a loss because of the surpassing worth of knowing Christ Jesus my Lord, for whose sake I have lost all things. I consider them garbage, that I may gain Christ.

The Lord is both the source and the goal of wisdom, so to find wisdom one must look to the Lord, because he is the one who gives it (6). The Lord's wisdom comes through the knowledge and the understanding that he communicates, particularly through his Word. The flow of this passage is that 'To seek true wisdom (vv. 1–4) is to find God (v. 5), and God gives wisdom that leads to himself (v. 6).'[7] Human teachers are important in assisting learners towards wisdom, so they deserve our careful attention and responsive attitude. Ultimately, however, true wisdom comes from the Lord, and we must seek it in him. The teacher's role is to point the learner towards the Lord, which is a process of spiritual direction or guidance. Wisdom does not find its ultimate source in the teacher, but rather the teacher guides the learner towards the Lord, in whom all wisdom finds its source.

A good example of this dynamic can be seen in the response by the Bereans to Paul's ministry to them in Acts 17:11: 'Now the Berean Jews were of more noble character than those in Thessalonica, for they received the message with great eagerness and examined the Scriptures every day to see if what Paul said was true.' The Bereans paid careful attention to their human teacher Paul as he instructed them, but then they evaluated all that he said by the standard of the Scriptures, because they rightly regarded the Lord, and not Paul, as their final authority. Not even as eminent a teacher as the apostle Paul could supplant the Lord as the source of knowledge for them. This is important for us to remember when prominent leaders can foster a cult of personality that exalts themselves rather than pointing their followers towards the Lord.

---

[7] Aitken, *Proverbs*, p. 30. Similarly, Fox, *Proverbs 1 – 9*, p. 114, states, 'God is the source of wisdom, and in seeking it one is in effect seeking him. Enlightenment draws its possessor toward the source of knowledge.'

In verse 7, the sage uses two images to communicate how the Lord gives wisdom. First, he *holds success in store*, or keeps it in readiness (cf. 1), for those who are upright, because they orient their lives according to the Lord's standard. This success is not the fleeting pleasure and prosperity that folly falsely promises to the youth in Proverbs 1:10–19, but it is *tûšiyyâ*, sound judgment that leads to abiding success.[8] Second, as a *shield* the Lord protects those who maintain a blameless walk before him. The Lord desires his people to walk before him and be blameless (as he called Abram to do in Gen. 17:1), that is, to live lives of integrity as they obey him consistently. This is not a life of moral perfection, because 'If we claim to be without sin, we deceive ourselves and the truth is not in us.'[9] It is, however, a life marked by a consistent pattern of obedience to the Lord. This is the kind of life that imitates the faithfulness of the Lord by its faithfulness to him and to his Word.

Continuing the image into verse 8, the Lord is actively involved in guarding and protecting his people along their way. In guarding them, the Lord keeps his people from danger and preserves them from damage.[10] The Lord's faithful people[11] are kept by his faithful protection, which is portrayed memorably in Psalm 121. That song of trust concludes on a reassuring note that evokes confidence in God's people:

> The LORD will keep you from all harm –
> he will watch over your life;
> the LORD will watch over your coming and going
> both now and for evermore.

Verse 9 begins with the same phrase as verse 5, *Then you will understand*. Here, searching for wisdom leads to understanding, or clear thinking about life and the ability to discern between competing alternatives. The Lord's wisdom and protection (6–8) enable the son to understand all the good values for life. Specifically, he understands what is *right*, what is *just* and what is *fair*,[12] and all of these qualities are

---

8 L. Goldberg, *TWOT* 1:413.

9 1 John 1:8.

10 Waltke, *Proverbs Chapters 1–15*, pp. 225–226.

11 The Hebrew term translated as 'faithful' is *ḥāsîd*, which is related to *ḥesed*, a frequent word in the Old Testament referring to the faithful, steadfast, loyal love of the Lord.

12 H. Olivier, *NIDOTTE* 2:567–568, discusses how the Hebrew term *mêšārîm*, translated here as 'fair', has the nuance of ruling with equity rather than partiality, as the Lord's rule is depicted in Ps. 9:8[9].

summed up as *every good path* or pattern for life. Elsewhere in the Old Testament, all of these behaviours of righteousness, justice and fairness are also stated as attributes of the Lord, because at its root wisdom is the imitation of God. Godly wisdom produces good character that reflects God's values.

The Lord gives his wisdom (6) to the one who searches for it (4). Wisdom then enters into the entire person (10), because the *heart* (*lēb* as in 2) encompasses the mind, the feelings and the will. Stated in parallel terms, the Lord's gift of *knowledge* gives pleasure to the *soul*, or the total inner person. The book of Proverbs has often been viewed as teaching success or shrewdness in life, and some have treated it as a handbook for how to succeed in business,[13] in relationships and in other human endeavours. Proverbs does speak to those subjects, but that is a superficial approach to the content of this wisdom book, merely the tip of the iceberg of its teaching. For example, verse 10 teaches far more than practical skill for making a living; wisdom leads to the joy of a delighted life.[14]

When the Lord's wisdom takes over the heart of a person, it provides protection for life. Using the same verbs as in verse 8, the sage says in verse 11 that the Lord works through his gifts of *discretion* and *understanding* to *protect* and to *guard* his people. Left to themselves, human beings are not skilful enough to resist the allurements of evil and folly, and the next section, 2:12–19, proceeds to describe the kinds of threats from wicked men and the adulterous woman that must be resisted and avoided. To do this, one needs to have discretion (*mĕzimmâ*), which along with understanding (*tĕbûnâ*) causes one to be resourceful, with clear thinking that leads to good choices in life.[15] By contrast, without the discernment and understanding that God's wisdom affords, we are left vulnerable to folly and wickedness that conspire to lead us into disaster. For this reason, Psalm 1:1–2 both warns against the wrong way and encourages towards the right way when it exclaims,

> Blessed is the one
>> who does not walk in step with the wicked

---

[13] See, for example, S. Marr, *Proverbs for Business: Daily Wisdom for the Workplace* (Grand Rapids: Revell, 2006).

[14] Verse 10 is reminiscent of the memorable words of the Westminster Catechism: 'The chief end of man is to glorify God and to enjoy him for ever.'

[15] J. E. Hartley, *NIDOTTE* 1:1112; Fox, *Proverbs 1 – 9*, p. 116.

or stand in the way that sinners take
  or sit in the company of mockers,
but whose delight is in the law of the LORD,
  and who meditates on his law day and night.

3. Learning in God's school

Proverbs 2:1–11 presents a vital emphasis that recurs throughout the book of Proverbs as it speaks about the role of the learner in God's school of wisdom[16] In the learning process, the teacher of wisdom has the great responsibility of guiding students towards skill in living as the Lord intends. Students, however, also play an essential role if they are to become wise as the Lord wants them to be. If we are going to learn what the Lord wants us to know and to live as he wants us to live, then we are going to need to accept our responsibility as good learners. The book of Proverbs shows us how to do that.

In Proverbs, it is clear that the learner must *receive* wisdom. This requires humility that is willing to learn from others who are wise. It begins with an attentive spirit (1–2), rather than a hostile attitude that refuses to listen or a proud attitude that thinks it has nothing to learn. As Proverbs 1:5 says, 'the wise listen and add to their learning'. By contrast, the refusal to listen leads to painful consequences, as personified Wisdom explains in Proverbs 1:30–33:

Since they would not accept my advice
  and spurned my rebuke,
they will eat the fruit of their ways
  and be filled with the fruit of their schemes.
For the waywardness of the simple will kill them,
  and the complacency of fools will destroy them;
but whoever listens to me will live in safety
  and be at ease, without fear of harm.

In addition to receiving wisdom, the learner must *respond* to wisdom, by joining living to listening. The sage says,

---

[16] This section is an abridged version of a chapter on the role of the student in D. J. Estes, *Hear, My Son*, NSBT 4 (Downers Grove: InterVarsity Press, 1997), pp. 135–149.

My son, do not let wisdom and understanding out of your sight,
  preserve sound judgment and discretion.[17]

It takes conscious effort to remember what has been taught. Learning requires active involvement, and not just passive awareness. The learner must take wisdom to heart, and then turn it into habits of behaviour. Wisdom is more than just knowing what is right; rather *what* we know should change *how* we act. Learning must transform living. For some Christians who have been around the teaching of God's truth for years, even decades, this can be a significant issue. Because they hear God's Word frequently and they are even conversant with theology, they may suppose that they are just fine in their spiritual lives. However, the Lord calls us both to learn and to live his Word. When we learn God's truth but do not live it, it is as though calluses begin to grow on our souls, so that we become increasingly insensitive to what God is teaching us and how he is reproving us. When this condition continues over an extended period of time, it will likely result in major spiritual problems in our lives.

Furthermore, the learner must *value* wisdom by loving the Lord's way wholeheartedly. When personified Wisdom speaks in Proverbs 8:10–11, she says,

Choose my instruction instead of silver,
  knowledge rather than choice gold,
for wisdom is more precious than rubies,
  and nothing you desire can compare with her.

Only the Lord's wisdom is worthy of our deepest love and delight, and if we love wisdom, then we must seek it diligently. Godly wisdom should not be viewed merely as an elective course or as a leisure pursuit, but it must instead become the passion of our lives, as the sage urges in Proverbs 4:5–8:

Get wisdom, get understanding;
  do not forget my words or turn away from them.
Do not forsake wisdom, and she will protect you;
  love her, and she will watch over you.

---

[17] Prov. 3:21.

The beginning of wisdom is this: get wisdom.
  Though it cost all you have, get understanding.
Cherish her, and she will exalt you;
  embrace her, and she will honour you.

Above all, as learners we must *assimilate* wisdom, so that we truly become wise. As we listen to wisdom, live it out and love it, we progressively develop an inner compass directed towards the Lord, which Proverbs describes as living in the fear of the Lord (1:7; 9:10). We develop a heart that respects and reveres the Lord throughout all of life (4:20–27), and that causes us to become men and women of integrity. Integrity means having all of one's life connected in a firm moral unity. Those who excel as learners in God's school of wisdom are people of integrity, because all the aspects of their lives are linked together by their commitment to revere the Lord. They do not live one way at worship and another way at work. Their lives Monday through Saturday are consistent with how they present themselves on Sunday at church. They are not hypocritical or inconsistent, but as they assimilate God's wisdom they increasingly manifest his values and follow his way in every part of their lives – in their actions, their attitudes, their motives, their ambitions – whether they are at home, at work or at play.

4. Concluding comment

To learn wisdom well, we must become good learners in the Lord's school. That means that we need to listen attentively to what our divine teacher says by maintaining regular time in his Word. It is not enough, however, just to show up at church on Sunday morning; we need to listen carefully to God's truth whenever it is proclaimed publicly, and also when we read it privately. When God speaks, we must hear and heed what he is saying to us. We must also respond to wisdom by living what we have learned from God's Word. Most of us know God's truth far better than we live it, so we need to become intentional about making *what* we know become *how* we live. Learning in God's school must not be done with an attitude of dull duty, as though it is the same old, same old message we have heard countless times before, but rather we must receive it with a sense of delight as we value his wisdom. Finally, we must commit ourselves to lives of Christian integrity as we welcome God's wisdom to take control of our entire lives. Wisdom is not just *knowing* what God wants us to know, or even *doing* what God wants us to do, but it is pre-eminently *becoming* what God wants us to be. In New Testament language, it is becoming conformed to the image of Christ (Rom. 8:29), which is God's plan for his people. We can be certain that the Lord will fully accomplish his role as our teacher of wisdom. The question is whether we will accept our role as learners of wisdom. To the extent that we are good learners in God's school of wisdom, we will become the kind of wise and godly men and women that the Lord desires us to be.

Proverbs 9

3. The contrasting paths of wisdom and folly

Proverbs 9, as it brings the prologue in Proverbs 1 – 9 to a rhetorical climax, presents a clear contrast between wisdom and folly, the two contrasting paths that lie before each person. Because the primary audience of Proverbs is the 'son', a young man on the verge of adulthood, wisdom and folly are poetically portrayed as two women who invite the youth to join them for a meal they have prepared. By this pair of literary images, the moral choice before the youth is presented in terms that capture well the powerful emotional forces that are in play both for the young man in the ancient world and for all people in every time in history, right down to the present day, when we are bombarded by marketing that is calculated to allure us.

The invitation by Woman Wisdom is heard first in 9:1–6, and then in 9:13–18 Woman Folly issues her invitation. In the central passage of the chapter, 9:7–12, wisdom and folly are contrasted, so that the issues at stake in this decision are made exceedingly clear. The youth must decide which invitation to accept, and the choice he makes will make all the difference in his life. This antithesis in Proverbs 9, coming at the end of the initial section of the book, sets the scene for the wisdom sayings that follow in Proverbs 10 – 31, most of which are presented as sets of contrasts. Sometimes the contrast is drawn between the person who is wise and the person who is foolish. Other times the emphasis is on the contrasting actions or attitudes that evidence either righteousness or wickedness. Frequently, the end result of either life or death is in view. In these various ways, the sayings in Proverbs 10 – 31 spell out in specific life experiences what the instructions in Proverbs 1 – 9 have developed as more general patterns. One commentator notes well the stark differences detailed in Proverbs 9:

> Wisdom is depicted as a noble patroness and Folly as a pretentious hostess. Both invite the gullible to their houses for a feast. Wisdom, out of true love, competes for the hearts of the uncommitted; Folly, out of erotic lust, competes for their bodies. Wisdom invites them to leave behind their old identification and become wise at her sumptuous feast; Folly lures those who have been going straight to turn aside, mindless of the consequences, at her profligate and self-indulgent meal. Those who accept Wisdom's invitation will live; the apostates will die.[1]

1. Invitation by Wisdom (9:1–6)

In verse 1, Wisdom is pictured as a woman who has built a luxurious house. This seven-pillared house suggests a stable, sizable and beautiful building, perhaps even a palace. It is likely that the number of pillars indicated the great wealth and high social status of the owner,[2] so Wisdom's house would qualify as a mansion. This opulent house has been carefully planned and expertly constructed to host many guests, as Wisdom appeals to *all who are simple* (4).

Wisdom has gone to great effort and expense to prepare for her guests (2). She prepared a sumptuous feast, featuring meat, which in the ancient world was a rare treat reserved for very special occasions. She also mixed wine, probably with spices (cf. Song 8:2), to drink with the meal. In addition, Wisdom set a lovely table, arranging it in order, not haphazardly,[3] another indication of the great care she invested as she prepared to invite her guests to join her. Everything about her table is done with the utmost care and propriety, because Woman Wisdom is the epitome of all that is good and right and lovely. Out of her goodness she prepares what is best for the young she invites to join her. Nothing is second-rate or careless or tawdry, but all she does is marked by excellence as she appeals to the best instincts of her anticipated guests.

---

[1] B. K. Waltke, *The Book of Proverbs Chapters 1–15*, NICOT (Grand Rapids: Eerdmans, 2004), p. 429.

[2] R. N. Whybray, *Proverbs*, NCBC (Grand Rapids: Eerdmans, 1994), p. 143.

[3] V. P. Hamilton, *NIDOTTE* 3:536.

With all preparations completed for the banquet, Wisdom sends out her maidens to invite the youths to come to her house (3; cf. Matt. 22:2–3). She herself calls out publicly from the highest point of the city, indicating that her invitation is public and is addressed to all who will come (cf. Prov. 1:21; 8:2–3). This is so different from the furtive solicitation by the adulterous woman in Proverbs 7:10–15:

> Then out came a woman to meet him,
> > dressed like a prostitute and with crafty intent.
> (She is unruly and defiant,
> > her feet never stay at home;
> now in the street, now in the squares,
> > at every corner she lurks.)
> She took hold of him and kissed him
> > and with a brazen face she said:

> 'Today I fulfilled my vows,
> > and I have food from my fellowship offering at home.
> So I came out to meet you;
> > I looked for you and have found you!'

By contrast, Woman Wisdom has nothing to hide and nothing of which to be ashamed. She has only the most honourable intentions in mind for those who will accept her invitation.

Verses 4–6 contain the words of the call by Woman Wisdom stated in verse 3. She invites all who are *simple* (*petî*, as in 1:4) to come to her house. This untrained youth is not yet a mocker, but rather is still teachable and able to learn.[4] These intended guests are also described as *those who have no sense*, literally, 'lacking of heart', because their incapability to make good decisions makes them vulnerable to temptation and manipulation (cf. 7:7; 12:11; 17:18). Youths like this are not yet set in their ways, and they can still choose to follow either the path of wisdom or the path of folly. Wisdom calls them to change their direction and to come to her house. However, if they decline her invitation, they may well set themselves up to accept the alternative offer from Folly (13–18).

---

[4] C.-W. Pan, *NIDOTTE* 3:715, concludes his detailed analysis of the Hebrew term, 'In summary, the *petî* is an ignorant and simple-minded person who does not hate knowledge but is receptive and always prepared to learn or be taught.'

All of the careful preparations by Woman Wisdom detailed in verse 2 culminate in her invitation in verse 5. She invites the youths to enjoy the lavish meal she has planned and provided for them, not just for the delectable food she has prepared but even more for the table fellowship she has envisioned. Her intentions are all and only good as she calls the youths to dine with her. In effect, she is inviting them to enter into a loving relationship with her.

The youths to whom Woman Wisdom appeals must choose either to take the path of wisdom or to default to the path of folly. Unlike Peter Pan, they must not insist, 'I won't grow up!', but must assume adult responsibilities and make adult decisions, rather than clinging to an adolescent attitude that avoids commitment. In other words, the path of wisdom must be chosen, and that means leaving one's *simple ways* in order to *walk in the way of insight* (6).

2. Contrast between wisdom and folly (9:7–12)

Before the invitation by Woman Folly is articulated in verses 13–18, the middle section of Proverbs 9 contrasts the two paths of wisdom and folly that can be taken by the youth. It is crucial to reach youths while they are still pliable, because that time will pass. The further people proceed down the path of folly, the less they tolerate the voice of wisdom, and once they reach the point of being mockers or wicked, it is likely too late to reach them. The *mocker* 'is the person who will not live by wise and moral teachings and is not content to let others do so without his cynical mocking'.[5] The root of the mocker's resistance to reproof is pride (21:24), so one who tries to correct a mocker only gets insults in return (cf. 13:1; 15:12).[6] Wicked people hate wisdom and they abuse those who rebuke them. Because they reject the message, they also reject the messenger.

Do not rebuke in verse 8 continues and extends the thought of verse 7. The same words of reproof can provoke widely contrasting responses, just as the heat of the sun both melts wax and hardens clay. For well-intentioned parents, teachers and friends, there are times when reproof can be a waste

[5] A. P. Ross, 'Proverbs', *EBC*, vol. 5 (Grand Rapids: Zondervan, 1991), p. 949.

[6] M. V. Fox, *Proverbs 1 – 9*, AYB 18A (New Haven: Yale University Press, 2000), p. 307, observes: 'The lēṣ, arrogant and contemptuous of others, cannot tolerate rebuke. Such a man will react with ire and contempt to any affront to his self-image. Acceptance of criticism requires the wisdom of humility, meaning a recognition of one's own limitations.'

of time and has an unnecessary cost, because mockers are impervious and antagonistic to rebuke (cf. 26:4). By contrast, the wise receive and welcome rebuke (cf. 12:1), because 'The wise are shown to be wise by their openness and love of wisdom. So eager are they to learn that they regard those who correct them as their friends.'[7] Those who are wise accept rebuke, and they appreciate those who rebuke them for their benefit.

Verse 9 continues to speak of the wise person who sees beyond the immediate sting of reproof to welcome the long-term benefit it provides. As already noted in the initial invitation to wisdom in Proverbs 1:5, the truly wise person is teachable and therefore welcomes the opportunity to learn and to grow more. In contrast to fools and mockers who think they know it all and are indignant when they are reproved, the wise realize how much they need to learn and to accept additional instruction. As often in the book of Proverbs (cf. 10:31; 11:30; 23:24), in this verse *wise* is paralleled to *righteous* (see chapter 12). Those who are wise are righteous because they align their lives to the Lord's standard, and as a result they are lifelong learners in God's school of wisdom.

In verse 10, the motto of Proverbs expressed first in 1:7 is restated in similar language at the end of the initial section of Proverbs 1 – 9, only here the fear of the Lord is the beginning of *wisdom*, whereas in the earlier verse the fear of the Lord is the beginning of *knowledge*. As the beginning of wisdom, the fear of the Lord is not like the first stage of a space rocket that is later jettisoned, but rather it is the essence of every aspect of wisdom, as letters are the building blocks of language, and notes of music.[8] Wisdom teachers carefully observed the creation to derive lessons for life from it, and in that activity wisdom worships the Creator. One cannot disrespect the Lord and be truly wise, because that is the mark of folly. Fearing the Lord is knowing him and revering him as he really is. As one scholar states well,

> One fears a superior power, so to fear Yahweh means to acknowledge
> that Yahweh is vastly more powerful than oneself. It is to put oneself in
> a position that will elicit obedience. It is the beginning of wisdom, which
> suggests that there is no wisdom apart from Yahweh.[9]

---

[7] R. J. Clifford, *Proverbs*, OTL (Louisville: Westminster John Knox, 1999), p. 106.

[8] For an excellent theological discussion of the fear of the Lord, see H. Blocher, 'The Fear of the Lord as the "Principle" of Wisdom', *TynBul* 28 (1977), pp. 3–28.

[9] T. Longman, *Proverbs*, BCOTWP (Grand Rapids: Baker Academic, 2006), p. 219.

In verse 11, the initial conjunction is likely better translated 'surely' rather than 'for', because it does not introduce a reason for the previous verse. It is evident that wisdom leads to a more fulfilling life, which is consistent with Proverbs 9:6; 12:28; 19:23; 22:4. As a wisdom saying, this is a generalization, and it is not intended to cover every specific situation or every individual life, because there are observable cases in which wicked people do enjoy long lives (cf. Pss 49 and 73), and righteous people can suffer (cf. Job) and even die young.

Verse 12 relates directly to verses 7–9, and more indirectly to verses 1–6. As there are two invitations by Woman Wisdom and Woman Folly, so there are two responses that lead to two ends. How people respond to reproof reveals whether they are wise or foolish. Accepting the invitation by Woman Wisdom (4–6) will be rewarded, but scoffing at her invitation will only lead to harm. It is clear in Proverbs that the path of wisdom leads to reward, but the path of folly leads to regret. All individuals must bear the responsibility for their response to Woman Wisdom's invitation. What was true in the ancient world in which Proverbs was written is as true for us today in the twenty-first century. We, too, must choose to respond either to wisdom or to folly, and we too will experience the good or bad consequences of whichever invitation we choose to accept.

3. Invitation by Folly (9:13–18)

The woman who is described in verses 13–18 is the personification of folly, who appeared previously in Proverbs in chapters 2, 5 and 7, and who is the antithesis of personified Wisdom in 9:1–6. In fact, she is a parody of Woman Wisdom, because 'The author is less interested in her than in Wisdom and depicts her in pallid colors, with little narrative development. The motive for the creation of this personification is rhetorical, to create a symmetry between wisdom and folly.'[10] In contrast to Woman Wisdom, who prepares her banquet carefully (2, 5), Woman Folly is careless. Instead of teaching the simple ones (13; cf. 1:4), Woman Folly herself is *simple*. She *knows nothing*, so she can teach nothing; her speech is just a lot of noise.[11]

---

[10] Fox, *Proverbs 1 – 9*, p. 300.

[11] The term *unruly* is *hōmîyâ*, which as in Prov. 7:11 ('noise') refers to one who is loud, defiant and undisciplined. Cf. W. R. Domeris, *NIDOTTE* 1:1043.

Woman Folly as presented in this section is just trouble for the youth, a disaster waiting to happen.[12]

Woman Folly sets up her seat in a prominent place at the highest point of the city as a direct rival and alternative to Woman Wisdom. Both in her location (cf. 3) and in her call (cf. 4–6), Woman Folly tries to imitate Woman Wisdom. However, nothing in the description of Woman Folly in verses 14–15 is on a par with the careful preparation and tasteful invitation by Woman Wisdom. Instead of sending out her servants, Woman Folly seeks to solicit those who pass by her door. Woman Folly views everybody as a potential victim, with the open door behind her endeavouring to tantalize those who pass by. She targets those who are going *straight on their way*, perhaps as in Psalm 27:11 a reference to those who are on the Lord's way. Having no consideration for their welfare, she urges the youths to forsake the way of wisdom and to come over to her way of folly. While Woman Wisdom delights those who join her, Woman Folly distracts and destroys those who hearken to her call. Though the path of the youths may necessarily pass *by* her house, if they are discerning it should not lead *into* her house. To enter there is to get sucked into her vortex of sure disaster.

Verse 16 is identical to verse 4, as Woman Folly mimics the words of Woman Wisdom to the youths. Although the words sound the same, in reality her intention is starkly different, as Woman Folly uses a deliberate strategy to deceive those who are simple. She seeks to entice them to disaster, not to delight. Those who are young have a crucial decision to make as they decide which invitation to accept. Because Woman Wisdom and Woman Folly speak with the same words, the youths must discern beyond the sound of the words to grasp the intention that animates them.

In contrast to the lavish banquet of meat and wine prepared by Woman Wisdom in verses 2 and 5, Woman Folly has not prepared properly for her guests. She offers only water instead of mixed wine, and the entrée on her menu is nondescript food instead of meat. She even brazenly acknowledges that what she offers is stolen, and yet she insists that it is sweet. This sweetness, however, may well be only a temporary sugar high (cf. 20:17) and lead to disappointment. When read in the light of Proverbs 5:15–20 and Song of Songs 4:15, her stolen water likely has an illicit sexual

---

[12] Drawing from the broader depiction of the woman of folly in Prov. 1 – 9, Waltke, *Proverbs Chapters 1–15*, p. 444, concludes: 'Without moral knowledge she also necessarily lacks benevolent shrewdness and discretion (see 8:12, 14). She has no clear concept of her goals because she has no sure values. As a result, she is left to her own will to pleasure and power, determined not to know that the end thereof is death.'

reference, which is reinforced when she speaks of bread eaten in secret (cf. 30:20). Woman Folly allures the youths with what they know is bad and wrong, as she appeals to their baser instincts. Nevertheless, even though it is a set-up for disaster to accept a tawdry invitation like this, this is precisely what so many people do as they choose the path of folly rather than the path of wisdom. Drawn in by their senses rather than directed by good sense, they succumb to Woman Folly's siren song, and like Odysseus they pay her terrible price.

The sage concludes in verse 18 that what Woman Folly offers is all sizzle and no substance, which is the classic bait-and-switch scheme used by hucksters and con artists. In accepting the invitation by Woman Folly, the youths are ignorant, perhaps willingly ignorant, of what the facts really are, and that ignorance proves to be their fatal flaw. Folly has not been honest, because in the house behind her open door are the dead. This is not the kind of party the youths expected, because in reality her house 'is not a home but a mausoleum', and 'if you enter it you will not leave it alive'.[13] Just as Woman Wisdom's invitation leads to life (6), so Folly's invitation eventuates in death (cf. 2:18–19; 5:5; 7:26–27).[14] Those who enter her house must abandon all hope, because their destruction is assured.

4. The fear of the Lord is the beginning of wisdom

Embedded in Proverbs 9 is the key concept of the book of Proverbs, that *The fear of the LORD is the beginning of wisdom* (10). The expression *fear of the LORD* occurs at the beginning of Proverbs in 1:7, at the end in 31:30, and a total of eighteen times throughout the collection. It also occurs in other wisdom writings, such as Job 28:28; Psalm 111:10; and Ecclesiastes 12:13. This principle is rooted in Old Testament law (Deut. 10:12; Josh. 24:14), and it is reaffirmed in the prophets. Proverbs 2:5 indicates that the fear of the Lord is both the starting point and the final goal of wisdom. It is the ethical principle that guides human beings along the path of wisdom that leads to life.

The Hebrew term for *fear* (*yir'â*) refers to overwhelming awe that causes human beings to tremble before the Lord in dread or to turn to him in

---

[13] R. L. Alden, *Proverbs* (Grand Rapids: Baker, 1983), p. 80.

[14] For a succinct discussion of death in the Old Testament, see D. Kidner, *Proverbs: An Introduction and Commentary*, TOTC 17 (Nottingham: Inter-Varsity Press, 2008 [1964]), pp. 51–52.

reverence. It is the appropriate stance humans should take before the awesome Creator of the universe, in contrast to the Greek concept of *hubris*, in which prideful humans like Achilles and Oedipus rebel against the deity. When we fear the Lord, we embrace what he desires and we avoid that of which he disapproves because we reverence who he is, and therefore 'To fear the LORD is to hate evil.'[15] The book of Proverbs does not just give practical advice about how to be a nice and successful person, but rather it grounds all of wisdom ultimately in one's relationship with the Lord. The person who fears the Lord humbly submits to his word and faithfully follows his way, because the foundational principle of wisdom is reverence for the Lord that causes one to obey what he says. Of far greater consequence than our position, power, fame and achievements is how we regard the Lord. No matter how much we may attain and accomplish in life, all pales in comparison to the central issue: Do we truly revere the Lord?

5. Concluding comment

With its two contrasting invitations in verses 1–6 and 13–18, and its central section describing two contrasting responses in verses 7–12, Proverbs 9 demonstrates that the wise person reveres the Lord by valuing even the reproof of wisdom above the enticements of folly. Although the sayings of this collection are especially directed towards the young, they require a response from readers of all ages. Every person every day receives numerous invitations both from voices of wisdom and from voices of folly, and each of the invitations calls for a response either to accept it or to reject it.

In evaluating these invitations, if we simply lean on our own understanding we will certainly default to the way of folly, because as Proverbs 14:12 observes,

> There is a way that appears to be right,
> but in the end it leads to death.

To choose the way of wisdom, we must examine everything through the lens of the fear of the Lord, asking if the alternative we are considering

---

[15] Prov. 8:13.

reveres the Lord by obeying his Word, or if it disrespects the Lord by disobeying his Word. When the Bible does not speak specifically about the matter, we must ask what course of action is consistent with the character of the Lord as revealed in his Word, because all that the Lord commands flows out of who the Lord is.

Ultimately, we must not live to do as we please or to please other people who influence us. Rather, when we fear the Lord we seek to please him by obeying what he says and by following his example, because that is the way of wisdom. To disobey his Word and to diverge from his example is to disrespect him, and that is the way of folly.

Proverbs 8

4. The personification of wisdom

Several times in Proverbs 1 – 9 wisdom is personified and is pictured as calling out to people, particularly the youth, to respond to her. Wisdom speaks in Proverbs 1:20–33, and she issues an invitation in Proverbs 9:1–6, which is then parodied by Folly in 9:13–18. The most extensive passage in which personified Wisdom is heard is Proverbs 8, and this long speech is worthy of our careful reading. As important as it is for us to hear *about* wisdom, it is even more crucial that we hear *from* Wisdom as she speaks to us. Even now in the twenty-first century, her voice speaks to us today as Wisdom calls us to listen to her and to keep her ways. In these days when we are inundated by the sound of so many voices clamouring for our attention on television, radio and the Internet, it is vital that we attend carefully to what Wisdom says in this chapter.

1. The call of Wisdom (8:1–5)

Before the voice of Wisdom is heard beginning in verse 4, the sage introduces her in verses 1–3. In this chapter, Wisdom is personified as a woman who acts as a teacher and speaks in the tone of a prophet. Like a town crier ringing a handbell and shouting 'Oyez', Wisdom is portrayed as calling out to all people (cf. 4) as she initiates communication with human beings, all of whom need to heed her voice. This in fact is the voice of God, because Wisdom 'is the divine summons issued in and through creation, sounding through the vast realm of the created world, and heard on the level of human experience'.[1]

In verses 2–3, Wisdom calls out in the centre of life, as five places in the ancient city are cited. It is significant that

> Wisdom does not recoil from the rough and tumble of the market-place with its busyness and noise. She does not reserve her discourse for a learned audience or esoteric circle, claiming immunity from the cut and thrust of a less exalted and refined level of debate and disdaining to mix with the crowd.[2]

Rather than waiting for people to seek her out, Wisdom goes to where the people are. Wisdom, then, is not truth that is confined only to the temple precincts or examined in the scholar's study, but truth that is intended to be learned and lived out in the world.[3] Rather than yielding the field to folly (cf. 7:12), Wisdom fights for every inch as she appeals to all people to hear and to heed her words. The *gate* was the strategic centre of the ancient city, and it is there that Wisdom *cries aloud*, the Hebrew verb *rnn* having the nuance of a loud, enthusiastic yell.[4] Nothing about Wisdom's call is secret, because she has nothing to hide and everything to proclaim publicly.

Beginning in verse 4, Wisdom speaks, as in the opening scene of a movie when the camera zooms in and the voice-over is heard for the first time. The words *To you* signal a direct, emphatic appeal. Wisdom makes a broad, universal call as she appeals to all people everywhere to listen to her. Her call is not limited to a specific group, but is intended for all human beings. Wisdom has the universal answer for a universal audience. In particular, her call in verse 5 is directed to the *simple* youth (*petî* as in 1:4; 9:4, 16) and the *foolish*. Wisdom urges even those who seem uninterested to listen to her, because apart from her they will not *gain*

---

[1] R. E. Murphy, *The Tree of Life: An Exploration of Biblical Wisdom Literature*, 3rd edn (Grand Rapids: Eerdmans, 2002), p. 138.

[2] W. McKane, *Proverbs*, OTL (Philadelphia: Westminster, 1970), p. 344.

[3] D. Cox, *Proverbs with an Introduction to Sapiential Books*, Old Testament Message 17 (Wilmington: Michael Glazier, 1982), p. 148, states that Wisdom's 'imperative is not delivered in the atrium of the temple, but in the ambient of secular affairs. Wisdom is competing for attention in precisely that arena where people live their lives, and where they are already preoccupied with affairs. Wisdom's place is thus not the ivory tower, but the arena of daily life, and she wishes to become involved with mankind at every level.'

[4] T. Longman, *NIDOTTE* 3:1129.

prudence (ʿormâ), the ability to navigate life successfully by using reason and forethought.[5]

2. The credibility of Wisdom (8:6–11)

In appealing to people to listen to her, Wisdom indicates that those who hear her must choose to become learners with responsive attitudes towards her (6). Wisdom is not crass in what she says, as Woman Folly is (9:13–18), but she speaks what is *trustworthy* and *right* (cf. 23:16). Wisdom evidences all of the best values, in contrast to how Folly appeals to the baser instincts of the youth in 1:10–19 and 9:16–17.

What Wisdom says is *true* (7), that is, it is reliable and faithful (ʾĕmet), a term used often in the Old Testament for the trustworthiness of the Lord's character and his word.[6] She does not make common cause with wickedness, because she detests it as an abomination, as the Lord does (6:16–17). In contrast to our contemporary world, in which it is often difficult to distinguish between genuine and fake news, for Wisdom there is a clear line separating truth from wickedness, and Wisdom always takes the side of what is true. Similarly, what Wisdom says is always *just*, and never *crooked or perverse* (8). Nothing that Wisdom says diverges from the Lord's righteous standard,[7] but she always leads in the Lord's straight way (cf. 2:12–15).

How the voice of Wisdom is perceived varies depending on the people who hear it (9). Those who have found knowledge by fearing the Lord (1:7) discern Wisdom's words as plain and straightforward, and they 'have no difficulty in understanding Wisdom's teaching'.[8] In fact, as Proverbs 9:9 indicates, those who are discerning are able to value and to understand the message of Wisdom and to gain more learning. Starting down the path of wisdom leads one to greater insight for life.

---

[5] T. Longman, *Proverbs*, BCOTWP (Grand Rapids: Baker Academic, 2006), p. 200, explains that 'prudence describes one's ability to use reason, in context and under the fear of God, to navigate the problems of life. Prudence carefully considers a situation before rushing in. It implies coolheadedness. Prudence is closely associated with wisdom and is the cure for simplemindedness.'

[6] R. W. L. Moberly, *NIDOTTE* 1:428.

[7] J. A. Kitchen, *Proverbs*, Mentor Commentary (Fearn, Ross-shire: Christian Focus, 2006), p. 180, explains the sense of ʿqš: 'The word for "perverted" is used elsewhere in Proverbs 2:15; 11:20; 17:20; 19:1; 22:5; 28:6, 18. The word pictures that which has been twisted or distorted from its original design. It has become a parody or caricature of the original. Words are not intended to be used in "crooked" ways, that is, to mislead. Wisdom's words, thus, are pure and in accord with God's original design. They do not mislead.'

[8] R. N. Whybray, *Proverbs*, NCBC (Grand Rapids: Eerdmans, 1994), p. 123.

Wisdom continues to call out to all people (cf. 4–5) to value her instruction more than riches (10–11). In language that echoes Job 28:15–19, Wisdom describes herself as worth far more than silver and the finest gold (cf. Ps. 19:10; Prov. 3:14; 16:16). People typically choose to pursue what they most value, and that choice inevitably shapes their lives. Wisdom is so much more valuable than the lesser values to which many people devote their lives. To seek wisdom is to seek the best that the Lord has for one's life; anything else is bound to disappoint. When human beings value material riches above wisdom, they in fact settle for a bad deal, because 'If one loves riches . . . wisdom will withdraw herself, leaving the person at best a rich fool for a while but headed for eternal death.'[9] How crucial it is to accept as credible the call of Wisdom, and to choose to respond to her and to value her above all.

3. The character of Wisdom (8:12–21)

Personified Wisdom continues to speak in the first person, as she also does in 1:20–33 and in 9:1–6. In verse 12 she describes her moral dimension, as she possesses and produces a prudent and discreet life. The term translated *discretion* is *mĕzimmâ*, which speaks of resourcefulness reflecting careful planning. This word is used elsewhere in a negative sense to refer to sinful schemes (cf. 12:2; 14:17; 24:8), but here, as in 2:11 and 5:2, it has a positive sense of having discretion and being circumspect.[10] Wisdom, then, equips a person to live capably in the world.

Wisdom does not blur the line between good and evil, because the fear of the Lord entails hating what is evil (13; cf. 16:6). In other words, one cannot at the same time both revere the Lord and befriend evil. Just as the Lord himself loves righteousness but hates wickedness (Ps. 45:7), so his people should as well (Ps. 119:163; Amos 5:15). Here the abstract *evil* is made concrete as the specific behaviours of *pride, arrogance, wickedness* and *perverse speech*. It is evident that evil affects a person's attitudes, actions and words, and all of these unrighteous behaviours are antithetical to the Lord's wisdom.

The qualities characteristic of the skilled person, such as *counsel, sound judgment* and *insight*, come from Wisdom (14), and not from human

---

9 B. K. Waltke, *The Book of Proverbs Chapters 1–15*, NICOT (Grand Rapids: Eerdmans, 2004), p. 399.

10 M. V. Fox, *Proverbs 1 – 9*, AYB 18A (New Haven: Yale University Press, 2000), p. 34.

expertise. To attain these beneficial qualities, one must receive them from Wisdom, because without Wisdom human beings default to unclear thinking. Wisdom also possesses *power*, the ability to accomplish what it knows is best. This is not power to do as one pleases, which is what the fool craves, but rather the Hebrew terms translated here as *wisdom* and *power* are used in Job 12:13 and Isaiah 11:2 to refer to attributes of God, and therefore it is power employed for the best purposes.[11]

The reference to *power* in verse 14 implies the language of government, and this leads into verses 15–16, where Wisdom declares that all human rule functions under the aegis of God's own wise rule. Although human kings may suppose they are autonomous, acting as though they are a law unto themselves, in reality they function under the authority of the sovereign Lord (cf. Dan. 2:20–21). The Lord evaluates rulers according to his own standard of justice, and holds them accountable for how they rule. It is by justice that a king gives a country stability (Prov. 29:4). To define leadership apart from wisdom is to miss the essential point, and poor leadership results when those in high position lead by folly rather than by wisdom.[12] Human leaders, then, are best evaluated by the criterion of wisdom, and not by lesser pragmatic measures. In nations in which citizens have the privilege of electing their leaders, this standard should direct God's people as they vote.

In verse 17, Wisdom speaks to the heart of the learner, as she declares that she loves those who love her (cf. 21). In the book of Proverbs, wisdom must be *learned* and *lived*, but it also must be *loved* (cf. 4:6; 29:3). Those who truly love wisdom will seek it until they find it (2:4–6), and this loving search for wisdom is equated to choosing to fear the Lord in Proverbs 1:28–29.

Perhaps echoing the Lord's gifts of wealth and honour to Solomon in 1 Kings 3:13, Wisdom states in verse 18 that she is the source of *riches and honour, enduring wealth and prosperity*. As a blessing from the Lord, Wisdom provides the kind of wealth that endures (cf. 3:10; 10:22). Unfortunately, wealth and power are often corrupted and perverted by human beings who try to gain by unjust means what Wisdom desires to give legitimately; 'The paradox is that when wealth is the chief end of life

---

[11] Kitchen, *Proverbs*, pp. 184–185.

[12] For a more detailed discussion of what the book of Proverbs teaches about wise leadership, see D. J. Estes, 'Proverbial Lessons: Leadership in the Proverbs', in B. K. Forrest and C. Roden (eds.), *Biblical Leadership: Theology for the Everyday Leader* (Grand Rapids: Kregel Academic, 2017), pp. 163–171.

it corrupts, whereas when it is subordinated to wisdom it may be enjoyed as an aspect of welfare and honour.'[13]

Picking up the comparative language of verses 10–11, Wisdom claims in verse 19 that the gold and silver that humans seek is nothing compared to her surpassing value. *Fine gold* is gold that has been highly purified from alloys, or what would approach 24-carat gold today. The fruit of wisdom exceeds even that precious treasure. Wisdom has so much to offer, if only people would love and seek it (cf. 17). Valuing anything above wisdom is a tragic miscalculation. It is a poor investment of a life, and yet how many people in our contemporary world choose to give their lives to the pursuit of wealth instead of the pursuit of wisdom.

Wisdom is not ethically ambiguous, because it is always aligned with *righteousness* (20). As the Lord rules in righteousness and justice (cf. Ps. 89:14), so Wisdom walks in them. The Lord and Wisdom, then, are always in lockstep with one another, and their way of righteousness is true life (cf. Prov. 12:28). Taking the path of Wisdom is following God's righteous way that leads to life in all of its dimensions. To diverge from the way of righteousness is both to abandon wisdom and to forsake the Lord.

Because Wisdom is better than riches (cf. 10–11, 19), she enriches all those who love her (21). She gives them a rich inheritance, which speaks not of a temporary benefit but of a permanent transfer of ownership. It is comparable to the bequeathing of a person's wealth to children in 13:22, and it is contrasted with wealth that is gained improperly and that will not endure in 20:21; 23:4–5; 28:18, 22.[14] The material riches craved and sought by human beings cannot hold a candle to what Wisdom gives. Wisdom is lavish with her generosity, as she fills the treasuries of those who love her. In the light of this reality, not to seek and love Wisdom is totally foolhardy and self-defeating.

4. The credentials of Wisdom (8:22–31)

Wisdom is not independent from the Lord, but instead has been with him from the beginning (22). Before the Lord created the world and before anything else existed, the Lord had Wisdom with him, such that Proverbs 3:19 says that it was by wisdom that the Lord laid the earth's foundation

---

[13] McKane, *Proverbs*, p. 350.

[14] Fox, *Proverbs 1 – 9*, p. 278.

(cf. Ps. 104:24). In this passage, wisdom is poetically personified so that it is presented vividly with the features of a human, but it is not a hypostasis (the essential being) of an actual heavenly person, because Wisdom speaks *about* the Lord, rather than being equated *with* the Lord. As exalted as wisdom is portrayed in this passage, it is still subservient to the Lord who made it. The language of Proverbs 8 was developed in later Jewish wisdom literature in ways that are reflected in the New Testament in Hebrews 1:1–4; Colossians 1:15–20; and John 1:1–18, because 'The reuse and development of Jewish thought about personified Wisdom gave the New Testament writers the concepts and language to speak of Jesus as the incarnation of the pre-existent Word/Son who was the agent in creation.'[15] Nevertheless, Kaiser argues cogently,

> The case for wisdom as a messianic theme certainly falls short of being a *direct* argument for the Messiah. And it is not clear that it is an *indirect* argument or a type for the Messiah either. Had it not been for Paul's statement in Colossians 1:16, it is doubtful if any connection would have been made between the coming Messiah and wisdom, Instead, we see wisdom as a personification of a quality or attribute of God.[16]

In verse 23, Wisdom elaborates on what she said in the previous verse, as she states that she was *formed* by God in antiquity at the very beginning, using the same verb (*skk*) that in Psalm 139:13 and Job 10:11 describes the prenatal weaving of the embryo by the Lord. Wisdom was not an afterthought, but was essential to the Lord's creative plan, as verses 24–31 will detail. This ancient pedigree of Wisdom indicates her pre-eminent value to the Lord, and it provides the rationale for why human beings should also value wisdom.

In the highly poetic depiction of the creation that follows beginning in verse 24, Wisdom came into existence before the watery depths. If this is a reference to what is narrated in Genesis 1:2, where the Spirit of God is hovering over the waters, then before the days of creation beginning in Genesis 1:3, and even before the scene described in Genesis 1:2, the Lord gave birth to Wisdom.

---

[15] E. C. Lucas, 'The Book of Proverbs: Some Current Issues', in D. G. Firth and L. Wilson (eds.), *Interpreting Old Testament Wisdom Literature* (Downers Grove: IVP Academic, 2017), p. 59.

[16] W. C. Kaiser, *The Messiah in the Old Testament*, Studies in Old Testament Biblical Theology (Grand Rapids: Zondervan, 1995), p. 91.

Continuing her thought in verse 24 into verses 25–26, Wisdom strongly affirms that she preceded all that human beings know in the world in which they live. She came into existence before the mountains were settled into their places. Wisdom existed before the Lord made the world, the fields and the dust from which human beings later were made (Gen. 2:7). In wisdom thought, the youth is taught by the elder, so by stating her antiquity Wisdom is likely indicating that human beings need to learn from her, their expertly qualified teacher.

In verses 27–29 Wisdom poetically depicts some of God's creative acts that are narrated in Genesis 1. Wisdom says that she was there when God set the heavens in place (cf. Gen. 1:6–8). Her reference to God marking out the horizon likely refers to the seashore, when by the word of God the land emerged from the sea (Gen. 1:9–10), or perhaps to the horizon between the land/sea and the sky. In this section, the Lord is likened to an artist as he creates the world. Nothing happened by chance, but all by divine direction and agency. As a skilful craftsman, the Lord knew exactly what he was doing as he constructed the world, even in hanging the clouds in the sky. Although the ancient Hebrews tended to fear the sea[17] (cf. the vivid description in Ps. 107:23–28), the deep (*tĕhôm*, as in Gen. 1:2) was no threat to the Lord, but rather he controlled it for his own purposes. Everything about the creation was determined and done by the Lord, who in verse 29 is described with the image of an architect and builder (cf. Job 38:4–7; Ps. 102:25). Even the location of the seashore was not arbitrary but divinely ordered, as the Lord set a limit on how far the sea could encroach upon the land (cf. Ps. 104:9; Jer. 5:22).

Verse 30 contains a difficult textual problem, as the Hebrew term *'āmôn* is rendered in various ways by different versions, all of which require a change of vowels from what the standard Hebrew text reads.[18] The NASB reads the term as 'master workman', in keeping with the building images in verses 27–29 (but those verses refer to the Lord, and not to Wisdom, as here in v. 30) and parallel to Song of Songs 7:1 and Jeremiah 52:15. Some commentators argue for a meaning of 'little child' in keeping with the language of birth in verses 22–25.[19] The option taken by NIV is *constantly*,

---

[17] *DBI* 200–201.

[18] For a detailed discussion of the interpretative options, see Waltke, *Proverbs Chapters 1–15*, pp. 417–422.

[19] Fox, *Proverbs 1 – 9*, p. 285, concludes, 'Wisdom is declaring that while God was busy creating the world, she was near him, growing up on his care and giving him delight.'

which is parallel to *always* (literally, 'at all times') in the final line of the verse, and this may well be the best rendering of the term. Wisdom describes herself in the most winsome terms, as she constantly delighted in the Lord and in his creative work.

Wisdom's delight reached a peak on the sixth day of creation, when the Lord made human beings (31; cf. Gen. 1:26–28). This grand finale in the divine activity of creation caused Wisdom to delight in the same spirit as the angels who sang for joy at the creation (cf. Job 38:7). This enthusiastic response by Wisdom to what the Lord did in creating the world sets the stage for her appeal in verses 32–36, as she challenges her students to find their delight in her, as she had found her delight in the Lord.

5. The challenge of Wisdom (8:32–36)

After her long soliloquy in verses 12–31, in verse 32 Wisdom again addresses her audience as *my children*, using the familiar tone of a teacher as she calls them to listen to her. These *children* mean all human beings, as she indicated in verse 4 when she said, 'I raise my voice to all humanity.' This verse begins the challenge to which her whole discourse has been heading. Wisdom wants all human beings to *keep* her ways, not just to *know* them. Those who keep the ways of wisdom are blessed, or happy (cf. Ps. 119:1), just as Wisdom found her own constant happiness in the presence of the Lord (30–31).

By heeding Wisdom's instruction, people will become wise, but those who disregard her teaching will become foolish (33; cf. 13:18; 15:32). By listening to Wisdom they will also become happy (34), as they wait with eager desire to learn from her. This response evidences genuine acceptance of Wisdom, not just grudging acquiescence to her words. Such a proactive response characterizes good learners who value wisdom.

The conjunction *For* in verse 35 introduces the reason why those who wait eagerly for Wisdom are happy. In finding Wisdom, one finds life, which is a great benefit. There is more, however, because this good life is a *favour from the* LORD. Wisdom does more than just enable one to achieve a successful life. Wisdom leads to the kind of life that pleases the Lord, and the Lord longs to bestow his blessing on those who accept his way of wisdom. In the words of Jesus, a life of godly wisdom culminates with the divine commendation, 'Well done, good and faithful servant! . . . Come and share your master's happiness!'[20]

Verse 36 is the antithesis to verse 35, as Wisdom concludes her long address by laying out two alternatives as a stark contrast. The choice is clear and consequential. Loving Wisdom leads to life (cf. 17), but hating Wisdom leads to death. Those who fail to find Wisdom harm themselves, and in effect they love death. As Proverbs teaches repeatedly, every person gets what he or she truly loves, along with the resulting good or bad consequences

6. Concluding comment

History and literature are punctuated by stirring speeches that seek to challenge, to inspire and to motivate people to some great endeavour. From the funeral oration by Pericles to Henry V's charge to his army at the Battle of Agincourt, Winston Churchill's entreaty to Britain to stand fast during the dark days of the Second World War and John F. Kennedy's inaugural address urging his fellow Americans to ask what they could do for their country, great orators have endeavoured to rouse the people of their times to wholehearted commitment for truly transcendent causes.

When Wisdom addresses all people in Proverbs 8 (v. 4), she presents a compelling challenge that surpasses even the most memorable speeches by the greatest of human leaders. Unlike prominent human orators, all of whom are flawed, Wisdom has impeccable credibility, always speaking what is true and just (7–8), so we can trust completely all that she says to us. History is littered with the broken promises and deceitful deceptions of leaders, but Wisdom hates what is evil and holds to what is good. Wisdom will never lead us astray or manipulate us by insincere words, but will direct us on the way of righteousness and justice (20). Human leaders may try to impress us with their credentials, so that we will place our faith in the political, military and economic prowess they claim to possess, but so often their actual ability is insufficient to meet the challenges that arise. By contrast, Wisdom has pre-eminent credentials, because she has functioned with the Lord even from the beginning of his activity in the creation of the world (22–31).

---

[20] Matt. 25:21, 23.

As Wisdom concludes her powerful address in Proverbs 8, we are left with a momentous decision to make. Will we take Wisdom at her word and accept her call, or will we dismiss her, as though what she says is flawed, unappealing or irrelevant to us? Wisdom has made her case, and what a compelling case it is; but we must choose to listen to what she declares and to live as she demands.

Part 2
The context of wisdom

Deuteronomy 30:15–20

5. Choose life

Our investigation of the message of wisdom has begun in the book of Proverbs, which is the logical place to start in the Bible for this important theme. Wisdom, however, is not confined to what is included in the book of Proverbs, because wisdom language appears throughout both the Old Testament and the New Testament. In the Old Testament, wisdom can be found in the law, in the historical narratives, in the prophetical literature and in the Psalms. In all of these sections of the Old Testament, we find the language, themes, images and emphases that we have seen in the book of Proverbs. Wisdom, then, is not a minor voice in the Old Testament, but rather it plays a prominent role in its theology and teaching, like a recurrent motif woven throughout a symphony.

Deuteronomy is the fifth and final book of the Pentateuch, or the law of Moses. Deuteronomy concludes the Pentateuch with the farewell addresses of Moses to the Israelites. For forty years, Moses led the people of Israel in their exodus from Egyptian bondage and then throughout the wilderness wanderings (Exodus, Leviticus, Numbers). As they were poised to enter the Promised Land of Canaan, and he was about to die, Moses in the book of Deuteronomy reminded the Israelites of some crucial truths. Towards the end of the book, in Deuteronomy 28, Moses emphasized that obedience would result in blessing by the Lord, but disobedience would bring curses from him. The Israelites would need to be committed to obeying the Lord, or they would face dire consequences. In Deuteronomy 29, Moses predicted the future defection and dispersion of the nation of Israel, and indeed in its subsequent history Israel did disobey the Lord, and that caused the people to be taken into captivity. However, Moses reassured them that dispersion would not be the end of the story, and in in Deuteronomy 30 he looks forward to a more distant time, when repentance can lead to restoration, because the Lord is compassionate. Moses anticipates this future deliverance in Deuteronomy 30:1–3 when he says,

> When all these blessings and curses I have set before you come on you and you take them to heart wherever the LORD your God disperses you among the nations, and when you and your children return to the LORD your God and obey him with all your heart and with all your soul according to everything I command you today, then the LORD your God will restore your fortunes and have compassion on you and gather you again from all the nations where he scattered you.

In verses 1–10 of Deuteronomy 30, Moses speaks about repentance and restoration. The Lord's judgment of Israel is not his final word, because he longs to bless his people when they obey him. This leads into Moses' encouragement to the people to obey the Lord in verses 11–14. When Israel come under divine judgment, they must not suppose that the Lord's word is beyond their reach, so that they are beyond hope. Rather, God's covenantal word 'is in your mouth and in your heart so that you may obey it'.[1] As one scholar explains,

> These were not remote, abstract, esoteric principles but a word that was among and within them. The 'word' (v. 14) is the commandment (*miṣwâ*) of the Lord, that whole body of stipulations that Moses was commanding that very day (v. 11). This single word 'commandment' occurs regularly in Deuteronomy as a term denoting the entire covenant text.[2]

The chapter culminates in verses 15–20, in which Moses issues a stirring challenge to the nation of Israel to choose life and blessing, rather than death and curses. The language Moses uses clearly parallels the description of the two ways of wisdom and folly described in the book of Proverbs, as he exhorts Israel to choose the path of obedience leading to life in the Promised Land instead of the path of disobedience that leads to dispersion from the land. So much is at stake for the nation of Israel, so

---

[1] Deut. 30:14.
[2] E. H. Merrill, *Deuteronomy*, NAC 4 (Nashville: Broadman & Holman, 1994), p. 391.

Moses presses them to make a wise decision, and he makes it exceedingly clear what will happen if they do not choose wisely. In effect, Moses functions as a master teacher as he clarifies the issues facing Israel, and points them towards the path they should take.

1. Call to obedience that leads to life (30:15–16)

After gazing into the remote future in verses 11–14, Moses returns to the situation in his own day as the Israelites prepare to end their wanderings in the wilderness and to enter the Promised Land of Canaan. At this auspicious moment, Moses makes a strong rhetorical appeal to the nation, as 'this powerful summary of the whole book reaches its climax charged with evangelistic energy, emotion, and urgency'.[3] By using second person singular pronouns (*you*), Moses crafts a strong personal appeal to the individuals in the nation. This is not just a general address broadcast to the nation as a whole; rather Moses endeavours to speak incisively and persuasively to the heart and conscience of every person. He also emphasizes that there is great urgency about the decision he is calling them to make *today* (cf. similar language in Deut. 4:39; 11:26; Josh. 24:15). His challenge echoes what the Lord said through Moses to the previous generation at Sinai in Exodus 19:5–8, when Moses following the Lord's instructions challenged the people of Israel to obedience. At that time, the Lord said to Israel,

> Now if you obey me fully and keep my covenant, then out of all nations you will be my treasured possession. Although the whole earth is mine, you will be for me a kingdom of priests and a holy nation.[4]

When Moses set these words from the Lord before the people, they responded, 'We will do everything the LORD has said.'[5] To the present generation poised to enter Canaan, Moses makes it evident that this is a call that cannot safely be ignored, but by all means must be heard and heeded by the Israelites. What was true for the Israelites in Moses' day is equally applicable to God's people today. God's Word often contains strong warnings

---

[3] C. J. H. Wright, *Deuteronomy*, Understanding the Bible Commentary Series (Grand Rapids: Baker, 2012), p. 291.

[4] Exod. 19:5–6.

[5] Exod. 19:8.

which, like a fire alarm, we ignore at our great peril. We, too, must learn and live God's Word, and if we do not there will be costly consequences.

Moses speaks in stark terms as he lays before the people a clear set of alternatives. On the one hand there is the path of *life and prosperity*, and on the other hand there is the path of *death and destruction.* These contrasting destinations are the same as the destinations to which wisdom and folly lead as detailed in Proverbs, and they are also found in the Lord's message to the nation of Judah through his prophet Jeremiah: 'see, I am setting before you the way of life and the way of death'.[6] Moses will go on in this passage to call Israel to commitment to accept the Lord's path that leads to life and to avoid the path of disobedience that will lead to death. The challenge Moses directed to his nation is equally relevant to all people at every time in history, because

> readers of Deuteronomy then and now are all confronted with one of the most explicit calls for a decision that the Bible presents. Whether one stands before God in the context of worship or hears the instruction of the Lord or simply reads through this presentation of it, one cannot step aside or put the text away as if all that has been done, said, or read is simply information.[7]

Moses, like personified Wisdom in Proverbs 8, presses Israel to make a decision to follow the Lord's path, and the decision they make will have profound consequences for them. No less than life or death hangs in the balance for Israel as they must choose whether to obey or to disobey the Lord.

The theme of command runs throughout Deuteronomy 30 (cf. 2, 8, 10, 11), and Moses continues that emphasis in verse 16 when he says, *For I command you today.* As in verses 11, 15, 18 and 19, there is intense urgency to his command, as Moses focuses on what he is exhorting them to do *today,* or this day. This is not just his recommendation or suggestion to the Israelites, but it has the force of law, as Moses calls on the Israelites to love and to obey the Lord their God in terms that echo Deuteronomy 6:5: 'Love the LORD your God with all your heart and with all your soul and with all your strength.' Loving the Lord is more than just having positive affection for him, because it also entails walking in his ways and keeping his word. God's word that is to be obeyed includes his *commands* (*miṣwôt*),

---

[6] Jer. 21:8.

[7] P. D. Miller, *Deuteronomy*, Interpretation (Louisville: John Knox, 1990), pp. 213–214.

his *decrees* (ḥuqqôt) and his *laws* (mišpāṭîm), which together constitute his specific covenantal stipulations that have been detailed in Exodus, Leviticus, Numbers and Deuteronomy.[8] The Israelites must *keep* what the Lord has commanded. They must pay careful attention to what he requires, not just knowing what he said but being committed to obeying it. Their responsive attitude is what the Lord demands and what Moses urges the Israelites to make their determined commitment.

If the Israelites will obey the Lord, they will *live and increase* as they experience his blessing in the Promised Land of Canaan. This prospect of life and blessing is reminiscent of what is said of the way of wisdom in Proverbs 2:20–22:

> Thus you will walk in the ways of the good
>   and keep to the paths of the righteous.
> For the upright will live in the land,
>   and the blameless will remain in it;
> but the wicked will be cut off from the land,
>   and the unfaithful will be torn from it.

Both covenantal obedience in the book of Deuteronomy and walking in the way of wisdom in the book of Proverbs lead to divine blessing. In both texts, living in the land under the blessing of the Lord is the ideal, as the Lord's obedient people thrive under his blessing and experience true life as he intends. Similarly, in the New Testament Jesus assures his disciples in John 15:10–11,

> If you keep my commands, you will remain in my love, just as I have kept my Father's commands and remain in his love. I have told you this so that my joy may be in you and that your joy may be complete.

2. Caution that disobedience leads to death (30:17–18)

The conjunction *But* that begins verse 17 indicates that the prospect of blessing for Israel is not unconditional and guaranteed. Moses has

---

[8] Merrill, *Deuteronomy*, p. 392, observes that the three terms used in v. 16 are also found in Deut. 6:1; 7:11; 8:11; and 11:1 to refer to the particulars of the covenant.

commanded the people of Israel to love the Lord, to walk in obedience to him and to keep his covenantal requirements, but now he raises the possibility that Israel will turn their hearts away from the Lord and towards disobedience. As the subsequent history of Israel narrated in the historical books demonstrates, this was not just a hypothetical possibility but a clear and present danger, a genuine threat facing the nation. And so it always is for God's people, because our sinful nature within and the many sinful influences all around us conspire to lead us away from obedience to the Lord. Drawing from the cautionary tale of Israel's disobedience (1 Cor. 10:1–11), Paul gives a warning to the Corinthians in the first century that is equally relevant to Christians in the twenty-first: 'So, if you think you are standing firm, be careful that you don't fall!'[9] Paul, however, hastens to reassure God's people,

> No temptation has overtaken you except what is common to mankind. And God is faithful; he will not let you be tempted beyond what you can bear. But when you are tempted, he will also provide a way out so that you can endure it.[10]

Moses makes it clear that the problem of disobedience begins in the heart, for as Jeremiah 17:9 exclaims,

> The heart is deceitful above all things
>   and beyond cure.
>   Who can understand it?

In these final words to the nation he has led for forty years, Moses warns them against their hearts being drawn away from the Lord, so that they worship other gods. This defection would in effect repudiate the Lord who has been so gracious and generous to them. When this admonition by Moses is read along with the narrative of Solomon in 1 Kings 11:4, it is evident that even that wisest of kings wandered into the path of disobedience, as 'his wives turned his heart after other gods, and his heart was not fully devoted to the LORD his God'. If even a man as wise as Solomon was in danger of defecting from the Lord, how at risk was the entire nation of

---

[9]   1 Cor. 10:12.
[10]   1 Cor. 10:13.

Israel, and how vigilant must we all also be against the allurements and encroachments of sin in our lives?

In verse 18 Moses states unequivocally that if the Israelites are disobedient and defect from the worship of the Lord, their penalty will be disastrous. He makes a strong statement of certainty because the calamity he predicts will indeed happen, no doubt about it. Israel must not carelessly presume on the Lord's past goodness to them. Even though the Lord graciously initiated a covenant with their ancestor Abraham and set forth his legal stipulations for the nation at Sinai, how Israel respond to the Lord will make all the difference in the future. If they disobey, their disobedience to the Lord will bring destruction from the Lord. Just as the Lord will graciously direct Israel in the conquest of Canaan and their possession of the Promised Land, so he will in his justice disperse them from it if they defect from him. Instead of experiencing life and prosperity, when Israel sins it will taste death and destruction (cf. 15), and the people will 'be evicted from the land given as its possession (v. 18b), a curse that reverses the blessing of long life there (vv. 15–16)'.[11] What a high price there will be to pay for their disobedience to the Lord!

3. Choosing life in the Lord (30:19–20)

As Moses brings his challenge to the people of Israel to its conclusion, his rhetoric paints the picture of a vast courtroom. He calls upon the heavens and the earth to serve as witnesses to what he has communicated to the nation (cf. Deut. 4:26; 31:28; Isa. 1:2). Although other Ancient Near Eastern treaties used this kind of language to invoke their gods to witness a legal agreement, in the Old Testament only Yahweh is God, so this language 'has been reduced to a metaphorical level, where the heavens and earth are personified or stand by metonymy for the watching world'.[12] With this expansive set of witnesses in place, Moses articulates his powerful closing summation by which he endeavours to persuade the nation of Israel to wholehearted commitment to the Lord. With great clarity and conviction Moses states definitively what Israel must do in responding properly to

---

[11] Merrill, *Deuteronomy*, p. 392.

[12] R. B. Chisholm, *NIDOTTE* 3:336. Similarly, J. G. McConville, *Deuteronomy*, AOTC 5 (Downers Grove: InterVarsity Press, 2002), p. 430, notes, 'This corresponds to a formal element in the treaty conventions of the ANE, while refusing the usual polytheism.'

the Lord, as well as the gravity of the consequences should they respond improperly to him.

As in verse 15, the expression *This day* evokes a sense of great urgency. The decision facing Israel must not be deferred to another day, but needs to be made immediately. As Moses frames the issue, the choice before Israel and its consequences could not be clearer or more compelling. As with the invitation by Woman Wisdom in Proverbs 9:6, this is a call to choose life. The choice that the Israelites make will result either in life and blessings for them, or in death and curses. Both in the ancient world and in our contemporary culture, human beings may suppose that there are many ways by which their lives can become prosperous and secure, but 'the Bible insists without qualification that there is really only one way to find life and good and well-being . . . It is the Lord's way. So choose that way, follow that Lord.'[13] Choosing life is in reality choosing the Lord and his way by obeying him. This choice set forth by Moses has profound consequences, both for his present generation poised to enter the Promised Land of Israel and in the future for their children who will come after them. It is vital that the right decision be made, for 'Choosing life, which is nothing less than choosing Yahweh and loving him with all of one's heart and soul, involves blessing, prosperity, and longevity. Choosing death, which is rejecting Yahweh, involves cursings, constant dread and uncertainty, and destruction.'[14]

It is important to recognize that not to choose is not an option. We all know people who are averse to making commitments. Either they cannot come to a decision, or they want to keep their options open or they just fear making a bad choice, so they make no choice at all. As Moses in Deuteronomy 30 and as Wisdom in Proverbs 8 set forth their cases, not to choose life is actually to choose death, just as not following the path of wisdom is by default to follow the path of folly. We must not deceive ourselves by supposing that we can avoid or defer making the decision to choose God's way today, because every day we do not choose what is right we have in reality chosen what is wrong. It is imperative that we *choose*, that we choose *wisely* and that we choose wisely *today*.

Verse 20 concludes both the thought of verse 19 and Moses' powerful appeal in verses 15–20. Choosing life in verse 19 means commitment to

---

[13] Miller, *Deuteronomy*, p. 215.

[14] T. L. Brenslinger, *NIDOTTE* 2:109.

love the Lord, to *listen* to his voice and to hold fast to him in *loyalty*. In listening to the Lord's voice (cf. Deut. 28:1), the Israelites will commit themselves to following all of his commands; and in holding fast to him (cf. 4:4; 10:20), they will devote unswerving loyalty to him. Choosing life is in fact choosing the Lord, and that will result in his blessing, which for the Israelites involved longevity in the land promised to their forefather Abraham in Genesis 12:7 and 13:17, and later reaffirmed to Isaac and to Jacob. The Lord had made a covenant with the patriarchs, and now their descendants are challenged by Moses to choose to opt into the agreement by keeping the covenant stipulations given by the Lord through Moses. In this arrangement the Lord 'is the life of his people because he has created and redeemed them, but he is also their life insofar as they capitulate to his sovereignty and live out their lives in compliance with his gracious covenant mandates'.[15]

Like the Israelites, Christians have also received an inheritance from the Lord. As Peter explains,

> In his great mercy he has given us new birth into a living hope through the resurrection of Jesus Christ from the dead, and into an inheritance that can never perish, spoil or fade. This inheritance is kept in heaven for you, who through faith are shielded by God's power until the coming of the salvation that is ready to be revealed in the last time.[16]

The people of Israel in the time of Moses were preparing to enter into their earthly inheritance in the land of Canaan, but Christians anticipate their heavenly inheritance that God has prepared and protected for us. For Christians today, just as for the ancient Israelites, it is essential that we love the Lord, listen to what he has said to us and hold fast to him in loyalty, because he is our life and our hope.

4. Concluding comment

The key idea in Deuteronomy 30:15–20 is that choosing life means committing to obey the Lord, who is the giver of life. This principle was true for Israel as they prepared to enter into their inheritance in the land

---

[15] Merrill, *Deuteronomy*, p. 394.

[16] 1 Pet. 1:3–5.

of Canaan, but it is also true for all people at every time. No response from Israel to the challenge of Moses is given in the text of Deuteronomy, but the Old Testament narrative goes on to trace the sad history of the subsequent defection and disobedience of the nation. This was the tragic pattern throughout the period of the judges as the people of Israel repeatedly abandoned the Lord, and it became the predominant downward trajectory during the period of the monarchy. Eventually the Israelites' disobedience to the Lord caused them to be defeated and dispersed from the Promised Land as they were led into captivity, the northern kingdom of Israel by Assyria and the southern kingdom of Judah by Babylon. For a nation that had such a high calling, their poor choices brought them exceedingly low.

As we read this passage today in the twenty-first century, we also have to decide whether we will choose the Lord's path of life taught in Proverbs, in Deuteronomy and in many other passages throughout the Bible, or if we will choose the path of death. Choosing God's path of life requires obedience and loyalty to him, and it leads to his blessing. Choosing the path of death entails disobedience to the Lord, and it results in his judgment. For us, as for the Israelites, there is a momentous decision before us, and the choice we make will make all the difference. No individual and no nation, no matter how powerful and prosperous, can evade the judgment of the sovereign Lord when they fail to choose his path of obedience and life.

As a loving Father, the Lord's desire is to bless his people, but his blessing is conditioned on our obedience to him. Human parents know well how sometimes their good plans and intentions are thwarted by the failure of their children to behave well and to respond positively to them. When that occurs, parents in sadness have to substitute discipline in place of what could have been a delightful family experience. Similarly, the Lord desires to lavish upon us his good gifts (cf. Jas 1:17), but when we refuse to listen to him he must discipline us, because that is what a truly loving parent does, as the sage states in Proverbs 3:11–12 (cf. Heb. 12:5–6):

> My son, do not despise the Lord's discipline,
>   and do not resent his rebuke,
> because the Lord disciplines those he loves,
>   as a father the son he delights in.

Just as the choice that the generation of Moses made had consequences for their descendants, so other people will be affected by the choice we make for or against the Lord. For so many reasons, we must be careful to follow his way, because many people will be either helped or harmed by what we choose to do. Each of our lives is like a pebble tossed into a pond. When the pebble touches the water, ripples begin to spread across the surface. In the same way, a life lived for God inevitably touches other people for good, first family, then friends, and eventually more casual acquaintances. In contrast, a life that rejects God will adversely influence others whom it touches. We all have a measure of influence on others through the choices we make for life or for death. The only question is *how* our influence will affect others around us. Will our lives direct them towards God's blessing, or will they lead them away from it? God desires that his people inherit his blessing so that they can be a channel of his blessing to others, but all of that depends upon our obedience to him. It is vital that we too choose life today.

1 Kings 3:5–15; 4:29–34

6. Solomon, the prototype of wisdom and folly

It is impossible to speak of wisdom in the Bible without considering Solomon. This great king of Israel is featured in the opening verses of the books of Proverbs, Ecclesiastes and Song of Songs, and he also appears in Proverbs 10:1 and 25:1. The superscriptions of Psalms 72 and 127 mention him, indicating that the earliest interpretative comments available connect him with these psalms, and Psalm 127 contains wisdom themes that are reminiscent of both Proverbs and Ecclesiastes.

In both the Old Testament and the New Testament, the wisdom of Solomon is widely recognized. For example, in 1 Kings 10:1–10, the queen of Sheba came to evaluate for herself the reports she had received about Solomon's wisdom, and she concluded, 'Indeed, not even half was told me; in wisdom and wealth you have far exceeded the report I heard.'[1] The narrator goes on to exclaim, 'King Solomon was greater in riches and wisdom than all the other kings of the earth. The whole world sought audience with Solomon to hear the wisdom God had put in his heart.'[2] Jesus alluded to this passage in Matthew 12:42 (cf. Luke 11:31), when he compared himself to Solomon: 'The Queen of the South will rise at the judgment with this generation and condemn it; for she came from the ends of the earth to listen to Solomon's wisdom, and now something greater than Solomon is here.'

---

[1] 1 Kgs 10:7.

[2] 1 Kgs 10:23–24.

In the biblical record, Solomon is portrayed as the ideal of wisdom as a result of the Lord's gift. However, sad to say, he also becomes a cautionary tale of folly. This king who was given so much from the Lord departed from the path of wisdom and defected to the path of folly. Solomon knew wisdom far better than he lived by it, and because of that he functions both as a prototype of wisdom and as a prototype of folly. From his life we can learn how to live skilfully in the Lord's world, but we are also warned how far away from God's way we can go if we do not continue to walk in wisdom.

1. Gifted by the Lord with wisdom (3:5–15)

The scene for this narrative about Solomon is set in verses 3–4, as Solomon went to Gibeon to offer sacrifices and to burn incense at the great high place there. The temple in Jerusalem was not yet constructed, and Gibeon, about 4 miles north-west of Jerusalem, was the site of the tabernacle and therefore the appropriate place to worship the Lord. There at Gibeon the Lord took the initiative to appear to Solomon in a dream at night. Revelation from God through dreams occurs numerous times in the Bible – for example, in Genesis 26:24; 28:10–17; Judges 7:13; 1 Samuel 3; Daniel 2:4; 7:1; and Matthew 1:20; 2:13, 22.[3] This was not something that Solomon sought, decreed or manufactured, but rather it represented the Lord's gracious act towards him.[4] In this dream, God gave to Solomon a no-strings-attached offer, urging him, *Ask for whatever you want me to give you* (5). How Solomon replies and what he requests from the Lord will reveal volumes about what Solomon values.

Solomon responded to the Lord with a tone of profound and humble gratefulness. Using familiar covenantal language that echoed the Davidic Covenant in 2 Samuel 7:7–16, Solomon extolled the Lord's great *kindness* (*ḥesed*) to David his father and to him (6). He described the walk of David before the Lord as *faithful*, *righteous* and *upright*, as David had lived consistently according to the laws established by the Lord. Solomon affirmed that the Lord, by enabling him to succeed his father on the

---

[3] D. J. Wiseman, *1 & 2 Kings*, TOTC 9 (Downers Grove: InterVarsity Press, 1993), p. 84.

[4] W. Brueggemann, *1 & 2 Kings* (Macon: Smith & Helwys, 2000), pp. 46–47, suggests, 'In that ancient world, a dream is understood not as a random offer of the unconscious but as an intrusion of the deity into one's affairs. The dream reported is a powerful claim for legitimacy, because what God gives in a dream is beyond human control or exploitation or manipulation or resistance.'

throne, had continued his great kindness to David. The Lord had been faithful in fulfilling his covenant, and David had set a high bar of faithfulness in his commitment to the Lord and his way. The question the reader asks is, will Solomon be able to live up to his father's example of godliness? History is full of examples of the children of political leaders, athletes, musicians and artists who try unsuccessfully to match the achievements of their parents. Would that be the case with Solomon?

In verse 7, Solomon acknowledged that it was the Lord who had made him king, just as the Lord had previously chosen Saul (1 Sam. 9) and David (1 Sam. 16) to rule over Israel. As Solomon had referred to his father David as the Lord's servant (6), so he also regarded himself as the Lord's servant who now served in the place of his father as king. Solomon was also well aware that he was young and inexperienced; the historical narrative indicates that he was likely in his early twenties,[5] the same age as Elizabeth II was when she succeeded her father as the monarch of the United Kingdom. In wisdom thought, wisdom resides with the elders rather than with the young, and in both Proverbs and Ecclesiastes it is the youth who is the stated learner of wisdom. Solomon called himself a *little child*, and one who did not know how to carry out his duties as leader. His admission, literally, 'I do not know how to go out or to come in', refers to his public life or his daily business and was 'an idiom referring to the skills of leadership'.[6] Specifically, Solomon lacked military experience, which was traditionally the means by which an ancient king proved his mettle and worth as a leader (cf. Deut. 28:6–7; 31:2–3).

As Solomon continued to speak to the Lord in verse 8, he was humble and honest about the formidable challenge facing him as king over Israel. Not only was he *a little child* but he had been placed over *a great people*. The Lord had chosen to set his affection upon Israel out of his love for them and because of the covenant he had made with their ancestors (Deut. 7:6–8). Now Solomon recognized the overwhelming responsibility that the Lord had given to him to rule over the Israelites, who could not be numbered, despite the ill-fated effort by David to do that in 2 Samuel 24. As Solomon viewed what the Lord called him to do, he was well aware that

---

[5] Solomon was born from the liaison between David and Bathsheba narrated in 2 Sam. 11 – 12, which likely occurred at about the halfway mark in David's reign. Solomon ruled over Israel for forty years (1 Kgs 11:42), and his successor Rehoboam was forty-one when he acceded to the throne (1 Kgs 14:21), so Solomon must have been a young man when he became king.

[6] *GKC* 114c; P. R. House, *1, 2 Kings*, NAC 8 (Nashville: Broadman & Holman, 1995), p. 110, lists parallels in Num. 27:17; Josh. 14:11; 1 Sam. 18:13, 16; 29:6; 2 Kgs 11:8.

his responsibility was great and that he was not, and this realization prompted his request for divine wisdom.

In verse 9 Solomon stated his request in response to the Lord's invitation in verse 5. He was aware that in himself he was not adequate for the calling he had received to rule over Israel. Far from claiming his royal right to do as he pleased, Solomon asked the Lord to give him discernment to govern as the Lord desired. He requested from the Lord a hearing or listening heart, the kind of discerning mind that would be able to govern the Lord's people rightly. Here, as often in the Old Testament, the Hebrew term *lēb* (*heart*) refers primarily to his intellectual dimension, because Solomon realized that he 'must be attentive, receptive, and discriminating if he is to render true justice'.[7] The verb *špṭ* is often rendered 'judge', but NIV rightly translates it as *govern*, which is broader than the judicial aspect alone, because it encompasses both the making of just laws and the coming to just decisions.[8] The subsequent episode in 1 Kings 3:16–28, in which Solomon has to decide between the competing claims of two prostitutes about which of them is the mother of a live baby and which of a dead baby, illustrates the kind of extraordinary discernment he would need. In this request, Solomon chose to accept the pattern of kingship enunciated in the Mosaic law (Deut. 17:14–20) and practised later by godly kings such as Hezekiah (2 Kgs 18:5–6) and Josiah (2 Kgs 23:25), in which 'the king is God's servant, a loyal vassal in a covenant relationship. The goal of this sort of kingship is the welfare of God's people, not the glory of the king.'[9]

In his reply to Solomon's request, the Lord was clearly delighted with him (10). Solomon did not ask selfishly, but rather wisely and righteously. In valuing what the Lord valued, Solomon pleased him. In verse 11, the Lord explained why Solomon's request met with his approval. Solomon had asked for the right thing, and he did not ask for wrong things. Seeing the bigger picture of the needs of the nation, Solomon did not squander this opportunity by thinking only of himself. He did not ask for personal blessings to make himself comfortable, successful and honoured, but he requested the wisdom he would need to rule the nation in a just way. Solomon wanted the Lord to equip him for the great task to which he had been called, so that he could fulfil his calling as king over Israel.

---

[7] S. J. DeVries, *1 Kings*, WBC 12 (Nashville: Thomas Nelson, 2003), p. 52.

[8] J. T. Walsh, *1 Kings*, Berit Olam: Studies in Hebrew Narrative & Poetry (Collegeville: Liturgical Press, 1996), p. 75.

[9] R. Nelson, *First and Second Kings*, Interpretation (Louisville: John Knox, 1987), pp. 31–32.

Continuing his reply to Solomon, the Lord said in verse 12 that he would go well beyond what Solomon requested, and although it is not reflected in the NIV, the repetition of the Hebrew conjunction *hinnēh* suggests the Lord's excitement as he spoke to the young king. The Lord affirmed that he would give to Solomon the *wise and discerning heart* he asked for, but also so much more. Solomon would receive not just adequate discernment to govern his people, but also extraordinary wisdom, *so that there will never have been anyone like you, nor will there ever be.* More than a keen intellect, this was a supernatural gift from the Lord, 'wisdom from above, not below'.[10] As will be spelled out in the subsequent episodes, this wisdom was for Solomon's rule as king, but it also extended across many areas of study (especially in 1 Kgs 4:29–34). This was the Lord's response that was immeasurably above all Solomon had requested, because the Lord made him wise both in his political duties, for which he asked, and in intellectual fields of endeavour, which surpassed his request in verse 9.

The initial word in verse 13, *Moreover,* signals that the Lord continued to pour out his gifts on Solomon. Although Solomon requested from the Lord a modest and selfless gift, the Lord in his pleasure gave to Solomon the *wealth and honour* he had not requested. During his lifetime, Solomon's wealth would be unmatched (cf. 1 Kgs 4:20–25), so that he was 'greater in riches and wisdom than all the other kings of the earth',[11] and his reputation would extend internationally (cf. 4:34; 10:24). Instead of gaining victory over his enemies in battle (11), Solomon came to exceed them in his possessions and prestige. This lavish gift, making him the Bill Gates or Jeff Bezos of the ancient world, was a measure of the generosity of the Lord from whom every good and perfect gift comes (cf. Jas 1:17).

After stating his generous intentions in blessing Solomon in verses 11–13, the Lord added a big *if* to what he said. The Lord desired to bless Solomon lavishly, but for Solomon to enjoy these benefits he must walk in the way of the Lord, which is defined as *obedience* to his *decrees and commands.* In reality, what the Lord required of Solomon is what he had previously stated as his requirement for the nation of Israel, because once Israel entered into covenant with the Lord, 'the expectation was that they walk according to its statutes (Lev 26:3; Deut 8:6; 11:22). If they did,

---

[10] I. W. Provan, *1 & 2 Kings*, Understanding the Bible Commentary Series (Grand Rapids: Baker, 1995), p. 49.

[11] 1 Kgs 10:23.

they could anticipate success in the Conquest and occupation of the Promised Land (Deut 11:23–25).'[12] Solomon had started well by walking according to the instructions he had received from his father David (3; cf. 2:3), but his continued blessing is conditioned on his obedience to the Lord over the long haul, because 'he must make a good choice all along the way, the choice of listening and obeying, for it is in choosing obediently that Israel and its king choose life'.[13] The Lord always insists on obedience as the necessary and proper response to his gracious offers. That was true for Solomon, and it is equally true for us today.

2. Wisdom in observing life (4:29–34)

This passage is a narrative vignette that describes the intellectual activity of Solomon. With the vast wisdom, insight and understanding he had received as a gift from the Lord, Solomon embarked on extensive observations of life, which he articulated as wisdom teachings. From this paragraph, it is evident that Solomon had both depth of discernment and breadth of investigation: 'This wisdom has to do with both depth and range, including such matters as insight, intellectual acumen, wide-ranging knowledge, skills of various sorts, and good judgment.'[14] Unlike chapter 3, which focuses on Solomon's exemplary discernment in governance, this section in chapter 4 details his extraordinary intellectual prowess. The Lord fully kept his promise in 3:12, because Solomon's understanding was *as measureless as the sand on the seashore* (29), a biblical expression for an incalculable amount, which also echoes the Lord's covenantal blessing on Abraham in Genesis 22:17.

When Solomon is described as having wisdom that exceeded that *of all the people of the East* and *of Egypt* (30), this is high praise indeed. By the standards of excellence of his day, Solomon had no intellectual peer. The people of the East would have included sages such as Job and his friends, indicating that Solomon had an international reputation, comparable to Nobel Prize recipients today. More specifically, his wisdom surpassed even that of the Egyptian sages, who had a long tradition of

---

[12] E. H. Merrill, *NIDOTTE* 1:1033.

[13] Brueggemann, *1 & 2 Kings*, p. 49.

[14] T. E. Fretheim, *First and Second Kings*, Westminster Bible Companion (Louisville: Westminster John Knox, 1999), p. 37. He continues to conclude with reference to chapter 10, 'His knowledge, including "scientific" knowledge, is so extensive that people travel to Israel to hear him speak.'

wisdom going back to the time of Ptah-Hotep around 2450 BC.[15] Again, it was evident that the Lord had fulfilled his promise to Solomon in 1 Kings 3:12, when he said, 'I will give you a wise and discerning heart, so that there will never have been anyone like you, nor will there ever be.'

Verse 31 adds to the previous verse by citing specific evidence to support the assessment of Solomon's superior wisdom. The individuals cited (Ethan, Heman, Kalkol and Darda) were apparently well-known exemplars of wisdom in Solomon's time, even though their prowess is not attested elsewhere, with the exceptions of the superscriptions of Psalm 88 (attributed to Heman) and of Psalm 89 (attributed to Ethan). These individuals were likely intellectuals and not political rulers. By objective measures, Solomon's wisdom stood out among his peers in wisdom teaching. Solomon had asked the Lord for discernment for governing his people (1 Kgs 3:9), but the Lord had given him so much more.

In addition to his effective rule over Israel that brought to the nation extensive peace, prominence and prosperity (4:20–28), Solomon also excelled as a scholar, poet and musician (32). His vast scholarly productivity featured three thousand proverbs. The book of Proverbs states that it contains proverbs of Solomon (1:1; 10:1; 25:1), and in it are about five hundred wisdom sayings, many of which are a single verse in length, while some are a good deal longer. Evidently the majority of the proverbs penned or collected by Solomon are not included in the biblical book of Proverbs. A window into how wise men like Solomon crafted their sayings is opened in Ecclesiastes 12:9–10, as the Teacher 'pondered and searched out and set in order many proverbs', and then polished his sayings with just the right words to make them concise and memorable and therefore especially effective in teaching truth. In addition, Solomon wrote 1,005 songs. The Song of Songs is linked with Solomon (Song 1:1), but other than that Solomon's songs are not included in the Bible, and they have not survived to the present day.

The proverbs mentioned in verse 32 include Solomon's observations drawn from a vast range of life (33). His wisdom and knowledge were encyclopaedic, as following the pattern exemplified in Proverbs 6:6–11 he derived wise sayings through careful observation of the world. Solomon spoke in proverbs relating to plants, from the great cedar trees of Lebanon to the tiny hyssop. He also had wisdom sayings relating to animals, birds,

15 *BBC*, pp. 360–361.

reptiles and fish, and Proverbs includes examples of these areas of observation and teaching. One scholar notes,

> Solomon's wisdom, moreover, embraces all branches of scientific learning, trees and every species of animal life. It is evident that the list in v. 33 is congruent with the primary categories of Genesis 1:20–25. That is, Solomon's learning is commensurate with all of creation.[16]

The procedure used by Solomon was later employed by Jesus in his teaching ministry – for example, when he points to the birds of the air and the flowers of the field to instruct his disciples about God's ample provision for the needs of his children (Matt. 6:25–34).

Solomon's extraordinary wisdom drew widespread attention (34), and later in 1 Kings 10:24 the narrator states, 'The whole world sought audience with Solomon to hear the wisdom God had put in his heart.' The people who came to listen to Solomon's wisdom came from *all nations*, and this included the queen of Sheba (1 Kgs 10), as well as messengers sent from various kings. Not only did this attest to Solomon's premier intellectual standing, but it also fulfilled the Lord's promise of unequalled honour in 1 Kings 3:13.[17]

3. Solomon, the prototype of folly

The Bible is painfully honest as it traces the life of Solomon and reveals that Solomon's vast wisdom did not insulate him from acting foolishly, and because of this Solomon 'offers a potent paradigm for right action, as well as a powerful illustration of the consequences of a choice for evil'.[18] In the narrative in 1 Kings, as well as in the parallel in 2 Chronicles, there are numerous explicit statements and implied clues that indicate that Solomon often adopted the way of folly rather than consistently pursuing the way of wisdom. For example, Solomon made an alliance with the pharaoh of Egypt by marrying his daughter, and he tolerated the people

---

[16] Brueggemann, *1 & 2 Kings*, p. 68.

[17] In 1 Kgs 4:21 it is stated that Solomon ruled over all the territory from the Euphrates River to the border of Egypt, and that all of these nations brought tribute to Solomon as his vassals. The *kings of the world* in 4:34 who heard of Solomon's wisdom appear to extend beyond the scope of Solomon's political control. This would definitely be the case for the queen of Sheba.

[18] G. H. Wilson, *NIDOTTE* 4:1233–1234.

worshipping at the high places, as he himself did (1 Kgs 3:1–3). He spent nearly twice as long building his own palace as he did constructing the temple of the Lord, which could imply that his values were misplaced (6:37 – 7:1). He accumulated a large number of chariots and horses, and he also entered into international commerce in these military assets (10:26–29), a practice that contrasts with the sentiment of the psalmist in Psalm 20:7, who trusts in the Lord rather than in military resources. Solomon also loved many foreign women, despite the Lord's prohibition of intermarrying with them, and they turned his heart away from full devotion to the Lord (11:1–13). Because of this, the Lord told Solomon, 'Since this is your attitude and you have not kept my covenant and my decrees, which I commanded you, I will most certainly tear the kingdom away from you and give it to one of your subordinates',[19] a threat that came to pass when Jeroboam wrested ten tribes away from Solomon's son Rehoboam (12:1–16).

By his foolish and sinful behaviour, Solomon failed to live up to the Lord's standards for the king stated in Deuteronomy 17:14–20. In particular, Solomon specifically violated the Lord's commands in Deuteronomy 17:16–17:

> The king, moreover, must not acquire great numbers of horses for himself or make the people return to Egypt to get more of them, for the LORD has told you, 'You are not to go back that way again.' He must not take many wives, or his heart will be led astray. He must not accumulate large amounts of silver and gold.

Solomon was also guilty of the very abuses that Samuel warned against in 1 Samuel 8:10–18, when the people of Israel demanded a king. His reign, though in many ways prosperous and powerful, fell far short of the ideal stated in royal psalms such as Psalm 72. When viewed against the messianic expectations in Isaiah 11:2–5, Solomon's failure points ahead to the need for the greater Son of David to come as the perfect King, because when he comes,

> He will judge the world in righteousness
> and the peoples with equity.[20]

---

[19] 1 Kgs 11:11.
[20] Ps. 98:9.

4. Concluding comment

The life of Solomon indicates that great wisdom is no permanent guarantee of the Lord's blessing, so we must not presume on it. Every day in many ways we stand at a crossroads, where we must choose between the wise way that honours God and the foolish way that dishonours him. Choosing wisely is a challenge we must face daily, because no matter how long we have lived for God we are not immune to the siren call of sin. The tragedy of Solomon is that he knew wisdom far better than he lived by it, so that

> at a certain point in his life, Solomon gave up the pursuit of wisdom and therefore lost it. As a result, his life can be read as a warning to others not to find the meaning of life in anything other than God.[21]

That the wisest man who ever lived fell into folly is a cautionary tale for all of us that we need to be circumspect and consistent in living according to the Lord's wise way, or we too will succumb to the temptation of folly.

In recent years, Christians have been saddened to hear numerous news accounts of their spiritual leaders who have fallen morally, financially and theologically. These leaders were highly gifted, well educated and deeply experienced in ministry, and yet they made bad choices that destroyed them personally and professionally. We also may be aware of many other cases that do not make the headlines but are equally devastating for those who are close to them.

It took only a faulty O-ring to cause the *Challenger* spacecraft to explode in flight. In the same way, major personal collapses typically can be traced back to compromises and decisions that may have appeared trivial and insignificant at the time, but set into motion a pattern of choices that led to worse and worse consequences.

We are kidding ourselves if we think that we would never do what Solomon did. To guard against following his example into folly, we must pray in the words of the psalmist,

> Search me, God, and know my heart;
> > test me and know my anxious thoughts.

---

21 T. Longman, *The Fear of the Lord Is Wisdom: A Theological Introduction to Wisdom in Israel* (Grand Rapids: Baker Academic, 2017), p. 107.

> See if there is any offensive way in me,
>   and lead me in the way everlasting.[22]

In addition, wise people invite trusted godly friends to hold them account-able, because others can see when our sin blinds us to our own faults, and they can speak the truth that our sin tries to silence.

---

[22] Ps. 139:23–24.

Jeremiah 8:8–10; 9:23–24

7. The distortion of wisdom

Just as the themes and language of wisdom occur in the Mosaic law (cf. Deut. 30:15–20) and in the historical narratives of the Old Testament (cf. 1 Kgs 3; 4), so the Old Testament prophets also speak of wisdom. Many times, however, the prophets do not speak of wisdom in a positive sense, as is typical in Proverbs and elsewhere. Rather, they tend to view wisdom in a negative sense, as they decry people who exalt their own insight and knowledge above the way of the Lord. This is not the wisdom of God, but an alternative and distorted human wisdom. Although it may use the same vocabulary, it is not legitimate wisdom that finds its source in the Lord. Following this distortion of wisdom is in fact taking the path of folly that leads to death.

Anything that the Lord intends for good can be distorted for evil purposes. The food God gives can be the object of overindulgence, with resulting medical complications. The material blessings he provides can become idols and obsessions. The joys he grants can become addictions that distract us away from the Lord. Even wisdom can be distorted, and that has been the case ever since the Garden of Eden. When the serpent tempted Eve to eat of the forbidden tree, she 'saw that the fruit of the tree was good for food and pleasing to the eye, and also desirable *for gaining wisdom*', so she took and ate of it (Gen. 3:6, emphasis added). That initial distortion of wisdom has continued ever since throughout human history. Among a number of Old Testament prophets who condemned this false notion of wisdom was Jeremiah, who called out those in his day who were distorting the wisdom of the Lord into something quite different from what the Lord intended. Over two thousand five hundred years later, Jeremiah's warning echoes down the corridor of history to caution us today, as contemporary men and women are also all too prone to embrace what God calls evil and to depart from what God calls good.

1. The Lord's rejection of the falsely wise (8:8–10)

The Lord, speaking through his prophet Jeremiah (cf. 4), poses an incriminating question to the sages of Judah in verse 8:

> How can you say, 'We are wise,
>   for we have the law of the Lord,'
> when actually the lying pen of the scribes
>   has handled it falsely?

The people to whom Jeremiah spoke claimed to be wise, and as evidence they pointed to the fact that they were teachers of the law of the Lord. As Jeremiah will go on to say, the sages were confusing knowledge of God's word with true wisdom. One commentator explains,

> An important feature of Jeremiah's indictment of Israel was that mere possession of the law of God, a fact so highly prized in popular religious and national feeling, could never of itself guarantee that Israel's behavior was pleasing to God. More was needed than simply knowing what was right; it was necessary to do it![1]

They claimed to have the law of the Lord, but in reality they were not living according to the Lord's requirements in his law, as he indicts them in verses 6–7:

> I have listened attentively,
>   but they do not say what is right.
> None of them repent of their wickedness,
>   saying, 'What have I done?'
> Each pursues their own course
>   like a horse charging into battle.

---

[1] R. E. Clements, *Jeremiah*, Interpretation (Atlanta: John Knox, 1988), p. 57.

Even the stork in the sky
knows her appointed seasons,
and the dove, the swift and the thrush
observe the time of their migration.
But my people do not know
the requirements of the LORD.

In referring to *the lying pen of the scribes*, Jeremiah indicates that the writing produced by their stylus was a far cry from the instruction the Lord had given in his word. The scribes in the time of Jeremiah avoided the Lord's requirements by misinterpreting them and explaining them away. This was not a careless slip-up; rather it was their conscious strategy of deception as they handled God's law falsely. The very people who were entrusted to teach the people had failed in their responsibility. Instead of teaching God's truth, as Ezra and the Levites of his day did (cf. Ezra 7:10; Neh. 8:7–8), they followed a long and sinful pattern of false teaching that emerged before the exile (Hos. 4:6; Zeph. 3:4) and continued during the exile (Jer. 2:8; Ezek. 22:26)[2] and afterwards in the post-exilic and inter-testamental periods. By the time of the earthly ministry of Jesus in the first century AD, false teaching was so entrenched in the religious leaders of Israel that some of Jesus' strongest denunciations were directed at the teachers of the law and the Pharisees, to whom he said, 'You shut the door of the kingdom of heaven in people's faces. You yourselves do not enter, nor will you let those enter who are trying to';[3] and

You are like whitewashed tombs, which look beautiful on the outside but on the inside are full of the bones of the dead and everything unclean. In the same way, on the outside you appear to people as righteous but on the inside you are full of hypocrisy and wickedness.[4]

The scribes were the pastors, seminary professors and Bible teachers of ancient Israel. They were learned in the law of God, but they did not

---

[2] P. Enns, *NIDOTTE* 4:896, observes, 'The task of teaching and proper execution of *tôrâ* was entrusted to several groups of people, most notably the priests and scribes (2 Chron 15:3; Ezra 7:6, 10; Neh 8:7; Mal 2:6–8). In view of their high responsibility, it was incumbent on these individuals to perform their tasks with faithfulness and integrity. This was not always the case, and some harsh words are reserved for those who failed to execute their high office properly (Neh 9:34; Jer 2:8; 8:8; 18:18; Ezek 7:26; 22:26; Hos 4:6; 8:12; Zeph 3:4).'

[3] Matt. 23:13.

[4] Matt. 23:27–28.

always live according to what they had learned. In Jeremiah's day these scholars by their teachings and their practices distorted the written law of the Lord. They along with *prophets* and *priests* (10) are condemned by the Lord through his prophet Jeremiah because of their deliberate manipulation of God's word. Their guilt was great, because 'The entire public leadership is guilty of acting only in self-interest. The covenantal foundations of communal life have been completely jettisoned by the entire leadership apparatus.'[5] Rather than fearing the Lord, which is the fundamental principle of wisdom, their misuse of the Lord's instruction displayed their arrogant disrespect for him. Their perverse speech and arrogant attitudes were the antithesis of the essence of wisdom (Prov. 8:13). The scribes were royal and priestly scholars, the intellectuals of their culture,[6] so what they said and wrote had great influence. Though they claimed to be wise, their actions proved they were not, and their false teaching led the people of Judah astray from the Lord by their lies, as also did the prophets, about whom the Lord said, 'Indeed, I am against those who prophesy false dreams . . . They tell them and lead my people astray with their reckless lies, yet I did not send or appoint them. They do not benefit these people in the least.'[7]

After the Lord's indictment of the wise men of Judah in verse 8, Jeremiah pronounced the divine sentence of condemnation against them in verses 9–10. By handling the law *falsely* (8), the scribes had in fact *rejected the word of the Lord* (9). By rejecting the word of the Lord, they demonstrated that they had no true *wisdom*. Their purported 'wisdom' was a total sham, and in fact it was unworthy to be called wisdom. Jeremiah's assessment of them is devastating, as he charges,

> They have added things that are against God's will, which will lead the people astray. Such wisdom is not wisdom at all. The wise are not worth their name, and they will be condemned and put to shame, instead of being honoured.[8]

By their misuse of the law the so-called sages of Judah had rejected the word of the Lord, and this was an act of abject contempt and arrogant rebellion

---

[5] W. Brueggemann, *A Commentary on Jeremiah: Exile and Homecoming* (Grand Rapids: Eerdmans, 1998), p. 88.

[6] W. L. Holladay, *Jeremiah 1*, Hermeneia (Philadelphia: Fortress, 1986), p. 282.

[7] Jer. 23:32.

[8] H. Lalleman, *Jeremiah and Lamentations*, TOTC 21 (Downers Grove: InterVarsity Press, 2013), p. 116.

against him. They had treated the law of the Lord as a text to manipulate, and not as the Lord's authoritative word that they were obligated to obey. What the wise men of Judah did was a practice that has recurred throughout history to the present day. Jeremiah was

> putting his finger on a very relevant temptation that has never gone away – the perverse ability of God's people to pay lip-service to the text of the Bible while living in disobedience to it, and to find clever ways of interpreting it in such a way as to justify their disobedience.[9]

Although Jeremiah spoke to the specific situation of his day, he addressed a problem that afflicts the contemporary church as well, so what he said needs to be heard and heeded today. The church in the twenty-first century has access to more books, journals, videos, podcasts and blogs about the Bible than ever before. We have a surfeit of materials that present themselves as God's truth, but the sad reality is that mixed with the truth there is error that needs to be detected and discarded. Not all that we read in print or online is faithful teaching of God's Word. Rather, some who write and speak about the Bible have distorted what God has revealed and have shaped it into communication that they think is more palatable and appealing to contemporary preferences. Paul's warning in the first century is equally timely today: 'For the time will come when people will not put up with sound doctrine. Instead, to suit their own desires, they will gather round them a great number of teachers to say what their itching ears want to hear.'[10]

Those who have been too proud to live by the Lord's instruction will be humbled. Jeremiah said that they would be *put to shame*, using the Hebrew term *bwš*, which in the Old Testament often refers to the disgrace of a military defeat due to divine judgment (cf. Jer. 46:24; 48:20; 50:2). The significance of this language is that

> The defeated enemy would not only experience shame, but they would be an object of ridicule and horror to others (cf. Jer 48:39). Scorn, mocking, and ridicule were common shaming techniques and were employed to depict the misery of the defeated enemy. The defeat is often viewed as part of the divine judgment.[11]

---

[9] C. J. H. Wright, *The Message of Jeremiah*, BST (Downers Grove: InterVarsity Press, 2014), p. 125.

[10] 2 Tim. 4:3.

[11] P. J. Nel, *NIDOTTE* 1:624.

The wise men of Judah may have supposed that they had the freedom to do with the word of the Lord whatever they pleased, but in reality their sense of liberation would actually ensnare them. Their folly would cause them to be dismayed emotionally and trapped experientially, hardly the future they had conceived for themselves. That is how it always is with sin. As the woman pictured as Folly in Proverbs 9:13–18 demonstrates, sin promises enjoyment and freedom, but it actually produces bitterness and bondage. The wisdom of this world, which is really folly, leads to death and not to life.

The general prophecy in verse 9 is spelled out in explicit detail in verse 10. Those who were called *wise* but did not live up to the description would suffer a tragic fate. In words that virtually repeat the oracle of judgment in Jeremiah 6:12–15, verses 10–12 describe the divine retribution that will be inflicted upon the wise men, and also upon the people, the prophets and priests, because *all* of them have been guilty of deceit.[12] The threatened judgment will be overwhelming and horrific, even extending to the *wives* they love being given to their invaders to enjoy, and the *fields* they value being forfeited to the enemy.

The scribes, who were supposed to be wise, led the whole nation to destruction by their false teaching as they rejected the word of the Lord. As a result, there was a total breakdown in Judah's spiritual leadership, because the scribes, the prophets and the priests all practised deceit. In Hosea 4:9, the Lord warned,

> Like people, like priests.
>   I will punish both of them for their ways
>   and repay them for their deeds.

Shortly after Hosea prophesied, his northern kingdom of Israel was taken into captivity by Assyria (cf. 2 Kgs 17:3–6), and during the time when Jeremiah prophesied, his southern kingdom of Judah went into captivity in Babylon (cf. 2 Kgs 25:1–12). In both of their prophecies, it is evident that as

---

[12] P. C. Craigie, P. H. Kelley and J. F. Drinkard, *Jeremiah 1 – 25*, WBC 26 (Dallas: Word, 1991), p. 134, observe, 'This oracle of judgment, paralleled by 6:12–15, declares judgment upon everyone, from people to wise men to prophet to priest. As the wisdom of the wise has been shown to be a lie, so are the words of the prophets who declared that everything would be all right and thus proclaimed, "Peace, Peace" . . . Because of the failure of the people to listen to Jeremiah's warnings, the same threat of invasion made earlier against the prophets and priests is now applied to people and wise men. No section of society will be exempt from the visitation of the Lord.'

the leaders went, so went the nation, because, as has often been said, for good or for bad everything rises or falls on leadership.

Instead of living and teaching the values of the law of the Lord, the spiritual leaders of Judah took the path of folly that leads to death. They were shameless in their sin, and instead of influencing the nation towards righteousness, they led it into wickedness, as Jeremiah discloses in verse 12:

Are they ashamed of their detestable conduct?
No, they have no shame at all;
they do not even know how to blush.
So they will fall among the fallen;
they will be brought down when they are punished.

Rather than living according to the fear of the Lord, which is the beginning of wisdom that leads to life, the leaders chose and modelled a path that brought Judah into judgment.

2. The Lord's reward of the truly wise (9:23–24)

This passage, Jeremiah 9:23–24, is not directly connected to the previous passage examined, 8:8–10. However, it is one of several texts in the book of Jeremiah that speak of people who are called wise or who suppose that they possess wisdom (for example, see also 9:12, which asks, 'Who is wise enough to understand this? Who has been instructed by the LORD and can explain it?'). These verses are framed as a specific communication from the Lord, as they are introduced by *This is what the LORD says* and conclude with *declares the LORD*. This, then, is a strong divine word of warning addressed to three groups of people, all of whom seem to have great resources, because they are *wise, strong* or *rich*. When read together with the narrative in 1 Kings, it is evident that these are the very features that marked Solomon's success, and yet they did not prevent his falling into folly. Through his prophet Jeremiah the Lord warns these prominent people in Judah not to boast of their intellectual, military or financial assets.

The term *boast* features in this passage, being used three times in verse 23 and once in verse 24. This is an uncommon form of the verb *hll*, which in its usual form is the familiar term for praising the Lord throughout the Old Testament, and especially in the book of Psalms. By using this play on words, the Lord indicates that when the wise boast of their wisdom, the strong boast of their strength or the rich boast of their riches, they are perverting the praise that should properly be directed to the Lord. Human assets become liabilities when they become the object of one's boasting, because only the Lord is truly deserving of praise. In their folly, human beings tend to place their confidence in their own resources, and to suppose wrongly that they are self-sufficient, when in fact they need to be dependent upon the Lord, who is the source of all true wisdom, strength and riches. By contrast, the faithful people of the Lord affirm in Psalm 20:7,

> Some trust in chariots and some in horses,
>   but we trust in the name of the LORD our God.

When people do not truly know the Lord (cf. v. 24), they are prone to distort wisdom into arrogance, strength into violence and riches into greed. If they shift their focus away from the Lord and place it on the resources they possess, they are replacing faith in the Lord with human arrogance, and that is folly indeed.[13] Although many people suppose that idolatry was an issue only in the ancient world, or perhaps exists only in remote areas of the world today, in reality there are many forms of idolatry that are pervasive even in the contemporary Western world. Whatever people trust in becomes their god, and human beings today, just as in the time of Jeremiah, are prone to trust in what they know, in the power they wield and in the possessions they own. All of these become idols when they take the place that rightfully belongs to the Lord alone, and to the extent that we place our confidence in them we are both foolish and idolatrous.

Verse 24 begins with *but*, which signals a profound contrast with verse 23. The Lord condemned human leaders in verse 23 because they boasted in their resources of wisdom, strength and riches. In verse 24, the Lord redirects his people to the proper object of boasting, or praise, and that is that they have *understanding* of him. The leaders of Judah were boasting

---

[13] *DBI*, p. 101, concludes well, 'Boasting in anything other than God affronts God with arrogant self-sufficiency. Such boasting symbolizes fallen humanity's natural inclination to trust in human wisdom, might and wealth rather than understanding and knowing God (Jer 9:23–24). Scripture depicts the rich and powerful who assume they are more clever and powerful than God and who boast in their affliction of the righteous and poor (Ps 52:1; 94:1–7). Their arrogant claims will dissolve in shame and judgment.'

about all the wrong things, but those who are truly wise know the Lord as he really is, because, as Proverbs 28:5 states,

> Evildoers do not understand what is right,
> but those who seek the LORD understand it fully.

Those who know the Lord are shaped by his values, rather than by bankrupt human values. Instead of boasting about their own resources, they know that the Lord is the one *who exercises kindness, justice and righteousness on earth*, and he is the example that they follow in their lives (cf. Mic. 6:8). Jeremiah's point is that 'Faithfulness or "loyal love" (*ḥesed*), justice and righteousness are part of God's character (cf. Exod. 34:6–7) and are reflected in those who know him . . . The focus of people's praise should be God and not themselves or their abilities.'[14] In the New Testament, Paul in 1 Corinthians 1:26–31 alludes to the theme of boasting in the Lord in this passage as he contrasts boasting in the Lord (cf. 2 Cor. 10:17) with human boasting in personal accomplishments and achievements (cf. 2 Cor. 11:18).[15] In fact, subverting human values,

> God chose the foolish things of the world to shame the wise; God
> chose the weak things of the world to shame the strong. God chose the
> lowly things of this world and the despised things – and the things that
> are not – to nullify the things that are, so that no one may boast before
> him.[16]

What a contrast this is to athletes who celebrate their triumphs, the wealthy who flaunt their possessions and the powerful who elevate themselves by pushing around those too weak to resist them.

---

[14] Lalleman, *Jeremiah and Lamentations*, p. 124. Similarly, J. A. Thompson, *The Book of Jeremiah*, NICOT (Grand Rapids: Eerdmans, 1980), p. 321, comments, 'True religion consists in acknowledging the complete sovereignty of God in life and allowing him to fill life with those qualities of steadfast faithfulness, justice, and righteousness which he possesses, in which he delights, and which he desires to find in his people.'

[15] L. C. Allen, *Jeremiah: A Commentary*, OTL (Louisville: Westminster John Knox, 2008), p. 121, states, 'The ironic exhortation "boast in the Lord" reappears twice in Paul's letters to Corinth as an echo of this text, at 1 Cor 1:31 in a contrast with human wisdom and power and at 2 Cor 10:17 in an attack on unjustified self-commendation on the part of rival missionaries who were boasting "according to human standards" (2 Cor 11:18).'

[16] 1 Cor. 1:27–29.

3. Concluding comment

Not everything that presents itself as wise actually is wise. Sometimes a person may be called a 'wise guy', but that is not at all the same as being someone who is genuinely wise. Rather, the wise guy is a caricature of the wise person, and is not truly wise at all. Similarly, the Greek word for wisdom is *sophia*, which is also the root of the word 'sophisticated'. What is sophisticated may appear as though it is in the know, up to date or edgy, but it is not actually wise. It is all appearance without the substance of wisdom.

Jeremiah points us to the importance of being wise as the Lord views it. Truly wise people do not distort what the Lord says in order to fit their own preferences; instead they obey his instructions. They accept God's Word as the direction for their lives, rather than manipulating it so that it suits their own purposes. If we are wise, we will not depend on our own resources, but will come to know the Lord and to accept his values for our own lives. This can be difficult, because even Christians have to contend with a sin nature that seeks to draw us away from the Lord. While the Spirit of God is working within us to produce his fruit of Christlikeness in our lives (Gal. 5:22–23), our flesh is ever seeking to cultivate its deeds in us (5:19–21). In so many ways, the godly life is like walking up the down escalator, and if we are not diligent about walking in the Spirit, we may well find ourselves falling into sin. This is not the way of wisdom, because even when it is painted to look as though it is 'wise', in reality it is thoroughly foolish in God's eyes.

It has often been said that the world has got more into the church than the church has got into the world. If we are to live wisely for the Lord, we must be people whose lives are shaped by the Lord's values, and who therefore manifest his qualities of kindness, justice and righteousness. We must not call ourselves Christians and yet live in a way that is derived from what our culture values rather than from what the Lord says is right and good. As in the days of Jeremiah, the people of the Lord must live wisely in the context of a world that is opposed to him. We will feel pressure from our sin nature within us and from our ungodly culture around us, both of which endeavour to deter us from the Lord's way. In the light of these threats, we must continue to work out with complete seriousness the salvation that God has given to us (Phil. 2:12). As we do this, we can be assured that God is empowering us, so that we will desire and be able to accomplish his good purpose (2:13).

Psalm 112

8. The blessings of fearing the Lord

Just as wisdom language and themes are found in the Mosaic law, the Old Testament narratives and the Old Testament prophets, so they occur in a number of the Psalms as well. Many psalms have minor or passing references to wisdom, but several have a sufficient concentration of wisdom language that they are commonly referred to as wisdom psalms. In their form, they are similar to other songs in the Psalter, but in their content they are reminiscent of the wisdom books, sometimes Proverbs (for example, Ps. 37) and at other times Ecclesiastes (for example, Pss 49 and 73).[1] Psalm 112 has several features that cause it to be included among the wisdom psalms.[2]

Proverbs 9:10 states, 'The fear of the LORD is the beginning of wisdom', and this declaration prompts two questions in our minds. First, what does the abstract concept of 'the fear of the LORD' look like in practical life? Second, why should we commit ourselves to the fear of the Lord rather than to some other life principle? Psalm 112 answers both of these important questions.

Although it is not evident in the various translations of the Bible into contemporary languages, both Psalm 111 and Psalm 112 are acrostic psalms, meaning that in the original Hebrew texts both of these psalms have lines that begin with the successive letters of the Hebrew alphabet. This careful structure suggests that these psalms are wisdom psalms that

---

[1] For a brief discussion of the wisdom psalms, see D. J. Estes, *Handbook on the Wisdom Books and Psalms* (Grand Rapids: Baker Academic, 2005), pp. 190–192.

[2] The discussion in this chapter has drawn from and adapted material from the exposition of Ps. 112 in D. J. Estes, *Psalms 73 – 150*, NAC 13 (Nashville: B&H, 2019), pp. 353–358.

make use of the same rhetorical pattern that is found in Proverbs 31:10–31, where the woman who fears the Lord is described and extolled in an acrostic poem. In addition, the expression *Blessed are those* that begins Psalm 112 is a standard wisdom phrase that occurs also in Psalm 1:1 and Proverbs 8:34. Because Psalm 112 is an acrostic, it does not have a clear logical structure, but is more like a kaleidoscope, as one commentator explains:

> The opening commendation formula creates the perspective of the whole psalm. It is used in wisdom literature to refer to an ideal to emulate; it is an implicit exhortation since it offers congratulations to those who comply. What follows in the rest of the psalm is a kaleidoscopic definition of the incentives and lifestyle of the person here praised. Respectful obedience of Yahweh's will revealed in the Torah is set forth as a worthwhile virtue to emulate.[3]

Or, to use another analogy, this psalm resembles an impressionistic painting by Claude Monet. Psalm 111 and Psalm 112 are closely related, as Psalm 111 concludes,

> The fear of the Lord is the beginning of wisdom;
>   all who follow his precepts have good understanding,

and then Psalm 112 picks up where Psalm 111 left off as it describes the behaviours and blessings of the person who fears the Lord. To view Psalm 112, we need to step back and view from a distance the pattern that emerges from it by seeing it as a whole, rather than analysing the consecutive verses of the psalm one after another.

1. The behaviours of the person who fears the Lord

Psalm 112 begins with the exclamation *Praise the Lord*, which is the Hebrew word that is transliterated as 'Hallelujah!' It could be that this word originally belonged to Psalm 111, as part of the exclamations of praise framing that psalm, because other descriptive praise psalms (for example, Pss 103; 104; 113; and 117) both begin and end with 'Praise the Lord'.

---

[3] L. C. Allen, *Psalms 101 – 150*, WBC 21, rev. edn (Nashville: Thomas Nelson, 2002), p. 130.

Whether or not that was the case, Psalm 112 immediately diverges into a wisdom teaching that describes the person who fears the Lord. Its striking parallels to the language of Psalm 111 suggest that Psalm 112 may well have been composed in imitation of the previous psalm. At the same time, the significant differences in style between the two psalms make it likely that they were written by two different psalmists. It seems best to conclude that the writer of Psalm 112 deliberately made use of the prior Psalm 111 text as his pattern. This could be likened to Sergei Rachmaninov who, in his 1934 *Rhapsody on a Theme of Paganini*, drew on what Niccolò Paganini, who lived from 1782 to 1840, had composed a century earlier.

Sprinkled throughout Psalm 112 are numerous descriptions of the kinds of behaviours that characterize the life of a person who fears the Lord. These behaviours answer the question, 'What does the fear of the Lord look like in life?' as they translate the abstract concept of the fear of the Lord into concrete actions and attributes. In verse 1, those who fear the Lord *find great delight in his commands*. Because they reverence the Lord they rejoice in his requirements, a spirit that is reflected also in Psalm 19:9–10:

> The fear of the LORD is pure,
>   enduring for ever.
> The decrees of the LORD are firm,
>   and all of them are righteous.
>
> They are more precious than gold,
>   than much pure gold;
> they are sweeter than honey,
>   than honey from the honeycomb.

Those who fear the Lord do not just know the word of God, or even obey it, but they delight in what it demands. That is to say, they are committed to learn, to live and to love his commands. They are enthusiastically devoted to what the Lord expects from them, so they find their joy in his way rather than insisting on their own way. For them, 'This life of honoring God and following God's commandments is not a drudgery but a delight!'[4]

---

[4] J. Limburg, *Psalms*, Westminster Bible Companion (Louisville: Westminster John Knox, 2000), p. 385.

Those who fear the Lord are *upright* (2), because they align their lives according to the Lord's character and his commands. They do not lean on their own understanding, but rather they trust in the Lord with all their heart (Prov. 3:5). They do not follow the path that appears right to them (Prov. 14:12), but they walk according to the way of the Lord. It is the Lord who is the standard for their behaviour. What the Lord has directed, they do, and how the Lord views matters is all-important to them, because they are devoted to doing what pleases the Lord. Similarly, in verse 3 they are righteous, because they have a commitment to the Lord's righteous standard that does not waver or swerve. Psalm 111:3 states that the Lord's righteousness 'endures for ever', and in Psalm 112:3 those who fear the Lord follow his commitment to what is right as the pattern for their lives. By living consistently according to the Lord's righteousness, they continue in the sphere of his blessing.

Continuing the parallels between Psalm 111 and Psalm 112, verse 4 describes the people who fear the Lord as *gracious and compassionate and righteous*, qualities of life that mirror the Lord, who is 'gracious and compassionate'.[5] The preposition translated as *for* is a Hebrew word that has a wide range of uses. In verse 4 it could have the sense of 'by', which would indicate that by imitating aspects of the Lord's character in their lives, they incarnate his values and bring his moral light into the sinful darkness of their culture. By their godly behaviour, the light of God's character penetrates the darkness of sin that pervades human experience. Instead of adopting and adapting the standards of the world, through their godly lives they shine God's light into a world that has turned away from him into the darkness of ungodliness, becoming 'a living testimony to and an indication of God's mercy, grace, and righteousness'.[6]

In Psalm 111:5, the Lord 'provides food for those who fear him', and in Psalm 112:5 his just people *are generous and lend freely*. Like the Lord, those who fear him are quick to see and to respond to the needs of others around them. As they have received freely from the Lord, so they give freely to other people, in keeping with the wisdom saying in Proverbs 19:17:

> Whoever is kind to the poor lends to the LORD,
>   and he will reward them for what they have done.

---

5 Ps. 111:4.

6 A. Weiser, *The Psalms*, trans. H. Hartwell, OTL (Philadelphia: Westminster, 1962), p. 703.

Christians are sometimes written off as being so heavenly minded that they are no earthly good, but this verse indicates that when the Lord's people share his values and priorities, they provide great earthly good. In their lending they are just; they endeavour not to take advantage of the poor, but rather to assist them in their need (cf. Pss 15:5; 37:21). There is a profound difference between how lending works in the contemporary world and how it functioned in the ancient biblical world:

> In Western society it mostly means people with resources increasing those resources by lending to people with none. In the OT lending is a means of the rich helping the poor, not helping themselves, and not making them the recipients of charity but giving them means of reestablishing themselves, after which they would pay back the loan (see, e.g., Exod. 22:25–27). Its ideology was closer to that of credit unions and building societies. Here, goodness includes being willing to use one's surplus wealth for the benefit of others. When they pay it back, it becomes available to help yet others.[7]

The lives of those who fear the Lord are marked by justice and generosity, and their godly behaviour is confirmed when it is scrutinized (cf. Job's defence in Job 29:11–16).

Reinforcing the description of those who fear the Lord in verses 4–5, verse 9 affirms,

> *They have freely scattered their gifts to the poor,*
> *their righteousness endures for ever.*

They are generous, not grudging, as they give to those in need, and in this they manifest the Lord's heart (cf. 111:5). Their righteousness, or living according to God's norm, is not an occasional event, but the consistent pattern of their lives that endures for ever (as also in v. 3). Because they revere the Lord, their lives align with the Lord's attributes and actions, in effect doing unto others as the Lord has done unto them. In this they live by the ethical paradigm propounded throughout the Bible, both in the Old Testament, where the Lord commands Israel, 'Be holy because I, the LORD

---

[7] J. Goldingay, *Psalms, Volume 3: Psalms 90 – 150*, BCOTWP (Grand Rapids: Baker Academic, 2008), pp. 311–312.

your God, am holy';[8] and in the New Testament, where Jesus charges, 'Be perfect, therefore, as your heavenly Father is perfect.'[9] At the most fundamental level, the standard for our human behaviour is rooted in the imitation of the Lord.

2. The blessings of the person who fears the Lord

Intertwined in the mosaic of Psalm 112 are the behaviours of the person who fears the Lord and the blessings that come to such a person. The causes (behaviours) produce the effects (blessings), and in this conjunction Psalm 112 answers the question, 'Why should we commit to the fear of the Lord?' Just as the behaviours are sprinkled throughout the psalm in no particular order, so the blessings are also presented without any discernible sequence. The meaning of the psalm emerges as we consider each of the blessings and then step back to see what the whole communicates.

In verse 1, those who fear the Lord *find great delight in his commands*, and as a result they are *blessed*. The Hebrew term *'ašrê* denotes the great happiness of those who esteem God's way rather than demanding their own way. In a world that desperately and vainly seeks happiness through achievements, possessions, status, thrills and so many other means, Psalm 112 points to true happiness as the consequence of fearing the Lord, which causes one to delight in his word.

Continuing the thought of happiness into verse 2, the blessing of those who fear the Lord extends to their descendants, as those who are upright leave a lasting legacy of blessing for the next generation. Their children will be *mighty*, or, better, 'prosperous', as the same term *gibbôr* is used in verse 3 and in Ruth 2:1.[10] In the language of traditional wisdom, as seen throughout the book of Proverbs, this indicates a general pattern of blessing, but it is not a certain guarantee or an ironclad promise, because there are other factors that can also come into play. For example, the children of Job were killed in the sudden catastrophe (Job 1:18–19) initiated by the adversary in his effort to undermine their father's commitment to the Lord. Also, Josiah, who was one of the godliest kings of Judah (2 Kgs 22:2), had three sons and a grandson who all met tragic fates in the

---

8 Lev. 19:2.

9 Matt. 5:48.

10 R. Alter, *The Book of Psalms* (New York: W. W. Norton, 2007), p. 401.

years culminating in the nation being taken into captivity by Babylon (2 Kgs 23:31 – 25:7).

In Old Testament wisdom, the blessing of the Lord brings wealth, as is stated in Proverbs 10:22:

> The blessing of the LORD brings wealth,
>> without painful toil for it.

Those who are righteous enjoy material prosperity and more as part of God's blessing, as personified Wisdom declares in Proverbs 8:18–19:

> With me are riches and honour,
>> enduring wealth and prosperity.
> My fruit is better than fine gold;
>> what I yield surpasses choice silver.

Similarly, verse 3 states of the righteous people who fear the Lord that *Wealth and riches are in their houses*. Although it is foolish to make the accumulation of wealth one's goal in life, wealth may be one of the Lord's benefits for those who seek him faithfully. Nevertheless, it should also be remembered that Psalms 49 and 73 teach clearly that there are wealthy and prosperous people who are not living as the Lord requires, so affluence is not proof positive that one is pleasing to him. What the Old Testament teaches is that

> Wealth is a blessing from God (Prov. 10:22), but to pursue wealth for its own sake is a recipe for discontent, loneliness, and emptiness (Eccl 4:8; cf. Prov 28:20) . . . Better than riches is a good name (Prov 22:1), and ultimately, real riches are to be found in the humility and fear of the Lord (22:4).[11]

In verse 6, the righteous have the benefit of stability, because they *will never be shaken*. In their own day, they will enjoy security, as Proverbs 10:30 observes:

> The righteous will never be uprooted,
>> but the wicked will not remain in the land.

---

[11] W. Domeris, *NIDOTTE* 3:560.

They also will be *remembered for ever*. Their commitment to justice prompts them to be generous (5), and this is a blessing that will be remembered with gratefulness for a long time by those who have benefited from their kindness; as Proverbs 10:7 notes,

> The name of the righteous is used in blessings,
>> but the name of the wicked will rot.

Those who fear the Lord do not fear evil threats that arise against them (7–8). Even when external situations are dire, they have internal stability, so they do not fear *bad news*. Even when life seems to go upside down for them, and injurious rumours about them are rampant, their faith keeps them firm. Their trust in the Lord sustains them through every trouble, because they share the confidence of the psalmist in Psalm 28:7:

> The LORD is my strength and my shield;
>> my heart trusts in him, and he helps me.
> My heart leaps for joy,
>> and with my song I praise him.

Human trust and divine deliverance are closely connected, although

> The Psalms do not specify the form in which the deliverance should take place. Indeed, they are probably nonspecific precisely so that the deliverance can in fact take a variety of different forms, depending on the situation and needs of the worshiper. But they are all clear about the intimate connection between trust and deliverance.[12]

Although their adversaries may seem to triumph over them in the short run, in the end those who fear the Lord will prevail (cf. Ps. 49:14) and *look in triumph on their foes*. This triumphant look may imply victory in battle, either literally (as in Ps. 91:7–8), or as a figure of speech portraying how they have transcended their adversity. Because they trust in the Lord to deliver them, they can view their present threats without fear.

In verse 9, the *horn* of those who fear the Lord *will be lifted high in honour*. Several times in Old Testament poetry a horn is a metaphor for

---

12   R. W. L. Moberly, *NIDOTTE* 1:646.

power drawn from the practice of a wild ox shaking its horns in triumph over its prey. For example, the psalmist exclaims in Psalm 92:10–11,

> You have exalted my horn like that of a wild ox;
>> fine oils have been poured on me.
> My eyes have seen the defeat of my adversaries;
>> my ears have heard the rout of my wicked foes.

Continuing the theme from verse 8, those who fear the Lord will enjoy the blessing of being exalted in honour by him. Instead of being defeated and shamed, they will be victorious and will enjoy the honour of the victor. By contrast, the wicked will be *vexed* when they see how the righteous are rewarded (10), even gnashing their teeth as they waste away in their defeat. As the *longings of the wicked* are frustrated, the desires of the righteous are fulfilled by the Lord (cf. Ps. 37:4).

The contrast between the exaltation of the righteous (9) and the devastation of the wicked (10) reflects the prominent teaching of the two ways of wisdom and folly in the book of Proverbs as well as in many other biblical passages, such as Psalms 1 and 37; Deuteronomy 30:15–20; and Matthew 7:13–14. In many respects Psalm 112 ends on the same note as Psalm 73, in which the psalmist concludes in verses 27–28,

> Those who are far from you will perish;
>> you destroy all who are unfaithful to you.
> But as for me, it is good to be near God.
>> I have made the Sovereign LORD my refuge;
>> I will tell of all your deeds.

3. The path to blessing

When the acrostic Psalm 112 is viewed as a unity, its key teaching emerges. It demonstrates that those who fear the Lord and obey his commands are blessed by him, and as a result they are a blessing to others. It also seems significant that Psalm 112 shares many links with the preceding Psalm 111, which is a praise psalm describing the Lord's greatness and goodness. The frequent parallels between the two psalms suggest strongly that the person who fears the Lord becomes like the Lord. In following the Lord's perfect pattern of righteousness and compassion in Psalm 111, the godly person in relating to other people increasingly becomes more and more like the Lord. Psalm 112, then, takes the abstract concept of the fear of the Lord and describes how it can be lived out through concrete actions and attitudes. Those who truly revere the Lord obey his commands and follow his example, and as a result they are blessed by the Lord, and thus they become a channel of the Lord's blessing to others as well. This is similar to Psalm 15, in which an initial double question is posed:

> Lord, who may dwell in your sacred tent?
> Who may live on your holy mountain?

The rest of the psalm answers the question by listing the kinds of behaviours that characterize the person whose life is pleasing to the Lord. All of these actions and attitudes bring blessing to other people as well.

4. Concluding comment

The wisdom that the Lord wants to develop in our lives is much more than just knowledge about him. It also entails reverence for him that causes us to obey what he says. Psalm 112, however, takes the message of wisdom even further, because in adopting the language of Psalm 111 that describes the Lord's attributes and using it to refer to the actions and attitudes of the one who fears the Lord, it teaches that the person who is truly wise follows the pattern established by the Lord himself. The commands of the Lord are rooted in the character of the Lord, because what he requires of his people is consistent with who he is in his own nature. The numerous textual links between Psalm 111 with its praise of the Lord and Psalm 112 with its description of those who fear the Lord

> is the psalm's way of teaching that the works of the Lord can and should shape the life of the righteous. The correlation is not a presumptuous claim that the upright independently and autonomously realize goodness. Rather, by their fear of the Lord, they enter into the works of the Lord, who works on and in and through their lives. Their goodness is godliness.[13]

---

[13] J. L. Mays, *Psalms*, Interpretation (Louisville: John Knox, 1994), p. 360.

Several years ago, there was a fad of wearing WWJD bracelets, with the letters standing for the question 'What would Jesus do?' Even though it often became trite and at times silly, this question does reflect the biblical sense of the wise life. Wise people who fear the Lord act righteously, because the Lord is righteous and they choose to follow his example. They delight in his Word, because they value it as the word of the Lord they respect and love. They are compassionate to those in need, because they are following the Lord's generous example. Although Psalm 112 never says it explicitly, as do Leviticus 19:2 and Matthew 5:48, when it is read together with Psalm 111 the imitation of God is clearly implied. This is the standard for God's wise people, and it is the kind of behaviour that the Lord delights to bless, as one commentator explains well:

> The foundation of the morally good life is reverence for Yhwh, which expresses itself in submission to Yhwh, and in an associated enthusiasm for Yhwh's commands. In relation to other people, the good life involves faithfulness, doing right by the people in our community. This expresses itself in bringing light to people when they are in darkness by being gracious and compassionate, not so much an attitude of sympathetic concern as a practice: we lend them what they need or give them what they need, and we do not merely start on such a project but complete it.[14]

Psalm 112 compels us to evaluate our lives to assess if our actions and attitudes validate that we truly revere the Lord. When we revere the Lord, our lives will follow his example, which is detailed in Psalm 111, and they will overflow in blessing to those around us. This is hardly just a strategy for self-improvement, but instead is the blessed result when the Lord becomes the focus of our lives. In New Testament terms, it is what the Lord wants to produce in us as he transforms us by the renewing of our minds, because then we will approve God's good, pleasing and perfect will for us (cf. Rom. 12:2).

---

[14] Goldingay, *Psalms 90 – 150*, p. 314.

Part 3
The conduct of wisdom

Proverbs 6:6–11

9. Wisdom in work

The book of Proverbs has much to say about learning to live well. In Proverbs, two paths are contrasted. The path of wisdom follows what is righteous according to God's norm, and it leads to life in all of its dimensions. By contrast, the path of folly diverges from what God requires, and it leads to death, with all of its disasters. The signpost that leads to wisdom and life is the fear of the Lord, reverence for the Lord that causes us to obey what he says, to value what he loves and to imitate his example.

The life that Proverbs describes parallels what Jesus says in John 10:10: 'I have come that they may have life, and have it to the full.' In Proverbs, we learn that the life God gives touches every area of our experience. There is no part of our lives that is merely secular and therefore unrelated to the Lord; rather all of life connects to the Lord and it all matters greatly to him. This includes even our work, that part of our lives from Monday through Saturday that often seems so far removed from our worship on Sunday. The wisdom of Proverbs teaches us how to work in a way that honours the Lord.

Although we tend to equate work with paid employment, with having a job, work is actually much broader than that. When Proverbs speaks of work, it actually encompasses how we make use of our time and opportunities, and that applies to everyone, not just to those who labour in what we typically consider the workforce. In addition to those who have paid employment, Proverbs speaks to children, to students, to homemakers, to the unemployed and to those who have retired from their careers. So, when Proverbs talks about wisdom in work, it is talking to all of us, no matter how our time is allocated. In the New Testament, Paul warns in

2 Corinthians 5:10, 'For we must all appear before the judgment seat of Christ, so that each of us may receive what is due to us for the things done while in the body, whether good or bad.' Because we all will have to answer to God for what we do in our work, it is crucial for us to learn what Proverbs teaches about wisdom in work, and then to live in the light of what we learn.

In this chapter, we will look especially at the text of Proverbs 6:6–11, but also at a number of other related verses scattered throughout the book of Proverbs. Unlike most of the other books of the Bible, which feature a sustained argument or narrative, much of Proverbs is like a jigsaw puzzle, with pieces that have to be sorted and then assembled. In order to learn what Proverbs teaches about the topic of work, we need to select the relevant verses, study them individually and then synthesize them. This chapter is the result of that procedure applied to about twenty verses in Proverbs that speak about how to work wisely.

Proverbs 6:6–11 speaks of wisdom in work by contrasting the ant (6–8) with the sluggard (9–11). In this pair of vignettes, the ant pictures diligence in work, which leads one on the path of wisdom to life. In contrast, the sluggard embodies laziness that avoids work, and this leads one on the path of folly to death. Throughout the book of Proverbs, these contrasting approaches to work appear numerous times.

1. Observe the ant, and be wise (6:6–8)

The historical narrative in 1 Kings 4:29–34 provides a window through which we can see how Solomon developed his wisdom sayings. He made observations of many different features of the Lord's world. From those observations he discerned patterns, often of causes and their effects, and from those patterns he developed lessons for life. The historical record states that Solomon spoke three thousand proverbs, some of which he may have learned from others and passed on as part of the wisdom tradition, and some that he himself authored. In the book of Proverbs there are several hundred sayings that are the finished product of this process of observation about life.

The approach to wisdom in Proverbs is also found in the teachings of Jesus, who in Matthew 6:28–30 counters worry by pointing to what observation of God's world of nature can teach:

And why do you worry about clothes? See how the flowers of the field grow. They do not labour or spin. Yet I tell you that not even Solomon in all his splendour was dressed like one of these. If that is how God clothes the grass of the field, which is here today and tomorrow is thrown into the fire, will he not much more clothe you – you of little faith?

Proverbs 3:19 states that 'By wisdom the LORD laid the earth's foundations', which suggests that he hardwired aspects of his wisdom into his world that can be observed by the attentive human eye. Wisdom is skill in living according to this moral order that the Lord embedded in his world, but folly departs from his moral order.

The two imperatives in Proverbs 6:6 are directed specifically to the *sluggard*, but they also speak more generally to the youth to whom the whole book of Proverbs is addressed (cf. 1:4).[1] The sluggard through laziness tries to defy the created order of the Lord. However, by observing the ways of the ant, the sluggard can become wise. This is not a fable, but rather observation of the actual habits of ants, comparable to the approach taken in Job 12:7; Isaiah 1:3; and Jeremiah 8:7. In this passage the ant is 'a model of wisdom in its foresight and activity in securing its food supply for the winter' and 'it acts on its own initiative and without the need for supervision'.[2] The Lord's wisdom is discernible in how the ant functions, and the sluggard needs to see and to learn from this small creature in the Lord's created world.

Proverbs 6:7–8 present the pattern of behaviour that is observed in the ant. In contrast to the sluggard (9–11), the ant is diligent. The ant does not need supervision, but is able to work on its own. One scholar expounds the three terms in verse 7 to draw out their specific meanings:

The three synonyms in this verse express different nuances of social influence: 'chief' [or 'commander'] is the trend-setter in society, the role-model figure, whom all slavishly copy; 'overseer' is the executive power which enforces the directives of the 'ruler', who dictates social norms,

---

[1] B. K. Waltke, *The Book of Proverbs Chapters 1–15*, NICOT (Grand Rapids: Eerdmans, 2004), p. 336, observes, 'The sluggard is the explicit audience, but the implicit audiences are the son and the gullible who are addressed in the book (see 1:4–5). They are being warned against laziness through the sluggard's chastisement (see 19:25).'

[2] R. N. Whybray, *Proverbs*, NCBC (Grand Rapids: Eerdmans, 1994), p. 97.

by force of law. The ant does not act under the impulsion of any of these forces.[3]

If ants can work without supervision, then certainly human beings should be able to do so. Although it is not stated in this verse, it may suggest as well that ants know how to work within the context of a group, which the sluggard also needs to learn.[4]

Continuing the thought into verse 8, the ant demonstrates industry and foresight. Rather than waiting for an easier or more convenient time, the ant grasps the present opportunity. Even in the intense heat of the summer (cf. Ps. 32:4; Prov. 30:25) the ant is working ahead, not taking a siesta, as the sluggard is prone to do. Unlike many people who are prone to procrastination, the ant does not wait until the last desperate moment to impel it to work, but it looks ahead, plans ahead and works ahead. That is a picture of diligence and prudence (cf. Prov. 10:5).

What careful observation of the ant evidences is diligence, which is a key component of wisdom in work. Although the word 'diligence' is not used specifically in Proverbs 6:6–8, it does appear numerous times in the book of Proverbs and is implied in this wisdom teaching drawn from the activity of the ant. There are three Hebrew terms used for 'diligence' in Proverbs, and each of these words suggests an important principle for wisdom in our work.

Proverbs 22:29 poses and then answers a question:

Do you see someone skilled in their work?
 They will serve before kings;
 they will not serve before officials of low rank.

The sage here calls the attention of the youth to one who is adept at work. The word rendered 'skilled' is *māhîr*, which is used of scribes in Ezra 7:6 and Psalm 45:1.[5] This wisdom saying is a challenge to excellence in work, for 'This is a verse for those unwilling to stop at what seems good enough in job

---

[3] A. G. Zornberg, *Malbim on Mishley: The Commentary of Rabbi Meir Leibush Malbim on the Book of Proverbs* (Jerusalem: Feldheim, 1982), p. 60.

[4] J. A. Kitchen, *Proverbs*, Mentor Commentary (Fearn, Ross-shire: Christian Focus, 2006), p. 138.

[5] The term *māhîr* has often been construed as 'speedy', but M. V. Fox, *Proverbs 10 – 31*, AYB 18B (New Haven: Yale University Press, 2009), p. 718, argues well for the nuance of 'adept, trained'.

performance and push on to doing it right.'[6] The high quality of one's work may well open up doors of opportunity, and Jesus taught in his parable of the talents in Matthew 25:21, 23 that one who is faithful in work will be given greater responsibility. When it is said that he will serve before 'kings', the plural form could suggest an international reputation as a reward for his diligence, as one commentator concludes:

> This proverb states that those who work hard and with skill will succeed in their careers. They will work for the most powerful and influential people in the society, while those who are not diligent will spend their careers working for people on the lower end of the social stratum.[7]

Because diligent people do not squander the opportunities that are within their grasp, they may well be given greater challenges, which lead to their distinction.

Proverbs 11:27 states,

> Whoever seeks good finds favour,
> but evil comes to one who searches for it.

Because the Hebrew noun *šaḥar* means 'dawn', the related verb *šḥr* has sometimes been rendered 'to seek early', but in its usage it means rather to seek eagerly (Job 24:5) or to seek with longing (Ps. 63:1), so in this verse it likely has the sense of seeking intently. For good or for bad, seekers are finders. Seeking what is good for others results in good consequences for oneself, and seeking to bring evil on others will boomerang on the perpetrator.[8]

Proverbs 21:5 states,

> The plans of the diligent [*ḥārûṣ*] lead to profit
> as surely as haste leads to poverty.

---

[6] D. A. Garrett, *Proverbs, Ecclesiastes, Song of Songs*, NAC 14 (Nashville: Broadman, 1993), p. 195.

[7] T. Longman, *Proverbs*, BCOTWP (Grand Rapids: Baker Academic, 2006), p. 419.

[8] Kitchen, *Proverbs*, p. 256, comments, 'The one who puts others first is, ultimately, seeking his own good as well, though he is not cognitively setting out to arrive at that point. In other words, his motives are not bent on pleasing himself by pleasing others. That is, it is a heavenly by-product that they unwittingly discover themselves to have been pursuing by their good will (cf. Prov. 11:17a).'

The term *ḥārûṣ* means 'sharp' and it is used of a threshing sledge in Isaiah 41:15, so it came to be used figuratively of someone who is decisive, prepared or diligent. This word 'does not always imply acting quickly. It refers rather to the carefully calculated move that succeeds.'[9] In many passages in Proverbs, diligence is contrasted with slothfulness, but here it is contrasted with haste.[10] Careful planning is profitable, in contrast to frenetic activity that leads to no good end. The plans of the hasty are not really plans at all, because the hasty person takes the fast and easy way, which typically leads to poverty.

Three times, *ḥārûṣ* is an antithesis to words speaking of slackness in work. In Proverbs 10:4,

> Lazy hands make for poverty,
>> but diligent hands bring wealth.

There is a predictable correlation between one's quality of work and quantity of wealth, but it also needs to be remembered that the general patterns in Proverbs are not intended to cover every specific case in life. In Proverbs 12:24,

> Diligent hands will rule,
>> but laziness ends in forced labour.

In Hebrew, the hand is often a metaphor for power or rule, and it is used both for the Lord and for human beings.[11] Diligent or adept people, then, are able to lead others, but one who is lazy will be controlled by others. Although lazy people may suppose that they are free, they are actually compelled to labour in menial tasks for others.[12] The general sense of this saying is that those who do not take the initiative to work will find that someone else will see to it that they do, and thus

---

[9] D. N. Freedman and J. R. Lundbom, *TDOT* 5:219.

[10] B. K. Waltke, *The Book of Proverbs Chapters 15 – 31*, NICOT (Grand Rapids: Eerdmans, 2005), p. 172, observes, 'Elsewhere the diligent person stands over against the lethargic sluggard (10:4; 12:24, 27; 13:4), but here he stands opposed to the rash and imprudent. The lazy are defective in action; the hasty, in thought. The prudence of the diligent now consists in his wise planning in contrast to ill-conceived and misdirected actions (cf. 11:24–28).'

[11] M. Dreytza, *NIDOTTE* 2:403.

[12] The term *mas* refers to forced servitude or involuntary labour in Exod. 1:11; 1 Kgs 5:13. Cf. G. Klingbeil, *NIDOTTE* 2:992–993.

'The diligent rise to the top and the lazy sink to the bottom.'[13] Proverbs 12:27 observes,

> The lazy do not roast any game,
> but the diligent feed on the riches of the hunt.

Diligence is a valuable asset, in contrast to laziness, which is a decided liability. The lazy person either avoids work altogether, or does not complete the job that has been started.

He thinks about hunting and providing food for his family, but it never ends up on the table. He is full of good plans and good intentions, but short on follow-through. He only roasts his game in his head. He only tastes roast game in his imagination. Even if he gets up off of the couch and actually bags his prize, he lacks the discipline to skin it out and cook it.[14]

These verses using *ḥārûṣ* indicate that diligence acts decisively. It is not impulsive or hasty, but it studies the opportunity and then grasps it wholeheartedly. However, the diligence encouraged in Proverbs should not be distorted into the workaholism that pervades so much of contemporary life. Psalm 127:2 speaks of the vanity of attempting to secure by our work alone what the Lord intends to give by his grace, and Jesus made it clear in his reproof to Martha in Luke 10:38–42 that he valued Mary's attentiveness to him more than Martha's distracted work in serving him.

2. Observe the sluggard, and don't be foolish (6:9–11)

Although Proverbs 6:6–8 describes the diligence of the ant, it is addressed to the sluggard (6). In the book of Proverbs the sluggard is a familiar picture of the lazy person who manifests folly in work (see 10:26; 13:4; 19:24; 20:4; 21:25; 22:13; 24:30–34; 26:13–16). It is evident in Proverbs 6:9–11 that the sluggard has problems getting started. The address to the sluggard links verse 9 with verse 6, where the sluggard is urged to consider the ways of the ant and be wise. Now the teacher has a tone of exasperation, asking

---

[13] A. P. Ross, 'Proverbs', *EBC*, vol. 5 (Grand Rapids: Zondervan, 1991), p. 973.

[14] Kitchen, *Proverbs*, p. 277.

How long . . . ? as he rebukes the sluggard.[15] Instead of bringing in the harvest, the sluggard is sleeping in bed. This is not the sleep of faith that trusts in the Lord's provision (cf. Ps. 3:5; 4:8; 127:2), but instead the slumber of indolence. The lowly ant that gathers its food at harvest (8) knows so much more than the sluggard. Apparently, the sluggard missed the memo about wise diligence that the ant had read!

Verse 10 contains the words of the sluggard's pathetic reply to the rebuke in verse 9. By a series of compromises, as though he is hitting the snooze button repeatedly, the sluggard loses all. This is his avoidance strategy by which he refuses to face the realities of life (cf. 26:13–14). By saying *a little* he makes it sound so reasonable and inconsequential, but actually sleep is the last thing he should be doing in harvest time, when there is urgent and vital work to be done.

The sluggard's laziness (9–10) will lead to his poverty (11). Like students who think it necessary to update their Facebook profiles, check their Twitter accounts and text their friends before starting on their assignments, the sluggard evades work, but he cannot avoid the consequences of that decision. In reality, he is his own worst enemy, because 'he robs himself by wasting away his time, talents, and earning power. Precious hours, important opportunities, and years of productivity are squandered because he lacks enthusiasm and initiative.'[16] He will not be able to defend himself against the adversary that will impoverish him, because he himself is his own worst enemy.

Even when the sluggard gets around to starting the job, he does not finish it. Proverbs 19:24 observes,

> A sluggard buries his hand in the dish;
>   he will not even bring it back to his mouth![17]

This saying pictures the sluggard beginning the process of eating, but by not finishing it he derives no nourishment. The sage pictures the sluggard 'as dozing off with his hand in the dish, so fond of sleep that he cannot stay

---

[15] The expression *'ad mātay* (*How long . . . ?*) introduces a rebuke in Exod. 10:3; 1 Sam. 1:14; 16:1; Prov. 1:22 and elsewhere in the Old Testament. Waltke, *Proverbs Chapters 1–15*, p. 338, observes, 'The rhetorical question implicitly admonishes the sluggard to repent of his foolish laziness and to get up quickly and redeem the time before it is too late.'

[16] R. L. Alden, *Proverbs* (Grand Rapids: Baker, 1983), p. 57.

[17] Similarly, Prov. 26:15 says, 'A sluggard buries his hand in the dish; he is too lazy to bring it back to his mouth.'

awake to eat'.[18] This may be an exaggeration, but its satirical description is not too far off! His laziness makes no sense at all, and his behaviour is totally ridiculous. Because he does not eat the food before him, his laziness only makes him weak and ineffective. This maxim can also be extended to apply to other matters besides eating, for 'Many opportunities for profit present themselves, but the sluggard refuses to make the slightest effort to take advantage of them.'[19]

Proverbs 22:13 indicates that the sluggard makes up excuses, as his inner thinking is disclosed:

The sluggard says, 'There's a lion outside!
  I'll be killed in the public square!'

It is evident from these words that the sluggard goes to extreme lengths to avoid his responsibility, as in his laziness he invents what he wants to believe.[20] He exaggerates the slightest possibility into a virtual certainty. There were indeed lions in ancient Israel (cf. Judg. 14:5; 1 Sam. 17:34; 1 Kgs 13:24), but they did not likely venture within walled cities with streets, and it is highly unlikely that lions would choose to attack a human being in the public square, where people congregated in ancient cities. The sluggard's rationalization would be hilarious if it were not so harmful. Even though it is clearly preposterous, it sounds convincing to him, because he supposes that it gives him cover for avoiding the work he should be doing.

In a portrait that parallels the picture of the diligence of the ant in Proverbs 6:6–8, the sage shows how the sluggard sets himself up for failure in Proverbs 24:30–31. The observation in verses 30–31 yields the lesson for life that follows in verses 32–34. The sage creates a true-to-life parable to teach his lesson (as also in Prov. 7), because everyone has seen this kind of abandoned property. He says,

I went past the field of a sluggard,
  past the vineyard of someone who has no sense;
thorns had come up everywhere,

---

[18] W. McKane, *Proverbs*, OTL (Philadelphia: Westminster, 1970), p. 530.

[19] Fox, *Proverbs 10 – 31*, p. 660.

[20] Kitchen, *Proverbs*, p. 501, notes aptly, 'When we do not want to do something, we can invent a multitude of reasons why it makes no sense. Laziness is fertile soil for paranoia and excuses.'

the ground was covered with weeds,
and the stone wall was in ruins.

His anecdote 'invites the reader to recall similar observations of homes in disrepair and to draw the same conclusions even while participating in the poet's disgust over the shameful condition of the lackadaisical man's home'.[21] In letting his vineyard go like this, the sluggard demonstrates that he has no sense, because in the ancient world a vineyard was a valuable asset from which a family derived its livelihood. In contrast to the wise woman in Proverbs 31:16 who plants a vineyard, the sluggard has failed to do the work necessary to maintain his field and the vineyard in it.

The description of his vineyard in verse 31 is a far cry from what a vineyard should look like. Vineyards are supposed to produce grapes, but the sluggard's laziness allows thorns to replace them. The ground of his vineyard is totally covered with weeds, nettles that make it unfit for human cultivation.[22] In addition, the wall is in ruins, leaving the vineyard open to predators, thieves and wild animals (cf. Isa. 5:5). For a farmer, this is a total failure, indicating that laziness is not a trivial matter but one that leads to catastrophic consequences.

3. Concluding comment

The book of Proverbs, in 6:6–11 and in other sayings spread throughout the collection, teaches that the wise person imitates the ant's diligence and not the sluggard's laziness. What Proverbs teaches about wisdom in work is part of a much larger story in the Bible. When God created the world in Genesis 1, he exclaimed that it was very good. God fashioned human beings and placed them in the Garden of Eden in Genesis 2, and his intention was that they should enjoy the life he had designed for them, including working in the garden as they cultivated and tended it. In Genesis 3, the serpent tempted Adam and Eve to disobey the Lord by suggesting an alternative wisdom which was actually folly (Gen. 3:5–6). To remedy their sin, the Lord had to provide his own Son as the perfect

---

[21] Garrett, *Proverbs, Ecclesiastes, Song of Songs*, p. 202.

[22] M. A. Grisanti, *NIDOTTE* 2:269, notes that the term *ḥārûl* occurs only in Job 30:7; Zeph. 2:9; and here in Prov. 24:31. In each case it signifies 'an undesirable weed that flourishes in untended ground', perhaps wild artichoke or chickpea.

substitute for them. Only by accepting God's gracious offer of salvation through the death of Jesus can we receive his gift of eternal life.

In addition to saving us through Christ, the Lord wants us to enjoy his abundant life today, and this is where the message of wisdom fits into God's good plan for human beings. What the book of Proverbs teaches is not moralism that tries to secure salvation by human effort apart from God. Rather, it teaches wisdom, which is skill in living according to God's way. In learning to be diligent like the ant in our work and to avoid the laziness of the sluggard, we come to experience life today as the Lord intended us to enjoy it, and that is part of his wisdom and the path to the abundant life he wants us to enjoy.

10. Wisdom in speech

The book of Proverbs is concerned with the cultivation of virtue. Many of its sayings serve to teach instrumental virtues, that is, skills for success in the various aspects of life. More than that, however, Proverbs teaches moral virtues, as it seeks to develop in us the kind of character that imitates and pleases the Lord.

In this collection there are many concrete examples drawn from nature and from human life that illustrate how wisdom and folly are evidenced in practical behaviour. Although these examples emerged from life nearly three thousand years ago in ancient Israel, many of them are so embedded in human experience that they are highly relevant to us today as well. By observing life and drawing lessons from it, these sayings illustrate what wisdom looks like in practice, and they point us towards the godly behaviour that the Lord wants to develop in us.

One of the most common subjects in the book of Proverbs is speech. About one in five verses in the collection relates to good or bad patterns of speech, because speech as a window on the heart evidences whether the speaker is wise or not. For example, Proverbs 16:23 states,

> The hearts of the wise make their mouths prudent,
>> and their lips promote instruction.

Wisdom in the heart overflows into wise speech, as our words reflect what we are thinking and how we are feeling. Similarly, Proverbs 10:31 contrasts the speech of the righteous with that of the wicked:

> From the mouth of the righteous comes the fruit of wisdom,
>> but a perverse tongue will be silenced.

A person who is righteous has a pattern of communication that is wise (cf. 12:14; 13:2; 18:20), but evil speech will be cut off, likely by the Lord,[1] rather than bearing good fruit.

Speech has the power of life and death, because it can either heal others or destroy them, as Proverbs 10:11 indicates:

> The mouth of the righteous is a fountain of life,
>> but the mouth of the wicked conceals violence.

For good or for bad, words have effects on others. What the righteous person says is a continual source of life to those who hear it. By contrast, a wicked person speaks what is destructive to life; the term 'violence' (*ḥāmās*) refers to 'the cold-blooded and unscrupulous infringement of the personal rights of others, motivated by greed and hate and often making use of physical violence and brutality'.[2] Proverbs 12:18 uses a vivid word picture to indicate how wise words heal, but foolish words harm:

> The words of the reckless pierce like swords,
>> but the tongue of the wise brings healing.

The speech of a fool is as dangerous to the people around as a sword wielded by one who is reckless and inconsiderate (cf. Ps. 57:4; 64:3; Prov. 25:18), because 'Like a mad man flailing away with a sword in a crowd of innocent people, so the person who does not measure and control his words wounds many innocent people.'[3] By contrast, the speech of the wise heals and helps others.

Proverbs addresses many aspects of verbal communication, and one of the most prominent features of wise speech in the book of Proverbs is truthfulness. Because we live in a time when fake news, abuses of social media and general dishonesty are pervasive, what Proverbs teaches about truthfulness is particularly relevant to life today. By contrast, in his book entitled *The Varnished Truth: Truth Telling and Deceiving in Ordinary Life*, philosopher David Nyberg argues that truthfulness has been overrated. He reasons pragmatically,

---

[1] The niphal form of the verb *krt* may well be a divine passive, indicating that the Lord will silence the speech of those who are wicked.

[2] I. Swart and C. Van Dam, *NIDOTTE* 2:178.

[3] J. A. Kitchen, *Proverbs*, Mentor Commentary (Fearn, Ross-shire: Christian Focus, 2006), p. 271.

Deception is not merely to be tolerated as an occasionally prudent aberration in a world of truth telling: it is rather an essential component of our ability to organize and shape the world, to resolve problems of coordination among individuals who differ, to cope with uncertainty and pain, to be civil and to achieve privacy as needed, to survive as a species, and to flourish as persons.[4]

What Nyberg endeavours to justify in philosophical terms is how many people live in practice. In our judicial proceedings, witnesses are required to swear to tell the truth, the whole truth and nothing but the truth, but that is not the standard adhered to by most people on a daily basis. Recent surveys in the USA document that upwards of 80% of university students admit to cheating; in addition, there are frequent news accounts of lying and deception by business and political figures, and claims to alternative truth are frequently heard. In contrast to the arguments made by Nyberg and the practice of a significant number of people in our contemporary culture, the message of wisdom in the book of Proverbs insists on the moral virtue of truthfulness.

1. The content of truthfulness

It is exceedingly clear in Proverbs 6:16–19 that the Lord hates lying, because it is antithetical to his character, which values what is true. In this enumeration of behaviours that are detestable to the Lord, at least three of the items pertain to speech that is not truthful:

There are six things the Lord hates,
seven that are detestable to him:
  haughty eyes,
  a lying tongue,
  hands that shed innocent blood,
  a heart that devises wicked schemes,
  feet that are quick to rush into evil,
  a false witness who pours out lies,
  and a person who stirs up conflict in the community.[5]

---

[4] D. Nyberg, *The Varnished Truth: Truth Telling and Deceiving in Ordinary Life* (Chicago: University of Chicago Press, 1993), p. 5.

[5] Emphasis added.

This is a representative list, not an exhaustive itemization, of what the Lord finds repugnant to his character and antithetical to his commands. These actions, including untruthful speech, are hated, loathed, by the holy Lord.[6] The Lord hates unjust behaviours of all kinds – in actions, words and attitudes. *Haughty eyes* view other people as lesser or unworthy compared with oneself (cf. Pss 18:27; 101:5; Prov. 21:4). A *lying tongue* is a metonymy by which the tongue represents the false words uttered by it. No part of evil behaviour escapes the Lord's notice and condemnation, because he detests both the intentions of the *heart* as it plans evil and the actions of the *feet* as they *rush* to carry out the wicked plans. Here, as in Proverbs 1:16 and Isaiah 59:7, 'running implies haste and active commitment to do something evil'.[7] In a court setting, witnesses are obliged to tell only the truth, but there are those who commit perjury by testifying falsely. The climactic result of these sinful behaviours, including failure to tell the truth, is that the spirit of community is destroyed, because the sins that the Lord loathes drive people apart rather than together as the Lord desires. This list of deplorable activities and attitudes indicates that the Lord abhors 'a self-regarding, manipulative, violent, and inherently malicious person',[8] and this is specifically the case for those who do not speak truthfully.

In contrast to the negative declaration in Proverbs 6:16–19 about what truthfulness is *not*, there are several sayings that speak positively about what truthfulness *is*. In Proverbs 8:6–8 personified Wisdom speaks truthfully, and this sets the pattern for all those who would be wise. In contrast to Folly, Wisdom speaks what is *right* (cf. 23:16), and seeks to teach all people to do the same. What Wisdom says is *trustworthy* and completely reliable. Wisdom draws a clear line between her truthful speech and the wickedness characteristic of Folly. All that Wisdom says is *just*, and none of her words distort or diverge from the Lord's righteous standard, unlike the words of 'wicked men'.[9]

Proverbs 30:5 describes God's word as the fixed standard for truthfulness when it says, *Every word of God is flawless*. There is no alloy of untruth in

---

[6] Of the verb *śn'* ('hates'), A. H. Konkel, *NIDOTTE* 3:1257–1258 explains, 'The anthropological language of hate is extended to God in a number of ways. God hates the abominable heathen practices (Deut 12:31; 16:22) as well as the ritualistic festivals observed amidst injustice (Isa 1:14; Amos 5:21); the Lord loves justice, but hates robbery with a burnt offering (Isa 61:8). God hates pride, arrogance, the way of evil, and perverted speech (Prov 8:13).'

[7] *DBI*, p. 745.

[8] R. J. Clifford, *Proverbs*, OTL (Louisville: Westminster John Knox, 1999), p. 77.

[9] Prov. 2:12–15.

what God says (cf. Ps. 12:6), because 'Like gold or other precious metal that has been thoroughly tried by fire, Yahweh's word is of proved authenticity and precious.'[10] The Lord is true to his word, and his promises of protection are a dependable *shield* for his people, so his truthfulness inspires us to place our trust in him.[11] In verse 6 a warning is added:

> *Do not add to his words,*
> *or he will rebuke you and prove you a liar.*[12]

By adding to God's words, human beings in effect reverse the smelting process, because what they say is dross. What God says can be counted on to be true, because he is truthful in his character (cf. Num. 23:19), but what human beings add to what God says may well introduce error, because they are intrinsically fallible, and indeed this has been evident countless times throughout history.[13]

2. The context of truthfulness

In our twenty-first-century culture, truthfulness, if it exists at all, is typically relegated to the private realm. For example, husbands and wives are expected to be truthful with one another and to their children. Wisdom, however, regards the Lord as the moral governor of the entire universe that he created, so his ethical standards apply equally to every inch of his domain, not just to close personal relationships. That means that truthfulness must permeate every area of life, both what is done in private and what is done in public, and this is clearly reflected in the book of Proverbs.

---

[10] R. Wakely, *NIDOTTE* 3:849.

[11] T. Longman, *NIDOTTE* 2:846, elaborates on the shield image as follows: 'The assertion that God is a shield is common in the Psalms, but occurs elsewhere as well (Deut 33:29). Enemies may attack God's people, but God intervenes so that their hostile plans do not prevail. God is a shield in actual battle and so protects Israel's army against the offensive weapons of their enemies. But he is also a shield against the emotional and spiritual hostility of those who seek to destroy God's people.'

[12] Cf. Deut. 4:2.

[13] Kitchen, *Proverbs*, p. 682, observes, 'People have added to God's word in many ways. The false prophets added their own interpretations and passed them off as of divine authority (Jer. 28:15–17; 29:21–22, 31–32; Ezek. 13:7–9). The Jews added their meticulous rules and regulations (Matt. 15:9). The pre-Gnostics of Paul's day added their observations (Col. 2:21–22). Some, even after the apostles, have laid their tradition alongside the Scriptures. Cults lay their leaders' books alongside the Scriptures and hold them to be of similar authority. Many today continue the trend in less formal ways, building their lives on a series of hunches, speculations and feelings, rather than upon the clear commands, prohibitions and principles of Scripture.'

Truthfulness should be evidenced in government, as is indicated by Proverbs 20:28:

Love and faithfulness keep a king safe;
through love his throne is made secure.

Both the term translated *love* (ḥesed) and the term *faithfulness* ('ĕmet) are used frequently in the Old Testament to describe the character of the Lord as possessing steadfast love and reliability (cf. Ps. 89:14). These same qualities, which imply truthfulness in dealings, are what made godly kings such as David (1 Kgs 3:6) and Hezekiah (2 Kgs 20:3) safe and secure in their rule. For kings, then, there is protection when they rule by godly values, because

Kindness and fidelity may be imagined as two guards on either side of the throne, which rests on a pedestal of kindness. If the king fails in his ethical duties, he is personally endangered, and his rule will crumble beneath him.[14]

Similarly, Proverbs 29:14 states,

If a king judges the poor with fairness,
his throne will be established for ever.

In many governments, poor people have no power or access, so they do not receive justice. The king God blesses has a moral core of truthfulness that drives his rule and determines his judicial decisions (cf. 22:22–23; 23:10–11), because he governs according to the divine standard of faithfulness ('ĕmet) and not by his own self-interest. By doing what is right and truthful, the king gains stability for his kingdom. Truthfulness, then, is a crucial element in effective political leadership (cf. Ps. 101:7). In our present age, we can become cynical about the lack of veracity in many of our political leaders, but the Lord requires truthfulness from them, and we should expect it from them as well. In fact, a potential leader's commitment to speaking truthfully is a key factor to consider as we decide how to vote.

---

[14] M. V. Fox, *Proverbs 10 – 31*, AYB 18B (New Haven: Yale University Press, 2009), pp. 677–678.

The book of Proverbs also speaks about truthfulness in the realm of business and commerce. Proverbs 20:14 pictures a scene that is as relevant today as it was in the ancient world:

> *'It's no good, it's no good!' says the buyer –*
> *then goes off and boasts about the purchase.*

The buyer claims that the produce is very bad, so that he can haggle down the price, but once he gets it at the lower price he boasts about what a great deal he got. This proverb does not prescribe how business *should* be done, but, sad to say, it describes how business often *does* operate. Just because this is common practice, however, does not make it right or wise, because 'Shrewdness is one thing, but deceitful misrepresentation in the deal in order to buy under value becomes unethical.'[15] Proverbs 20:23 insists,

> *The LORD detests differing weights,*
> *and dishonest scales do not please him.*

To the righteous Lord the practice of using two sets of balances (one when buying and the other when selling), or two sets of books or two prices, is unjust, and these business practices are loathsome to him (cf. Deut. 25:13, 15). God's people should live and love his ways, and not conform to accepted but dishonest practices in their business dealings. The Lord demands truthfulness in the marketplace, so common practices such as bluffing, which many would praise as a skilled business strategy in the art of the deal, are really offences against his holy character. People who are wise before the Lord do not compromise truthfulness in order to get a bargain or make a sale.

The major focus of truthfulness in the book of Proverbs is in the area of personal relationships. For example, Proverbs 3:27–28 instructs,

> *Do not withhold good from those to whom it is due,*
> *when it is in your power to act.*
> *Do not say to your neighbour,*
> *'Come back tomorrow and I'll give it to you' –*
> *when you already have it with you.*

---

[15] A. P. Ross, 'Proverbs', *EBC*, vol. 5 (Grand Rapids: Zondervan, 1991), p. 1044.

The resources that God places into our hands are to be used to assist those who are in need. In this proverb, however, a person brushes aside a friend with a phony, untruthful excuse. Perhaps this person hopes that someone else will meet the need before he or she has to do so, but such an insincere speech is not how a true friend responds to a need.

Moving into the legal court setting, Proverbs 24:28 again enjoins truthful speech. The sage admonishes,

> *Do not testify against your neighbour without cause –*
> *would you use your lips to mislead?*

Wisdom requires telling the truth in every area of life, and false testimony by an *ʿēd*, 'a legal witness to the truth of a matter',[16] is an abuse of speech that directly violates the ninth commandment (cf. Exod. 20:16). Similarly,

> *Like a club or a sword or a sharp arrow*
> *is one who gives false testimony against a neighbour.*
> (25:18)

All three similes are lethal weapons that are used to hurt and to kill an enemy. The verb used here (*ʿnh*, often 'answer') suggests that this *false testimony* is given in response to a question posed in a legal case, as the individual commits perjury rather than telling the truth, and by this means the witness harms and perhaps causes his or her neighbour to be executed as though guilty, when that is not the case. In several other Old Testament passages, such as Psalms 57:4; 64:3; and Jeremiah 9:8, lies are pictured as sharp and even poisoned arrows that have deadly force.

Several passages are set in more general, non-judicial contexts in life. Proverbs 16:28 observes,

> *A perverse man stirs up conflict*
> *and a gossip separates close friends.*

Perverse speech stirs things up with harsh words rather than settling things down with gentle words (cf. 15:1), turning God's moral order upside down with calamitous consequences. Falsehood wears many faces. In this verse,

---

16 R. B. Chisholm, *NIDOTTE* 3:337.

gossip will drive a wedge between even *close friends* as it betrays information given in confidence by disclosing it publicly. Lying deliberately tells a
story that one knows to be false. Deception selectively omits facts in order
to colour what others perceive or understand to be the truth. Innuendo uses
negative associations to imply guilt; for example, alleging that someone
who is offended by inhumane prison conditions is 'soft on crime'. Rumour
passes on unsubstantiated allegations as though they are true, sometimes
even by Christians under the guise of concern or a prayer request. In
Proverbs 26:18–19, a simile is followed by the reality it pictures:

> *Like a maniac shooting*
>   *flaming arrows of death*
> *is one who deceives their neighbour,*
>   *and says, 'I was only joking!'*

Such deceivers wield dangerous weapons in their untruthful words. To
compound the problem, they refuse to take responsibility for the harm their
falsehood has inflicted, choosing rather to dodge it by insisting that they
were just joking, blithely oblivious to the hurt they have inflicted on others.
The wise person realizes that deception is a serious matter, and not
something to laugh off as no big deal.

Another aspect of truthful speech is seen in Proverbs 27:5–6, which
says,

> *Better is open rebuke*
>   *than hidden love.*

> *Wounds from a friend can be trusted,*
>   *but an enemy multiplies kisses.*

Rebuke can bring great benefit, but only if it is spoken and then heeded. This
is far better than *love* that is *hidden* – that is, love that does not speak of
faults. A real friend will tell the truth, even if it hurts, because reproof can
be constructive, beneficial and life-enhancing. By contrast, an enemy does
not speak the truth; instead such a person deceives and manipulates by
playing on one's feelings rather than speaking the facts. As Judas demonstrated (Mark 14:43–45), a *kiss* can appear flattering, and yet not at all be
the expression of love it purports to be.

A final category of untruthful speech is seen in Proverbs 25:14:

Like clouds and wind without rain
  is one who boasts of gifts never given.

The land of Israel was dependent on rain, and without rain nothing grew. In the same way, talk is cheap if there is nothing to back it up. The person envisioned in this saying talks big, but he or she does not come through on these verbal commitments. People may be attracted by the promises that raise their expectations, but they are disappointed by this person's failure to deliver on what he or she has said.[17] This saying warns that we must be honest in what we say, not stretching the truth to impress others or making promises we will not or cannot keep. This holds true for political leaders seeking votes, people in business endeavouring to close a deal, donors pledging a financial contribution, and parents making commitments to their children.

3. The consequences of truthfulness

Is it really worth it to be truthful in a culture pervaded by untruthfulness? Proverbs resoundingly answers, 'Yes!' Truthful speech brings personal benefits, as is implied in Proverbs 12:13:

Evildoers are trapped by their sinful talk,
  and so the innocent escape trouble.

Falsehood has a way of coming back to haunt the one who speaks it, but truth keeps a person from *trouble*. The unstated assumption is that the Lord, who values truth, will reward truthful speech, just as he punishes *sinful talk*, as is taught explicitly in Proverbs 19:5:

A false witness will not go unpunished,
  and whoever pours out lies will not go free.

---

[17] B. K. Waltke, *The Book of Proverbs Chapters 15–31*, NICOT (Grand Rapids: Eerdmans, 2005), p. 324, explains, 'He boasts about the gift but intentionally distorts the factual reality to deceive another. The metaphor suggests that the boaster has loudly and with great fanfare promised his gift, exciting great expectations, and then sunk them in disappointment. It also connotes that the gift was essential for the well-being of the deceived.'

In the Old Testament law, a *false witness* was punished severely (cf. Exod. 23:1; Deut. 19:16–21), so telling a lie is never a good strategy; telling the truth is always the right thing to do.

The personal consequences of untruthfulness are also described in a vivid word picture in Proverbs 20:17, which states,

> *Food gained by fraud tastes sweet,*
> *but one ends up with a mouth full of gravel.*

Deception may seem *sweet* at first, but it inevitably leaves an unpleasant taste. Like *gravel*, it provides no nourishment or pleasure, and it may even break one's teeth (cf. Lam. 3:16), thereby preventing future enjoyment as well. Proverbs 12:19 contrasts truthful lips which endure for ever with a lying tongue that lasts only a moment. Truthful speech provides a long-term advantage, but false speech has a short shelf life and no staying power. In fact, 'The truthful man will go on from strength to strength for none of his words will fall to the ground, but the liar will speedily be detected and discredited.'[18]

More broadly, truthful speech has consequences for other people beyond the individual who speaks it. In the legal context, Proverbs 14:25 states,

> *A truthful witness saves lives,*
> *but a false witness is deceitful.*

For good or for bad, what people say affects others around them (cf. 6:19; 12:17; 14:5; 19:5). When a witness tells the truth, a just decision is made for the defendant, because 'the entire process of justice depends on the veracity of the witnesses'.[19] In the setting of education, the sage discloses,

> *My son, if your heart is wise,*
> *then my heart will be glad indeed;*
> *my inmost being will rejoice*
> *when your lips speak what is right.*
> (23:15–16)

---

[18] W. McKane, *Proverbs*, OTL (Philadelphia: Westminster, 1970), p. 445.

[19] Kitchen, *Proverbs*, p. 316.

The teacher longs to see a heart of wisdom in the learner, and righteous speech (16) is evidence of a wise heart (15). Truthful students bring great joy to their teachers, just as truthful children delight their parents (cf. 10:1; 15:20; 3 John 4).[20]

Speaking truthfully also has consequences before the Lord, because

The LORD detests lying lips,
> *but he delights in people who are trustworthy.*
(12:22)

The verb *detests* refers to what is repugnant to the Lord's very nature, as lying is. By contrast, the Lord *delights* in truthfulness that imitates his own faithful character as he describes it in Exodus 34:6. Truthfulness in speech brings joy to the Lord as it imitates his own values, but 'lying is a violation of the divine character and therefore an obnoxious offense to the God of truth'.[21]

4. Concluding comment

Many sayings in Proverbs teach the principle that the wise person imitates the Lord by speaking truthfully. In our contemporary culture with its prevalent moral relativism, truthful speech often seems as outdated as slide rules and polyester leisure suits. Sad to say, too often even Christians find themselves defaulting to our culture's pattern of falsehood when they say things that they know are not true, misrepresent other people and bring unjust criticism upon them, stand by silently while others are wrongfully accused, or refuse to take responsibility for the pain they have inflicted by their speech or failed to prevent by their silence. Christians should speak fervently about God's truth, but when they fail to speak truthfully about other people, their falsehoods have calamitous consequences.

Why is it so hard for us to be truthful? Truthfulness can fail for many reasons, but oftentimes it surrenders to fear. We fail to be truthful because we fear criticism, but then we end up looking like cowards when the truth

---

[20] Prov. 17:21 also teaches the opposite side of the issue: 'To have a fool for a child brings grief; there is no joy for the parent of a godless fool.' See also 17:25; 19:13.

[21] D. A. Hubbard, *Proverbs*, The Communicator's Commentary 15A (Dallas: Word, 1989), p. 185.

eventually comes out. We fail to be truthful because we fear responsibility, but we end up trapped in a web of our deceptions. We fail to be truthful because we fear the personal cost of getting hurt, but we end up enslaved to the guilty conscience pricked by our dishonesty. We fail to be truthful because we fear upsetting others, but we end up missing the chance to provide constructive reproof that would actually help them.

By contrast, truthful speech has the courage to follow the Lord's example, speaking truthfully to others as the Lord speaks truthfully to us. In our world in which falsehood too often is the norm, the Lord calls his people to live by his virtue of truthfulness. By speaking truthfully we evidence wisdom through our speech that pleases the Lord.

11. Wisdom in decisions

Every day we are faced with decisions we have to make. Many of these decisions are small, such as what to eat for lunch or what colour shirt to wear. Other decisions are much more consequential, because in those cases a wise decision can bring great benefits but a bad decision can invite disaster. We might like to avoid having to make decisions, especially difficult decisions, yet we all have to make them, like it or not.

The book of Proverbs has a lot to say about making decisions. The familiar words of Proverbs 3:5–6 give us general direction:

> *Trust in the Lord with all your heart*
> *and lean not on your own understanding;*
> *in all your ways submit to him,*
> *and he will make your paths straight.*

The book of Proverbs also contains many additional wisdom sayings that fill in the details, as they teach what leads to foolish decisions (leaning on your own understanding) and what leads to wise decisions (trusting in the Lord with all your heart). In these maxims, Proverbs gives reliable guidance to direct us towards God's good and wise way for our lives.

1. How to make foolish decisions

There are numerous verses in Proverbs that show how people make foolish decisions, and these provide negative examples to avoid. When we presume on the future, that attitude often leads to costly mistakes. For example,

> *For the waywardness of the simple will kill them,*
>   *and the complacency of fools will destroy them.*
> (1:32)

In Proverbs, the *simple* (*petî*) 'is an ignorant and simple-minded person who does not hate knowledge but is receptive and always prepared to learn or to be taught'.[1] Those who are simple run into trouble when openness to instruction morphs into careless complacency. They float in the stream, supposing that everything will work out fine, and then the waterfall comes! The sage points out what may not be evident at the time of their decision, namely where the path they take will end. Similarly, Proverbs 27:1 warns,

> *Do not boast about tomorrow,*
>   *for you do not know what a day may bring.*

Those envisioned in this saying have a cocky attitude towards the future, presuming that they can anticipate and control the factors that will arise, as did the merchant who is criticized in James 4:13–16. We cannot foresee what will come tomorrow, much less control it, so we should not act as though we can, for 'If the most immediate and most visible future is not under human control and is uncertain, how much less the distant future.'[2] The wise person, by contrast, lives one day at a time in a way that honours God.

Foolish decisions are also the result of taking hasty shortcuts. When Proverbs 21:5 says,

> *The plans of the diligent lead to profit*
>   *as surely as haste leads to poverty*

it causes us to think of the many get-rich-quick schemes that people are tempted to follow. This verse teaches the virtue of diligent, disciplined labour, because cutting corners means that we are probably trespassing on someone's lawn. The modern adage 'haste makes waste' is paralleled in Proverbs 19:2 and 29:20, with the sense that carelessness leads one to

---

[1] C.-W. Pan, *NIDOTTE* 3:715.

[2] B. K. Waltke, *The Book of Proverbs Chapters 15–31*, NICOT (Grand Rapids: Eerdmans, 2005), p. 373.

calamity. In these verses, 'The "hasty" settle for an approach that is quick and dirty, sloppily planned and halfheartedly implemented. Their accomplishment is "poverty", the lack of all the basics needed to support life adequately.'[3] Similarly, Proverbs 28:20 states,

> A faithful person will be richly blessed,
>> but one eager to get rich will not go unpunished.

How one achieves prosperity is important to the Lord. Faithfulness, that is, steadiness and perseverance, brings lasting blessing without regrets, so being slow and steady is much better than being swift and shady.[4] Being ambitious to prosper can prompt us to make bad compromises. It is far better to have a faithful life blessed by God than an affluent life purchased at the price of divine punishment for sin.

We also make foolish decisions when we neglect to get advice. Our neglect can lead to folly, because

> The way of fools seems right to them,
>> but the wise listen to advice.
> (12:15)

Fools cannot see where their paths are heading, and because they have not got the benefit of counsel from others they only suppose that they are wise in their own eyes (3:7; 21:2; 26:12). Such people are trapped by their own weakness and prejudices (16:2), because they have failed to draw from the insights of others. One commentator has noted well the predicament into which this leads them:

> The fool is so excessively self-opinionated that he is deaf to advice from any quarter and never entertains a shadow of doubt that his own courses may be wrong. He has no problems because he does not have the critical faculties to recognize them, and his unbounded confidence in himself is

---

[3] D. A. Hubbard, *Proverbs*, The Communicator's Commentary 15A (Dallas: Word, 1989), p. 344.

[4] A. P. Ross, 'Proverbs', *EBC*, vol. 5 (Grand Rapids: Zondervan, 1991), p. 1108, explains: 'The idea is that the first is faithful to his obligations to God and to other people; but the one who hastens to make riches is at the least doing it without an honest day's work and at the worst dishonestly. In a hurry to acquire wealth, he falls into dishonest schemes and bears the guilt of it – he will not be unpunished. The Targum adds an interpretation – probably a correct one – that he hastens through deceit and wrongdoing.'

a symptom of his lack of intellectual discipline and rigour and even his incapacity for these virtues.[5]

Neglecting to get advice also leads to failure, for

Plans fail for lack of counsel,
but with many advisers they succeed.
(15:22)

The Hebrew verb *prr*, translated by NIV here as *fail*, has the sense of 'frustrate' or 'thwart'.[6] Projects begun without counsel waste resources and potential, unexamined dreams get dashed and untested plans founder. As a general rule, the better the counsel, the better the consequences, although this is qualified by Proverbs 19:21, which states that the Lord's purposes transcend even the best of human plans. Similarly,

Whoever disregards discipline comes to poverty and shame,
but whoever heeds correction is honoured.
(13:18)

Our critics can be our greatest help, even though our ego may be tempted to discount them as inconvenient hindrances. Even when instruction comes as a correction, it is important to listen to it. Rebuke should be welcomed as a friend and not repulsed as though it were an enemy, because neglecting to get advice carries a steep price. It may well result in financial loss eventuating in *poverty*, along with the accompanying *shame* and social humiliation.

Failing to get advice leads to a fall, as Proverbs 11:14 teaches:

For lack of guidance [taḥbulôt] *a nation falls,*
but victory is won through many advisers.

The term *taḥbulôt* may picture counsel as the navigation for a ship,[7] or it may have the nuance of 'strategy',[8] but in either case without *taḥbulôt* one's

---

[5] W. McKane, *Proverbs*, OTL (Philadelphia: Westminster, 1970), p. 442.

[6] T. F. Williams, *NIDOTTE* 3:697.

[7] A. Wolters, *NIDOTTE* 4:285, links the six uses of this term in Job 37:12 and Prov. 1:5; 11:14; 12:5; 20:18; 24:6 to the term for 'rope', and suggests that it 'may have referred originally to the steering of a ship'.

[8] M. V. Fox, *Proverbs 10 – 31*, AYB 18B (New Haven: Yale University Press, 2009), p. 536.

venture will fail. It is also crucial to get the counsel of many people and not to ask only those you know will applaud whatever you want to do, because 'Through the diversity of their insights, one may begin to detect a pattern of common agreement. The proclivities of one and the opinions of the few are balanced by the collective wisdom of the many.'[9]

When we do not get advice, futility is inevitable. Proverbs 14:12 and 16:25 say,

> *There is a way that appears to be right,*
> *but in the end it leads to death.*

Not everything that *looks* good *is* good, because what we think we see may actually be a mirage or a fantasy. Just as in Genesis 3 what appeared right to Eve proved to be lethal, what looks right may well be the way of folly, for 'The way that seems so secure by human judgment *may* turn out to be not only erroneous, but unwise and leading to death!'[10] Good advice can help us to see the reality behind the appearance, and thus deter us from taking the path to futility.

Another way people often make foolish decisions is to get advice but then refuse to take the advice that has been received. This is implied in Proverbs 14:16 by a set of contrasts:

> *The wise fear the LORD and shun evil,*
> *but a fool is hotheaded and yet feels secure.*

Although *the LORD* is included in the NIV and is supported as the proper sense by some commentators, these words are not in the Masoretic Text, and they should not be added. The sense of the verse is that wise people are cautious because they fear the consequences of their actions, in contrast to fools, who are 'reckless, self-assured, and over-confident'.[11] Although fools are consumed by fury, they nevertheless feel a false sense of security that does not accurately assess the risks of their actions. Similarly, Proverbs 13:10 says,

> *Where there is strife, there is pride,*
> *but wisdom is found in those who take advice.*

---

[9] J. A. Kitchen, *Proverbs*, Mentor Commentary (Fearn, Ross-shire: Christian Focus, 2006), p. 248.

[10] R. E. Murphy, *Proverbs*, WBC 22 (Nashville: Thomas Nelson, 1998), p. 105.

[11] Ross, 'Proverbs', p. 987.

In contrast to wisdom, which is open to the ideas and suggestions of other people, pride insists on doing what it pleases as it strokes one's own ego. Good counsel is a gift that should not be spurned but taken seriously.

Foolish decisions also come from listening to bad advice. The sage warns in Proverbs 1:10,

> *My son, if sinful men entice you,*
> *do not give in to them.*

In this passage, the son hears the voices of both folly (the sinners) and wisdom (the father). He has to decide which voice to heed, and much is at stake. The sage encourages him to evaluate the character of those who are seeking to counsel him, and to maintain a fixed resolve not to give in to the sinful advice that emerges from their sinful character (cf. Ps. 1:1). In Proverbs 12:5 it is said that *the advice of the wicked is deceitful*. The term used here is *mirmâ*, which indicates a betrayal or fraud, as in Proverbs 11:1; 12:17; 14:8. If a person is wicked, then that will overflow into what he or she advises others to do, so it is important that we get past what may be an attractive facade to measure the adviser and the advice by God's righteous standard.[12] Proverbs 11:3 contrasts the upright who are guided by their integrity with the unfaithful who are destroyed by their duplicity. It is vital to anticipate the consequences of the advice you receive, and ask, 'Where will this take me?' Playing fast and loose with what God calls morally crooked leads to destruction.[13]

2. How to make wise decisions

When we think of making good decisions, we naturally focus on the actual point in time when the decision is made, but Proverbs reveals that wise decisions derive ultimately from good character. For this reason, Proverbs 4:23 urges,

> *Above all else, guard your heart,*
> *for everything you do flows from it.*

---

[12] Kitchen, *Proverbs*, p. 264, explains, 'The "righteous" are concerned first, and foremost, in all of their plans with what is right in the eyes of God and men. The "wicked" begin all considerations from the vantage point of what benefits them. The thoughts, plans and choices of each then proceed from these starting points.'

[13] Fox, *Proverbs 10 – 31*, p. 532, states, 'Words from the root s-l-p imply distortion and twisting of words and deeds. They can refer to a flaw in words, deeds, or character (Exod 23:8; Deut 16:19; Job 12:19; Prov 11:3; 19:3). In 21:12 and 22:12, s-l-p refers to undermining or ruin. In the present verse [Prov. 11:3] *selep* clearly means moral crookedness, because its consequence is destruction.'

In Hebrew, the *heart* (*lēb*) refers to the whole inner being, and everything in one's life is connected to the heart. From the heart come choices, decisions, motives, values, ambitions and delights. However, the human heart has been contaminated by sin (Jer. 17:9), so unless it is guarded it will default into evil. What is in our heart will drive our decisions, so we must attend to the source and not just manage the symptoms. This is why the psalmist prays,

> Search me, God, and know my heart;
> > test me and know my anxious thoughts.
> See if there is any offensive way in me,
> > and lead me in the way everlasting.[14]

Good character produces integrity, or a pattern of wise behaviour, and

> *Whoever walks in integrity walks securely,*
> > *but whoever takes crooked paths will be found out.*
> (10:9)

The *crooked path* diverges from the Lord's righteous way, and it will suffer punishment (Pss 1:6; 125:5). By contrast, the consistent walk of *integrity* leads to security, which includes wise decisions that produce one's security. This is among the good benefits that the Lord gives to those whose walk is blameless (cf. Ps. 84:11). A character marked by integrity has motives that are godly. Humans have a great propensity to construe their own ways as right, but *the Lord weighs the heart* (21:2). The Lord knows perfectly what drives our actions and decisions, and he evaluates *why* we are doing what we are doing. Godly motives are essential for making decisions that the Lord considers good and wise.

The book of Proverbs also teaches that practising routine obedience is important for making wise decisions; for example, in Proverbs 16:3,

> *Commit to the Lord whatever you do,*
> > *and he will establish your plans.*

This verse speaks of the commitment of our daily works to the Lord, or practising godliness in the daily choices of life. We may overlook the

---

[14] Ps. 139:23–24; cf. Ps. 19:14.

significance of the small details in our lives, but when we honour and trust the Lord in the details, then he causes the big picture of our lives to emerge well. In Proverbs 4:20–27, various parts of the body are used to make the point that it is crucial to be intentional about maintaining a wise pattern of life, and in verses 26–27 the sage counsels,

> *Give careful thought to the paths for your feet*
>   *and be steadfast in all your ways.*
> *Do not turn to the right or the left;*
>   *keep your foot from evil.*

In other words, pay attention to the routine, and the trajectory of your life will fall into place. When we form good habits, our path in life is established (cf. 12:28). This is not Aristotle's golden mean between two harmful extremes, but it is staying on God's right way,[15] because swerving either to the right or to the left forsakes God's path of wisdom and gets us into trouble (cf. Deut. 5:32; 17:11, 20; 28:14; Josh. 1:7; 23:6).

Wise decisions come from getting and following good advice. Proverbs 19:20 exhorts,

> *Listen to advice and accept discipline,*
>   *and at the end you will be counted among the wise.*

Wise people realize how much they do not know, so they ask someone who does know. They recognize that other people have wisdom that they need to hear and to heed. This proverb says that if we listen to the right people, we will end up in the right place in the future. Similarly, Proverb 15:14 states,

> *The discerning heart seeks knowledge,*
>   *but the mouth of a fool feeds on folly.*

The wise person has a taste for knowledge (cf. Jer. 15:16; 1 Cor. 3:1–2; 1 Pet. 2:1–2), but folly dulls the appetite for knowledge in general, and for counsel specifically. Those who are wise passionately seek[16] to learn more.

---

[15] B. K. Waltke, *The Book of Proverbs Chapters 1–15*, NICOT (Grand Rapids: Eerdmans, 2004), p. 301.

[16] Kitchen, *Proverbs*, p. 333, observes, 'The contrast is most noticeable in the verbs. The first verb "seeks" points to a quest characterized by passionate intention. The second verb "feeds" describes the arbitrary munching of domesticated animals.'

In addition to getting good advice, those who make wise decisions follow the good advice they have received. Several verses in Proverbs contrast listening and not listening to counsel. In Proverbs 11:14, victory comes from having abundant counsel that provides wise guidance, and without it a nation falls. Proverbs 12:15 clearly distinguishes between fools and the wise:

The way of fools seems right to them,
but the wise listen to advice.

Advice ('ēṣâ) here refers to 'a plan of action, both as it is conceived in the mind and as it is communicated to others'.[17] What this saying teaches is that 'Those who think they know it all are foolish, but those who look for guidance and knowledge are wise.'[18] Similar maxims include Proverbs 13:10, 18; and 15:22. All of these sayings emphasize that success comes from accepting wisdom from others who are in a position to provide good counsel. The general rule is that the better the counsel, the better the consequences. For this reason, wise people do not just pay lip service to the advice of others, but they act upon the good advice they receive.

In practical terms, in order to make wise decisions, it is important that we consider the facts. Proverbs 18:17 cautions,

In a lawsuit the first to speak seems right,
until someone comes forward and cross-examines.

Although this saying is set in the context of a lawsuit (*rîb*, as in Deut. 1:16; 19:16–18), it holds as well for evaluating assertions of all kinds, because 'The experience at court offers a lesson to all who make judgments about others. Truth appears gradually; one must listen to all sides.'[19] Anyone who has sat on a jury realizes that a reasonable case can be made by the plaintiff, but to believe one side of the story alone may well lead to misunderstanding. Some apparently persuasive arguments wither under cross-examination, so it is vital to hear the defendant as well. Proverbs 14:15 contrasts *simple* people who in their gullibility *believe anything*, with those who are prudent

---

[17] A. Wolters, *NIDOTTE* 2:490.

[18] D. A. Garrett, *Proverbs, Ecclesiastes, Song of Songs*, NAC 14 (Nashville: Broadman, 1993), p. 132.

[19] R. J. Clifford, *Proverbs*, OTL (Louisville: Westminster John Knox, 1999), p. 172.

and *give thought to their steps*. It is important to weigh carefully all of the evidence that God has made available to us. It is true that when making decisions we may well not have all the facts that we would like, but God has given us our minds to use, so we must give careful consideration to all the evidence that we do have.

The book of Proverbs in several passages teaches that the plans we make must be flexible, because ultimately it is the Lord's plan that will come to pass. For example,

> *To humans belong the plans of the heart,*
> *but from the LORD comes the proper answer of the tongue.*
> (16:1)

Planning is a legitimate human activity, but the Lord is able to transcend what human beings plan, even altering what they intend to say. Also,

> *In their hearts humans plan their course,*
> *but the LORD establishes their steps.*
> (16:9)

We plan the course of our lives, but only the Lord can make our steps secure and firm. Because of this, 'humankind is functioning at its best when we recognize that we are not in control of our own destiny, that we are not self-guides, and that such matters are best left to an infinitely wise God'.[20] Consequently, when we make plans, we should write them in pencil and not in stone, and be humbly attentive to how the Lord adjusts them as he establishes his plan in our lives. We may generate many plans, but it is the Lord's purpose that will endure (19:21). Wise people seek the Lord's purpose, rather than insisting on their own plans, which the Lord can frustrate (cf. Neh. 4:9; Ps. 33:10; Isa. 19:3; Jer. 19:7). We must not clasp our own plans so tightly that we resent the Lord if he diverges from them.

It is also important to anticipate future challenges and needs and to keep looking ahead down the road, because

> *The prudent see danger and take refuge,*
> *but the simple keep going and pay the penalty.*
> (22:3)

---

[20] V. P. Hamilton, *NIDOTTE* 3:824.

The wise person is alert to danger and changes direction to avoid it. By contrast, those who are clueless suffer calamity, paying a price for stumbling into what they should have foreseen, for 'The simple person is unwary, uncritical, and credulous; he is not equipped to survive in this world and so blunders into trouble.'[21]

Proverbs also teaches that it is vital to focus on the most crucial matters first, as is seen in Proverbs 24:27:

Put your outdoor work in order
and get your fields ready;
after that, build your house.

It is important to think through the sequence of steps, rather than getting allured by what seems easiest or most enjoyable. It is fine to build a house, but first one must make sure that there is food growing in the fields so that there will be something to eat in the house. Production, then, should come before consumption, and more generally this means that 'laying the groundwork is necessary before embarking on any great project'.[22]

Several sayings in the book of Proverbs indicate that there are aspects of our lives that we cannot understand, because they are of the Lord's doing. For example,

A person's steps are directed by the LORD.
How then can anyone understand their own way?
(20:24)

There is an element of mystery in wisdom, but what is mysterious to us is fully known by the Lord (cf. Job 42:2–3). The Lord understands his way with us more than we can understand it. Because our understanding is limited but the Lord's understanding is perfect, we must trust him for what we cannot understand. The Lord has ways of working that transcend what humans can manipulate, because

In the LORD's hand the king's heart is a stream of water
that he channels towards all who please him.
(21:1)

---

21 Ross, 'Proverbs', p. 1060.
22 Clifford, *Proverbs*, p. 218.

133

As farmers adjust their irrigation channels, so the Lord alters the plans even of kings, because they are under his control. In the biblical texts, the Lord counsels humans (Pss 16:7; 32:8), but humans never counsel him (Isa. 40:13; Rom. 11:34). Proverbs 21:30 states,

> *There is no wisdom, no insight, no plan*
>   *that can succeed against the LORD*

so even the best of human wisdom must yield before the all-knowing Lord.[23]

3. Concluding comment

Living in godly wisdom involves making wise decisions and avoiding foolish decisions. Every day we are confronted with decisions we have to make. Some of them are small, but others are substantial. Some decisions are clear, but others are complex. At times, even our best efforts to get good counsel do not give all the insight we need, and we always have to trust the omniscient Lord, because he alone knows all the factors. The book of Proverbs provides ample information about how to make good choices, but we must resolve to follow its teaching, so that as we make decisions we can learn to choose wisely.

---

[23] Waltke, *Proverbs Chapters 15–31*, p. 192, concludes, 'Before the LORD, who is infinite in his omniscience and omnipotence, human ability fails to even raise its head above the plain of human folly. Without him, and how much more against him, these significant skills on the human axis do not even exist on the vertical axis.'

12. Wisdom as righteousness

Can you imagine what it would be like to play a game with all the players making up their own rules? Or what it would be like to drive on a road with no lane markers, speed limit or traffic lights? Think how chaotic and confusing it would be to live in a community where everybody decides for themselves what is right and what is wrong.

Some people might call this freedom, but these are actually examples of the effects of relativism, when personal freedom becomes the primary focus. During the period of the judges in the Old Testament, the Israelites experienced the spiritual and social anarchy produced by relativism. The final verse of Judges concludes, 'In those days Israel had no king; everyone did as they saw fit',[1] a laconic comment that follows some of the most despicable scenes anywhere in the Bible. What the Israelites considered freedom was in reality the path to their moral collapse.

The wisdom literature teaches in Proverbs 3:19,

By wisdom the LORD laid the earth's foundations,
by understanding he set the heavens in place.

Not only did the Lord use his wisdom to create the world, but he also embedded in the world his moral order. As wisdom teachers observed various features of God's creation, they were able to discern patterns that led them to lessons for life (for example, in Prov. 6:6–11, as the patterns observed in the ant lead to a lesson about diligence in work). God's law, both that which he hardwired into the world and that which he has communicated in his word, is not intended to make life miserable, but to make it

---

[1] Judg. 21:25.

meaningful. To live by God's standard is righteousness, and to depart from it is wickedness. The wise person is characterized by righteousness, but those who reject God's righteous standard and insist on doing their own thing have taken the path of folly. As one commentator has noted,

> Throughout the book of Proverbs, righteousness and wisdom are interchangeable terms. One cannot be wise without being righteous. In the same way, folly and wickedness are inextricably intertwined. Foolish behavior is evil. If we understand this, we recognize the ethical dimension of wisdom.[2]

1. The road to righteousness

How do we find the Lord's righteous way for our lives? This is clearly answered in Proverbs 2:9, which says,

> *Then you will understand what is right and just*
> *and fair – every good path.*

The word *then* indicates that there is a cause that produces this effect, and that cause is spelled out in the earlier verses of the chapter. In this passage it is evident that we find righteousness by seeking it.

Proverbs 2:1–4 is introduced by *if* in verse 1, which is repeated in verses 3 and 4. This implies that the son has to make a decision to respond to the teaching he receives because he values what he hears. In other words, he must do more than *learn* wisdom; he must also *love* it so that he *lives* it. If the son values what his father teaches, he needs to listen to him attentively and accept eagerly what he says (2). This is his personal responsibility, and it is essential if he is to understand the Lord's righteous way. Verses 3–4 use vivid language to illustrate how the father's invitation to wisdom must be accepted. The son must *call out*, even *cry aloud*, for insight and understanding, because he recognizes his great need for them. In fact, he must regard them as treasures that require his diligent effort to acquire, because

> Neither silver ore nor wisdom is got in a day, or got without industry;
> but for miner and student alike, the prize is worth the toil. But toil there
> is; and so an earnest desire to obtain wisdom must be uppermost.[3]

---

[2] T. Longman, *The Fear of the Lord Is Wisdom: A Theological Introduction to Wisdom in Israel* (Grand Rapids: Baker Academic, 2017), p. 11.

[3] K. T. Aitken, *Proverbs*, DSB (Philadelphia: Westminster, 1976), p. 27.

Wisdom is actually better than treasures like silver and gold (cf. 3:14; 16:16), and to find what is right we need to seek it intently.

The conditions in verses 1–4 must be met if the consequences in verse 5 and following are to be realized. As in so many things in life, what we find depends on where and how we seek. The sage's teaching is like a compass that guides us to understanding the fear of the Lord, which is both the beginning and the end of wisdom (cf. 3:13; 9:10). The *fear of the Lord* in verse 5 is paired with the *knowledge of God*, which is 'to react ethically to his will, to follow his principles'.[4] Verse 9 repeats the words that open verse 5, *Then you will understand*, as it presents a second aspect of the consequences of meeting the conditions laid out in verses 1–4. Because *the Lord gives wisdom* and *protects the ways of his faithful ones* (6–8), the son will come to understand *what is right and just and fair* (9). These three particulars, which repeat what is said in Proverbs 1:3 and are all aspects of the Lord's attributes in other Old Testament passages,[5] are now summarized in one general category of *every good path*. This is the road of righteousness taken by those who are wise in God's eyes.

To find righteousness requires deep commitment, not just a casual interest, because

> *Whoever pursues righteousness and love*
> *finds life, prosperity and honour.*
> (21:21)

The key term here is *pursues*, which indicates a great effort, as in Matthew 6:33 when Jesus urges, 'seek first his kingdom and his righteousness'. Righteousness and love are both qualities that mark the Lord himself and that the Lord requires of human beings in Micah 6:8:

> He has shown you, O mortal, what is good.
> And what does the Lord require of you?
> To act justly and to love mercy
> and to walk humbly with your God.

---

[4] A. P. Ross, 'Proverbs', *EBC*, vol. 5 (Grand Rapids: Zondervan, 1991), p. 912.

[5] J. A. Kitchen, *Proverbs*, Mentor Commentary (Fearn, Ross-shire: Christian Focus, 2006), p. 62, observes, 'These three terms are oral synonyms, but if any distinction is to be seen it might be that they refer to the character, choices and equity of God now incarnate in the man of wisdom.'

This commitment to developing godly character results in great benefits as it leads to genuine life (cf. Prov. 19:23; 22:4). The term translated by NIV as *prosperity* in the second line is actually the Hebrew noun ṣĕdāqâ, which is usually translated as 'righteousness', as it is in the first line. Here, however, it is parallel to life and honour, so it is likely used as in Psalm 112:3 with the nuance of 'prosperity', and thus in keeping with the NIV rendering. Although several scholars argue for the more familiar meaning of 'righteousness', the two uses of ṣĕdāqâ in this verse may well be a Hebrew pun, because poets are fond of exploiting the full lexical potential of terms, even using familiar terms in unfamiliar but attested ways in order to make their points especially potent.[6]

2. The reality of righteousness

Proverbs speaks about how we must seek the road to righteousness, but what precisely *is* righteousness? The Hebrew term translated as righteousness is ṣĕdāqâ, which refers to action according to a standard. Just as the material world functions according to God's natural laws, such as gravity, so the Bible teaches that humans must live according to God's moral laws, and that is righteousness. The righteous life is the kind of life that meets the standard of the Lord's will, which ultimately reflects the Lord's own character. The key question for the righteous person is, 'How does the Lord evaluate what I am doing, planning, thinking or saying?'

Righteousness is marked by wisdom, as is seen when personified Wisdom speaks in Proverbs 8. Wisdom says in verse 8,

> All the words of my mouth are just;
>   none of them is crooked or perverse.

What Wisdom says is always righteous, because Wisdom never strays from the Lord's righteous norm. In verse 15, Wisdom declares,

> By me kings reign
>   and rulers issue decrees that are just.

---

[6] B. K. Waltke, *The Book of Proverbs Chapters 15–31*, NICOT (Grand Rapids: Eerdmans, 2005), p. 184. For arguments supporting the reading 'righteousness', see D. A. Garrett, *Proverbs, Ecclesiastes, Song of Songs*, NAC 14 (Nashville: Broadman, 1993), p. 183; and Kitchen, *Proverbs*, pp. 478–479. The LXX omits the second occurrence of the term as an accidental scribal error of dittography.

Throughout the Bible it is evidenced that the Lord rules by righteousness, and he evaluates human rulers by the same standard. Though human rulers may have great authority in their political domain, they must answer to the Lord for how they rule, and they will be held accountable by him. In verse 20, Wisdom affirms,

> I walk in the way of righteousness
>   along the paths of justice.

Because Wisdom walks in the righteousness that characterizes the Lord's rule (cf. Ps. 89:14), it is clear that the Lord and Wisdom are in moral lockstep in their commitment to living by the divine standard.

Righteousness is also marked by truthfulness, as is seen in Proverbs 12:17:

> An honest ['ĕmûnâ] witness tells the truth [ṣedeq],
>   but a false witness tells lies.

This saying teaches that truthfulness ('ĕmûnâ) and what is righteous (ṣedeq) go hand in hand, because one who is truthful tells what is right. In other words, when one tells the truth, it will be the right thing to say. The second line expands from the general situation of the first line into a legal setting, where a witness tells lies. In the Old Testament law, witnesses 'were not to withhold testimony (Lev 5:1) or bear false witness against an innocent man (Exod 20:16 = Deut 5:20; Exod 23:1)',[7] because 'The judicial system is viable only if people can, on the whole, be relied on to produce honest testimony.'[8] Whether in a formal legal context, or in life more broadly, righteousness does not bend or break the truth.

3. The rewards of righteousness

Living by the Lord's righteous standards may sound like a lot of rigour and too many restrictions by those who regard their own freedom as their highest value. Why, then, should we seek to cultivate righteousness in our

---

[7] R. B. Chisholm, *NIDOTTE* 3:337. He goes on to say, 'False witnesses received the same penalty as the falsely accused individual would have suffered if condemned as guilty (Deut 19:16–21)', indicating how crucial it was for legal witnesses to speak truthfully if righteous judgment were to prevail.

[8] M. V. Fox, *Proverbs 10 – 31*, AYB 18B (New Haven: Yale University Press, 2009), p. 555.

lives? Is it worth it to live by God's norms in a world that offers individual freedom and personal choice as an alternative?

It is clear in Proverbs 11:18–19 that righteousness yields a reward that lasts:

> *A wicked person earns deceptive wages,*
> > *but the one who sows righteousness reaps a sure reward.*
>
> *Truly the righteous attain life,*
> > *but whoever pursues evil finds death.*

Throughout the wisdom literature, *wicked* (*rāšā'*) and *righteous* (*ṣaddîq*) are a standard contrasting pair. In their forty-five uses, '*ṣaddîq* delineates loyal, reliable conduct based on a commitment to God and his covenant' and '*rāšā'* represents the opposite of *ṣaddîq*. It connotes disloyalty to Yahweh, rebellion against the covenant standards, and total disregard for the welfare of fellow citizens.'[9] In verse 18 what the wicked person earns is acquired fraudulently[10] and does not endure, in contrast to the person who sows righteousness (cf. Hos. 10:12) and thus reaps a reward that lasts. Ultimately, everything ties back to character, because *who* a person is determines *how* a person acts, and then *what* that person receives as a result. In verse 19 the larger implications of the actions in verse 18 are articulated. The path of righteousness leads to *life*, as do wisdom and the fear of the Lord (cf. 19:23; 22:4). In language that echoes the two alternatives laid out by Moses in Deuteronomy 30:19, the sage teaches that the values we adopt determine our destination, for good or for bad.

Some of the rewards of righteousness pertain specifically to the individual, as, for example, in Proverbs 11:5:

> *The righteousness of the blameless makes their paths straight,*
> > *but the wicked are brought down by their own wickedness.*

A blameless heart produces actions that are right, a pattern of life that is not perfect but which does manifest integrity. This pattern of righteous

---

9 E. Carpenter and M. A. Grisanti, *NIDOTTE* 3:1202–1203.

10 R. E. Murphy, *Proverbs*, WBC 22 (Nashville: Thomas Nelson, 1998), p. 83, notes that the Hebrew text contains a pun between *wages* (*śeker*) and *deceptive* (*śeqer*).

behaviour smooths out the wrinkles of life and makes our paths straight. In Proverbs 3:6 the Lord is the one who makes straight the paths of those who trust in him, and throughout the wisdom literature the straight path is an image of God's way.[11] By contrast, wicked behaviour contains the seed of its own destruction, as the *wicked* are *brought down* (the verb *npl* implies a disaster[12]), perhaps perishing in the pits they have dug in order to trap others (cf. 26:27).

Proverbs 16:8 declares,

> *Better a little with righteousness*
> *than much gain with injustice.*

In keeping with several other maxims in Proverbs, this verse states that doing what is right more than compensates for any lack of material wealth. In fact, righteousness is worth far more than riches. This principle is given a sharper point in Proverbs 10:2, which says,

> *Ill-gotten treasures have no lasting value,*
> *but righteousness delivers from death.*

Righteousness delivers us from the bankrupt values of our culture that applaud the accumulation of treasure, because to God *how* we get our treasure makes all the difference. Treasures gained by wickedness will not last, because 'Wealth is worthless in the day of [God's] wrath' (11:4), and 'treasures that are accumulated to ward off death are deceptive'.[13] By contrast, righteousness accomplishes what treasures gained by wickedness cannot, in that it leads to life rather than to death. Similarly, Proverbs 13:6 maintains,

> *Righteousness guards the person of integrity,*
> *but wickedness overthrows the sinner.*

Here, as in Proverbs 11:5, the blameless person aligns with God's standards and enjoys his protection. Often in Proverbs the adjective 'blameless' refers

---

[11] *DBI*, p. 819, states, 'The image of a straight path or way appears approximately twenty times (chiefly in Psalms, Proverbs and Ecclesiastes). Those who continue on the straight path are the ones whose walk is in accordance with God's walk, while those leaving the straight path are rebels against God and are therefore in danger of his judgment.'

[12] R. N. Whybray, *Proverbs*, NCBC (Grand Rapids: Eerdmans, 1994), p. 177.

[13] B. K. Waltke, *The Book of Proverbs Chapters 1–15*, NICOT (Grand Rapids: Eerdmans, 2004), p. 453.

to a life of integrity. This is not moral perfection but 'consistent and thorough conformity to God's ways. When we walk in conformity to God's ways, He guarantees us success and safety (Prov. 2:11; 4:6).'[14] The use of the same verb (*guard*) in Proverbs 22:12 indicates that it is the Lord who guards the person of integrity and overthrows those who are wicked. As demonstrated repeatedly in the narratives of the kings of Israel and Judah, the righteous way leads to safety and security, but the wicked way leads to danger and defeat.

Righteousness also leads to the reward of reputation, for Proverbs 16:13 observes,

> *Kings take pleasure in honest lips;*
> *they value the one who speaks what is right.*

Although righteousness may not always lead to popularity, it does typically lead to respect. When a king gets truthful counsel, he has the information he needs to make wise decisions. Of course, this is the ideal (cf. Ps. 101:7), but regrettably it is also the case that many human rulers have preferred sycophants who flatter them by saying only what they want to hear (cf. 1 Kgs 22:6). Eventually, however, they find out that 'a flattering mouth works ruin'.[15] It takes wisdom to be willing to hear inconvenient truth, but a righteous ruler will value the right kind of speech. More broadly, people who can be trusted because of their righteous behaviour are valued, and not just by rulers but by other people in general, including employers, colleagues, neighbours and friends.

Proverbs 16:31 states,

> *Grey hair is a crown of splendour;*
> *it is attained in the way of righteousness.*

The two lines of this proverb have an effect-to-cause relationship, because the honour due to one who is aged is caused by a long life devoted to righteousness. Age in itself is not regarded as a glory, but only if it reflects long-term adherence to the righteous path of life. The person in view is one who has walked wisely for a lifetime, and who now is able to reap the

---

[14] Kitchen, *Proverbs*, p. 284.
[15] Prov. 26:28.

proper reward of esteem (cf. 4:9; 20:29). Although most cultures throughout history have deferred to their elders, in our contemporary world youth is more often valued and the elderly are frequently disregarded. It is indeed possible to be old and not be wise (cf. Eccl. 4:13), but it is difficult to become wise without years of maturing. It takes time to develop a lifestyle of wisdom and righteousness, because 'Experience informs wisdom; the aged are more likely to be mature than the young. These are suppositions of wisdom literature of the OT . . . Thus, gray hair is a crown.'[16]

Pre-eminently, righteousness brings the reward of the Lord's pleasure, as is seen in Proverbs 15:9:

> The LORD detests the way of the wicked,
>   but he loves those who pursue righteousness.

How human beings live is supremely important to the Lord. On the one hand, as the parallel in the previous verse (v. 8) states, the Lord loathes the hypocritical sacrifice of those who are wicked, but by contrast in verse 9, he loves those who seek his righteous way. This does not speak of perfection, because no human being lives in an unfailingly consistent way according to the Lord's norm (cf. Ps. 14:3), but refers to a pattern of right living. As one scholar clarifies, 'It is not the perfection of every detail upon which God's pleasure hangs, but a consistent, steady, intense, purposeful, set direction toward His righteousness.'[17] The verb *pursue* indicates one who is intentional and persistent in going after righteousness; the Lord loves those who are firmly resolved to live according to his standard. Similarly, Proverbs 21:3 states,

> To do what is right and just
>   is more acceptable to the LORD than sacrifice.

Several times the Old Testament makes it clear that the Lord desires the righteousness of the heart much more than the religion of the hands (cf. 1 Sam. 15:22; Isa. 1:10–17; Mic. 6:6–8). The Lord sees what is in one's heart, and that is what matters most to him. Because the Lord wants human beings

---

16 T. Longman, *Proverbs*, BCOTWP (Grand Rapids: Baker Academic, 2006), p. 338.

17 Kitchen, *Proverbs*, p. 330.

to value what he values, that is, what is *right and just* in his eyes, 'Sacrifice must be accompanied by proper interior devotion.'[18]

Just as righteousness brings rewards to the individual, so it also provides rewards for society, because Proverbs 14:34 says,

> *Righteousness exalts a nation*
> *but sin condemns any people.*

Speaking probably in a moral rather than a political or economic sense, this saying indicates that doing what the Lord considers right is ennobling for a nation. By contrast, sin takes a nation down morally just as surely as righteousness lifts it up. To make this point, the sage uses the verb *ḥsd*, which is a homonym of the familiar term for the loyal love (*ḥesed*) of the Lord. This form of *ḥsd*, however, means to insult, reproach or disgrace, as in Leviticus 20:17 and Proverbs 25:10. By this startling word choice, the writer causes the reader to do a mental double take, thus arresting our attention.[19] Social problems are often the visible symptoms of spiritual disease, and a nation that is given over to sin has sown the seeds of its own destruction. No nation, however powerful and affluent it may be, can spurn God's laws and get away with it. What a sobering reality this is for the post-Christian cultures of the Western world that are blind to the fact that before the righteous Lord they are living on borrowed time.

Proverbs 16:12 observes,

> *Kings detest wrongdoing,*
> *for a throne is established through righteousness.*

It has often been remarked that as the leader goes, so go the people, and this has been seen many times in the Bible and throughout history. This saying indicates that effective leadership is built on righteousness, so to have a good end the king must make a commitment to what is right. It is right and not might that makes a throne secure. As the Lord rules in righteousness (Pss 89:14; 97:2), so a successful king must rule in imitation of the Lord's righteousness.[20] What is true for kings can also be applied broadly to

---

[18] Murphy, *Proverbs*, p. 159.

[19] Fox, *Proverbs 10 – 31*, p. 587.

[20] Waltke, *Proverbs Chapters 15–31*, p. 19, notes, 'The revulsion of kings against wickedness identifies them with the moral tastes of Woman Wisdom (8:7) and of the LORD (6:16; 15:9). What is said here of the king could also be said of the LORD (cf. 3:32; 11:1; 15:9; 16:12; 21:3, 15).'

leaders of all kinds, because 'Since most people wield authority in some direction, and are tempted to exchange the proper objects of abomination and delight, the proverb is of more than academic interest.'[21]

In Proverbs 25:4–5, the word picture in verse 4 is developed into a principle in verse 5:

> *Remove the dross from the silver,*
> *and a silversmith can produce a vessel;*
> *remove wicked officials from the king's presence,*
> *and his throne will be established through righteousness.*

A silversmith needed to have discernment to see the dross in the silver ore, and then diligence to give the effort necessary to smelt it out. As one commentator explains,

> To get the good metal, one had to separate it from the worthless metal. In the same way, one should remove wicked people from the presence of the king, which is probably a reference to the king's associates and advisers. If this is done correctly, then the king's reign (symbolized by his throne) will be characterized by righteousness.[22]

A king must exercise moral discernment to see the wicked character of officials in his regime, and then exercise courage in removing them. As Psalm 101:7 indicates, leaders who are committed to righteousness do not tolerate wicked subordinates around them, and as a result their rule is established.

4. Concluding comment

Every day we must choose whether to live by relativism or by righteousness. Relativism claims, 'I know what is best for me', and it craves the supposed freedom that our culture so often endorses. This 'freedom' of relativism, however, is not all it claims to be, even in our personal relationships, as sociologist Robert Bellah has observed:

---

[21] D. Kidner, *Proverbs: An Introduction and Commentary*, TOTC 17 (Nottingham: Inter-Varsity Press, 2008 [1964]), p. 113.

[22] Longman, *Proverbs*, p. 451.

freedom turns out to mean being left alone by others, not having other people's values, ideas, or styles of life forced upon one, being free of arbitrary authority in work, family, and political life . . . And if the entire social world is made up of individuals, each endowed with the right to be free of others' demands, it becomes hard to forge bonds of attachment to, or cooperation with, other people, since such bonds would imply obligations that necessarily impinge on one's freedom.[23]

What relativism calls 'freedom' is actually selfishness, which leads inevitably to the isolation and loneliness that is pervasive in contemporary life. This falls far short of what the Lord desires and what his righteous norm for life produces.

The Lord has a much better way that leads us out of the frustration perpetrated by moral relativism. As the book of Proverbs teaches, living by the Lord's righteous standard leads to peace with God, to respect and fellowship with others, and to personal contentment. Righteousness is living within the protective boundaries that the Lord has set up for our welfare. Only within the Lord's righteous boundaries can we find true freedom and fulfilment in life. The path of wisdom is the road of righteousness, and it is God's gift to human beings that enables us to enjoy life as he designed it to be. When we follow our own path of relativism, we will find that it leads to no good end, but when we follow the Lord's path of righteousness, it will lead us into the abundant life that he has planned for us.

---

[23] R. N. Bellah, *Habits of the Heart: Individualism and Commitment in American Life* (Berkeley: University of California Press, 2008), p. 23.

Part 4

The complexity of wisdom

13. Retribution and its limits

The book of Proverbs contains many sayings that distinguish between wisdom and folly. The path of wisdom demonstrates skill in living according to the Lord's moral order by righteous behaviour that leads to life in all of its dimensions. By contrast, the path of folly diverges from the Lord's moral order by wicked behaviour, so it leads to death in all of its dimensions. This standard pattern is called the retribution principle. Retribution reflects how the Lord administers justice in his world as he rewards what is good and punishes what is evil. As we look more carefully at the data in Proverbs and throughout the Bible, we come to understand that though there is indeed a pattern of retribution, there are also limitations to the general pattern that good things happen to good people and bad things happen to bad people. In the Lord's world, it is more complicated than that.

1. General retribution pattern

Retribution is a prominent principle in the book of Proverbs, and it is also found in many other biblical texts.[1] In his final address to the nation of Israel, Moses in Deuteronomy 28 – 30 emphasized that the Lord would bless them if they were obedient to him, but he would curse them if they disobeyed his law. The narratives in the book of Judges trace how the people of Israel received divine punishment when they departed from the way of the Lord, but when they returned to the Lord he blessed them

---

[1] For an excellent overview of the biblical theology of retribution, see J. R. Vannoy, *NIDOTTE* 4:1140–1149. He summarizes retribution as 'God's bestowal of rewards and punishments for the good and evil acts of human beings' (p. 1140).

with his deliverance. When Hosea prophesied against his sinful nation of Israel, he said,

> They sow the wind
>> and reap the whirlwind,[2]

and many of the other Old Testament prophets made similar declarations as they sought to bring their sinful nation back to obedience to the Lord.

This cause–effect relationship between human behaviour and divine response is also found in a number of the psalms. For example, Psalm 7:15–16 states,

> Whoever digs a hole and scoops it out
>> falls into the pit they have made.
> The trouble they cause recoils on them;
>> their violence comes down on their own heads.

Similarly, Psalm 37:14–15 uses a vivid word picture to speak of retribution:

> The wicked draw the sword
>> and bend the bow
> to bring down the poor and needy,
>> to slay those whose ways are upright.
> But their swords will pierce their own hearts,
>> and their bow will be broken.

Psalm 1 contrasts the wicked and the righteous, and it concludes,

> For the LORD watches over the way of the righteous,
>> but the way of the wicked leads to destruction.[3]

The retribution principle also appears in the New Testament. Jesus contrasts the two paths human beings can take in Matthew 7:13–14, when he says,

---

[2] Hos. 8:7.
[3] Ps. 1:6.

Enter through the narrow gate. For wide is the gate and broad is the road that leads to destruction, and many enter through it. But small is the gate and narrow the road that leads to life, and only a few find it.

Paul warns the Galatians, 'Do not be deceived: God cannot be mocked. A man reaps what he sows. Whoever sows to please their flesh, from the flesh will reap destruction; whoever sows to please the Spirit, from the Spirit will reap eternal life.'[4] The book of Revelation concludes with the righteous entering into eternal blessing with the Lord, but the wicked being consigned to eternal punishment away from the presence of the Lord.

One of the clearest statements of the retribution principle is found in Proverbs 26:27:

> Whoever digs a pit will fall into it;
>   if someone rolls a stone, it will roll back on them.

These actions illustrate the negative side of the retribution principle: that evil actions bring evil consequences. In this saying it is implied that the actions of digging a pit and rolling a stone are done with the malicious intent of harming others, as is stated explicitly in Jeremiah 18:22:

> they have dug a pit to capture me
>   and have hidden snares for my feet.

The reference to 'rolling a stone' may well indicate someone pushing a stone up a hill in order to send it down the hill on an enemy. However, 'as they roll it up the height, its weight proves too much, and it rolls back, crushing the wicked'.[5] What these examples indicate is that 'what goes around comes around', because 'the evil that one intends for others will come back on one's own head'.[6] What is stated as a maxim here is seen in the Old Testament narratives, as the evil schemes of Haman (Esth. 7:9–10) and of Daniel's enemies (Dan. 6:24) resulted in their own downfall.

Proverbs 11:18 views both sides of the retribution principle when it says,

---

[4] Gal. 6:7–8.

[5] T. Longman, *Proverbs*, BCOTWP (Grand Rapids: Baker Academic, 2006), p. 471.

[6] R. J. Clifford, *Proverbs*, OTL (Louisville: Westminster John Knox, 1999), p. 234. Cf. the similar language in Eccl. 10:8.

> *A wicked person earns deceptive wages,*
> *but the one who sows righteousness reaps a sure reward.*

For bad or for good, humans reap what they sow, with a wicked person receiving wages that that are not as good as he expected but a righteous person receiving wages that provide a genuine benefit.

Similarly, Proverbs 22:8–9 observes,

> *Whoever sows injustice reaps calamity,*
> *and the rod they wield in fury will be broken.*

> *The generous will themselves be blessed,*
> *for they share their food with the poor.*

The image of sowing and reaping is a frequent biblical picture of retribution as it draws a clear connection between acts and their expected consequences. However, we must also realize that 'not only does one reap much more than one sows, but often one reaps only long after one has sown. Thus act-consequence may have both an immediate and an eventual sequence.'[7] In verse 8, the *rod* wielded by the wicked is likely a flail used for threshing, as in Isaiah 28:27. This, then, is a vivid picture of one who oppresses the poor with the vigour of a farmer threshing grain, as he uses his power to beat down those who are too weak to resist him. Nevertheless, the rod wielded in fury *will be broken*, the passive form suggesting that human injustice will be counteracted by divine justice. This implication is supported by the fact that the verb *klh* (*broken*) is used frequently in the Old Testament for the wrath of God against evil nations.[8] In verse 9 the positive side of retribution is stated, as those who are generous give to those who are in need, rather than grasping their resources only for themselves. In being generous, they follow the pattern of the Lord, who gives to all generously (Jas 1:5). They consider themselves as channels of God's blessing to others who need it, and they are *blessed* for it, likely by the Lord (cf. 10:22).

Proverbs 13:21 focuses on the consequences of a person's behaviour when it says,

---

7 V. P. Hamilton, *NIDOTTE* 1:1152.

8 W. R. Domeris and C. Van Dam, *NIDOTTE* 2:642.

> *Trouble pursues the sinner,*
>   *but the righteous are rewarded with good things.*

Sinners receive negative consequences, as *trouble pursues* them. By contrast, those who do what is right and live according to God's norms receive *good* rewards. For bad or for good, a person's values are compensated, with the verb *šlm* (*rewarded*) suggesting a legal sense of repayment (cf. 2 Kgs 4:7).[9]

These verses from Proverbs indicate that it is the expected consequence that wisdom (righteousness) will lead to life, and that folly (wickedness) will lead to death. In a frequently cited article,[10] Klaus Koch formulated this into an impersonal linkage between act and consequence, in which the Lord does not function actively as the sovereign judge but simply ensures the outworking of a deeds–destiny process. In Koch's view, this is really a deistic notion, in which the Lord is like a clockmaker who starts a process that then functions without his personal involvement. Koch's mechanistic notion of retribution was revised by Patrick Miller, who rightly reasoned that

> while there is always a causal effect in the relationship between someone or some people's actions and the judgment they receive, that relationship is not necessarily internal but is perceived as resting in the divine decision and not happening apart from that decision or decree.[11]

In contrast to Koch and in agreement with Miller, it is better to say that the Lord actively intervenes to impose his blessing or punishment in response to the righteous or wicked behaviour of humans, as is clearly stated by Moses in Deuteronomy 7:9–10:

> Know therefore that the LORD your God is God; he is the faithful God, keeping his covenant of love to a thousand generations of those who love him and keep his commandments. But

---

[9] P. J. Nel, *NIDOTTE* 4:130.

[10] K. Koch, 'Gibt es ein Vergeltungsdogma im Alten Testament?', *ZTK* 52 (1955), pp. 1–42. English translation: 'Is There a Doctrine of Retribution in the Old Testament?', in J. L. Crenshaw (ed.), *Theodicy in the Old Testament*, IRT 4 (Philadelphia: Fortress, 1983), pp. 57–87.

[11] P. D. Miller, *Sin and Judgment in the Prophets: A Stylistic and Theological Analysis* (Chico: Scholars, 1982), p. 134.

> those who hate him he will repay to their face by destruction;
>> he will not be slow to repay to their face those who hate him.

Similarly, Saul's words to David indicated the activity of the Lord in bringing retribution, when he said, 'When a man finds his enemy, does he let him get away unharmed? May the LORD reward you well for the way you treated me today.'[12]

Numerous verses in Proverbs clearly present the Lord as the active agent of retribution. For example, Proverbs 3:33 states,

> *The LORD's curse is on the house of the wicked,*
>> *but he blesses the home of the righteous.*

In both lines of this verse the Lord is stated explicitly to be the one who curses and blesses, because while the book of Proverbs

> stresses the causal relationship between right living and a good life, it does so in a God-centered way. Thus, a secure, stable, and satisfied existence is not just the natural result of godly living, it also comes as a direct blessing of God, the tangible consequence of his favor.[13]

The wicked may erect what appears to be a secure house, but the Lord can destroy it; by contrast the Lord blesses even the temporary residence (*nāweh*, used elsewhere in the Old Testament for a shepherd's hut) of the righteous.

Proverbs 10:3 observes,

> *The LORD does not let the righteous go hungry,*
>> *but he thwarts the craving of the wicked.*

This verse details one of the ways in which the Lord causes righteousness (wisdom) to result in life and wickedness (folly) to result in death. What the righteous deeply need the Lord provides for them, as he had promised the nation of Israel in Leviticus 26:3–12. By contrast, what the wicked deeply crave the Lord will not give to them, as he warned in Leviticus 26:14–20.

---

[12] 1 Sam. 24:19.
[13] M. L. Brown, *NIDOTTE* 1:765.

The Hebrew verb *hdp*, translated here as *thwarts*, is used in Deuteronomy 6:19; 9:4; and Joshua 23:5 of the Lord pushing out the Canaanites before the Israelites, as he actively intervened on behalf of his people.

The saying in Proverbs 12:2 also demonstrates the Lord's involvement in bringing good and bad consequences upon human beings:

> *Good people obtain favour from the* Lord,
>> *but he condemns those who devise wicked schemes.*

As in Proverbs 14:14 and Micah 6:8, the Lord rewards those who share his commitment to what is good. By contrast, the Lord condemns those who devise what is wrong (cf. Deut. 19:16–19). The term translated *schemes* (*mĕzimmâ*) refers to evil plans that provoke the legal pronouncement of guilt from the Lord.[14]

Proverbs 15:25 reflects a specific example of wicked behaviour that is counteracted by the Lord when it states,

> *The* Lord *tears down the house of the proud,*
>> *but he sets the widow's boundary stones in place.*

The first line implies that what the proud possesses has been gained through injustice, as in Proverbs 16:19. The Hebrew word *gē'* (*proud*) refers to 'a fundamental attitude of self-sufficiency because of which a person throws off humility and pursues selfish desires',[15] and as a result rejects God's laws and limitations. One way in which the proud transgressed the Lord's requirements was by taking advantage of vulnerable people such as widows, who were 'the epitome of social vulnerability in ancient Near Eastern culture. In a predominantly patriarchal society, a widow had no one to represent her in society or in court, so she was often the victim of malicious people.'[16] The Old Testament prophets frequently decry the exploitation of widows and other vulnerable people like orphans and strangers (cf. Isa. 1:23; Jer. 7:6; Amos 2:6–7; Mic. 2:1–2). Because of this, the Lord intervenes to defend their rights, because he is 'A father to the fatherless, a defender of widows.'[17] In

---

[14] E. Carpenter and M. A. Grisanti, *NIDOTTE* 3:1201, observe that the hiphil form of the verb *rš'* denotes the pronouncement of judicial guilt in passages such as Exod. 22:9; Deut. 25:1; and 1 Kgs 8:32.

[15] G. V. Smith and V. P. Hamilton, *NIDOTTE* 1:787.

[16] Longman, *Proverbs*, p. 321.

[17] Ps. 68:5.

particular, unscrupulous people would rearrange the boundary stones with a neighbour in order to enhance their own property at the expense of one who was weaker, an action that clearly violated the law of the Lord (Deut. 19:14; 27:17; Prov. 22:28; 23:10). The Lord, however, exercises his prerogative by setting the misappropriated boundary stones back in their proper place.

The general pattern of the data in Proverbs regarding retribution is summarized well in this way:

> The book of Proverbs expresses a firm belief in justice at a personal level. The wise, righteous and good person will be rewarded, while the foolish, wicked and evil person will be sentenced. The timetable and details of how this justice will be executed is, however, in most cases left open and unspecified. Ultimately the belief in the retribution principle is built upon belief in a God who is active in the world and upholds justice in relation to both good and evil.[18]

2. Limitations to the retribution pattern

The Bible in general, and the book of Proverbs in particular, clearly affirms a general pattern of retribution in which good behaviours are rewarded with good consequences and evil behaviours receive evil consequences. However, there is more to what the Bible teaches about retribution, revealing other dimensions in the relationship between acts and consequences that must also be considered.[19] The standard approach of wisdom was to observe life carefully in order to discern patterns that could be expressed as lessons for life (e.g. Prov. 6:6–11). In the book of Proverbs, observation reveals the general pattern of retribution, but also yields counter-examples. There are a number of wisdom sayings that indicate that 'the sages were acutely aware that not all wealth was the result of wise and righteous living, but could accrue through greed and ruthless dishonesty'.[20] This is stated explicitly in Proverbs 11:16, which says,

---

[18] L. Boström, 'Retribution and Wisdom Literature', in D. G. Firth and L. Wilson (eds.), *Interpreting Old Testament Wisdom Literature* (Downers Grove: IVP Academic, 2017), p. 152.

[19] This qualification of the retribution principle is also seen in the New Testament, as clearly evidenced by Jesus' replies to questions in Luke 13:1–5 and John 9:1–3.

[20] G. H. Wilson, *NIDOTTE* 4:1281.

> A kind-hearted woman gains honour,
>> but ruthless men gain only wealth.

This antithetical parallel contrasts a woman who by her grace gains honour, with men who by their violence acquire wealth. The Hebrew term translated by NIV as *ruthless* is *'ārîṣîm*,[21] which in other Old Testament passages speaks of those who are fierce (Isa. 49:25), cruel (Jer. 15:21) or terrifying (Ezek. 28:7), all indicative of wicked people who nevertheless are able to gain wealth, in contrast to the expectation of the retribution principle.

In some cases, the divine justice that is foundational to the retribution principle is not activated immediately, but instead is postponed to a future time that lies beyond human observation at the present. This expectation of future divine retribution is at the heart of Old Testament faith, as people who cannot now see justice place their faith in the Lord, trusting that he will bring justice at some time in the future.[22] This future expectation of retribution is implied in Proverbs 13:22, which states,

> A good person leaves an inheritance for their children's children,
>> but a sinner's wealth is stored up for the righteous.

It is evident from legal stipulations such as in Numbers 27:1–11 and Deuteronomy 21:15–17 that in Israel land was inherited through the family. In fact, even when land was sold it was to revert to the original family in the year of jubilee. In this verse, however, the wealth of a sinner does not go to his or her descendants, as would be the case for the good person. Rather, the sinner's wealth is redirected to the righteous, who are implied as being the rightful owners of what has been wrongly appropriated by the sinner. Nothing is specified about how this will happen or when it will occur, only that 'divine justice determines the final disposition of one's inheritance'.[23] One scholar observes that though the sinner

> intended his wealth to serve his greed, under providence he ironically stored it up for those who serve God's universal kingdom. The proverb

---

[21] Following the LXX, M. V. Fox, *Proverbs 10 – 31*, AYB 18B (New Haven: Yale University Press, 2009), pp. 537–538, emends *'ārîṣîm* to *ḥārûṣîm* ('diligent'), but this seems to be special pleading that wrongly transforms the antithetical parallel into a synonymous parallel.

[22] See R. C. Van Leeuwen, 'Wealth and Poverty: System and Contradiction in Proverbs', *HS* 33 (1992), p. 34.

[23] A. P. Ross, 'Proverbs', *EBC*, vol. 5 (Grand Rapids: Zondervan, 1991), p. 981.

assumes that the wicked have their deceptive wealth for a season and that retribution is not bound strictly to a temporal order.[24]

Similarly, Proverbs 20:17 points out that falsehood may taste sweet at first (cf. 9:17), but in the end it disappoints, because *one ends up with a mouth full of gravel*. *Gravel* is just small pieces of rock, so it is definitely not appetizing or nutritious. In addition, Lamentations 3:16 notes that gravel breaks the teeth, which takes away one's ability to enjoy any food. Proverbs 21:6 contrasts the immediate perceptions of wicked behaviour with its longer-range realities:

A fortune made by a lying tongue
is a fleeting vapour and a deadly snare.

This saying states that treasures procured through deception are themselves deceptive, because to attain a fortune fraudulently is to acquire a short-lived asset that has no lasting value. Rather, it is a *fleeting vapour*, just 'a puff of smoke on a gusty day'.[25] Wealth gained by lying is bad, even lethal, and not at all a continuing benefit.

Proverbs 29:16 gives both a caution and an encouragement as it declares,

When the wicked thrive, so does sin,
but the righteous will see their downfall.

One commentator emphasizes,

This proverb could be read as a word of warning to the wicked: you may be strong now, but it won't last. The proverb is also a comfort to the righteous during a period when it appears that the lawless dominate.[26]

In the short term, sin may appear to be in the ascendency, but in the long run the righteous will see the fall of the wicked who presently thrive. The Hebrew expression *rā'â bě* here rendered as *see* has the sense of 'look with triumph, gloat over' in Psalms 22:17; 54:7; 118:7.[27] Here, as elsewhere in Proverbs, it is implied that the Lord will eventually bring justice that

---

[24] B. K. Waltke, *The Book of Proverbs Chapters 1–15*, NICOT (Grand Rapids: Eerdmans, 2004), p. 572.

[25] Fox, *Proverbs 10 – 31*, p. 681.

[26] Longman, *Proverbs*, p. 506.

[27] R. N. Whybray, *Proverbs*, NCBC (Grand Rapids: Eerdmans, 1994), p. 402.

will bring down the wicked who have prospered by means of their sinful actions. It takes faith in the Lord to look beyond the present injustice to his future intervention to bring 'the utter collapse in influence and strength of those whose hearts are set against the will of Him who created them'.[28]

The books of Job and Ecclesiastes as speculative wisdom texts extend the counter-examples to retribution in Proverbs into full-scale arguments. In Job, the title character learns to accept by faith his human limitations before the all-knowing Lord (Job 42:2–6). Job realizes that the retribution formula does not explain all that he has experienced, and he places his faith in the omniscient Lord, acknowledging,

> Surely I spoke of things I did not understand,
> things too wonderful for me to know.

Nevertheless, at the end of the book righteous Job is rewarded by the Lord, just as the retribution principle would maintain (see chapter 14). In Ecclesiastes the sage repeatedly demonstrates how life's experiences are *hebel*, an enigma, a puzzle, something that does not make sense. However, the book concludes with an epilogue that reaffirms that

> God will bring every deed into judgment,
> including every hidden thing,
> whether it is good or evil.[29]

In both Job and Ecclesiastes, as well as in the whole storyline of the Bible, there is a framework of retribution in which the Lord rewards righteousness and punishes wickedness. Within that framework, however, there are many details that are inscrutable, and for which the people of God must trust him to bring his justice in his time and in his way.

3. Concluding comment

The book of Proverbs teaches clearly that humans are finite as they live under the sovereign rule of the Lord, so are not able to comprehend all that the Lord does in his world. For example, Proverbs 20:24 follows a statement with a rhetorical question:

---

[28] D. A. Hubbard, *Proverbs*, The Communicator's Commentary 15A (Dallas: Word, 1989), p. 443.

[29] Eccl. 12:14; see chapter 15.

> A person's steps are directed by the LORD.
> How then can anyone understand their own way?

Numerous observations from life in Proverbs demonstrate that retribution is a valid general pattern, but the retribution principle must not be pressed into a fixed formula for every detail in the Lord's moral order for his world. That was the error of Job and his friends, whose focus on retribution had the effect of making the Lord totally predictable, rather than viewing him as he truly is, the active moral governor of his creation.

We, too, must accept humbly that there are some aspects of how the Lord works in the world and in our lives that must remain in the realm of mystery. We do not have to look far to see things that seem terribly unjust and out of kilter. The daily news is filled with reports of good people who suffer poverty, injustice and pain. We are troubled when evil people amass and flaunt great wealth and wield oppressive power over others. How do these things fit into the Lord's moral order in his world? Because of our inherent limitations as human beings who are both finite and fallible, we cannot see as the Lord sees or understand as he understands. Because we are limited, we must place our faith in the Lord who alone knows all things perfectly and who is committed to acting justly in his world. There will be puzzles in life that we cannot solve, there will be inequities that we cannot resolve and there will be present injustices that await future divine resolution, but when we trust the all-knowing and ever-just Lord, then we can exclaim with the apostle Paul,

> Oh, the depth of the riches of the wisdom and knowledge of God!
>> How unsearchable his judgments,
>> and his paths beyond tracing out!
> 'Who has known the mind of the Lord?
>> Or who has been his counsellor?'
> 'Who has ever given to God,
>> that God should repay them?'
> For from him and through him and for him are all things.
>> To him be the glory for ever! Amen.[30]

---

[30] Rom. 11:33–36.

Job

14. Wisdom resides in the all-knowing Lord

This chapter takes a different approach from that taken in the other chapters in this book. In investigating what the Bible teaches about the message of wisdom, our studies have focused either on a specific passage of Scripture or on a group of verses that all relate to a common theme. To grasp the massive book of Job in a short chapter, however, requires that we fly over it at thirty thousand feet so that we can survey it as a whole. What I will present briefly now can be supplemented by what I have written more extensively in my section on Job in *Handbook on the Wisdom Books and Psalms*[1] and in my commentary on Job.[2] For now, let's sit back, make ourselves comfortable and enjoy the flight over this fascinating but rarely preached biblical text, as we observe what it teaches about the message of wisdom.

1. The complexity of wisdom

The wisdom sayings in the book of Proverbs are typically called practical or traditional wisdom. Simply put, practical wisdom teaches that the path of wisdom is characterized by righteousness, and it leads to life in all of its dimensions. In contrast, the path of folly is characterized by wickedness, and it leads to death in all of its dimensions. This approach to wisdom that dominates Proverbs is called retribution theology, which views life in terms of the correlation between actions and consequences, with wisdom leading

---

[1] D. J. Estes, *Handbook on the Wisdom Books and Psalms* (Grand Rapids: Baker Academic, 2005), pp. 11–139.

[2] D. J. Estes, *Job*, Teach the Text (Grand Rapids: Baker, 2013).

to God's blessing and folly resulting in divine punishment. As the previous chapter has discussed in detail, retribution is a prominent principle of the book of Proverbs, and it is a theme that is also central to the Mosaic law in Deuteronomy and to the Old Testament prophets, who called the people of Israel back to obedience to the law of the Lord.

Retribution theology is undeniably taught in verses such as Proverbs 26:27, which observes,

> Whoever digs a pit will fall into it;
>> if someone rolls a stone, it will roll back on them,

and Proverbs 28:10:

> Whoever leads the upright along an evil path
>> will fall into their own trap,
>> but the blameless will receive a good inheritance.

However, if retribution theology is pressed too far, it begins to view God in a deistic sense, as only a clockmaker who set the world into motion, and not as the sovereign Lord who actively brings history to its end through his active providential direction. Even in the book of Proverbs there are hints that retribution, although clearly a general pattern, is not the fixed formula or rigid rule that fits every specific situation in life. There are also other factors at work in addition to the typical pattern of retribution.

Both within the book of Proverbs and in other biblical books there are texts that are often referred to as speculative wisdom. These speculative wisdom texts focus on situations in life in which the general patterns of retribution theology do not seem to account for all of life as it is actually experienced. For example, Psalms 49 and 73 ask the troubling question, 'Why do good things happen to bad people in God's world?' The book of Job as the premier example of speculative wisdom in the Bible asks, 'Why do bad things happen to good people in God's world?' In probing these complementary questions, the speculative wisdom texts are considering observable cases in which good acts are not always rewarded by good consequences and bad acts are not always punished by bad consequences. These are not just theoretical issues, but they are the troubling questions that we often find ourselves asking when life does not seem to work out as it should.

It is crucial to remember that both the practical wisdom texts and the speculative wisdom texts are included in the Bible as parts of the Lord's revealed truth. We do not have the luxury of accepting one and discarding the other, but we must read them together as equally truthful teachings revealed by God. Speculative wisdom, then, does not subvert what practical wisdom observes, but rather it supplements it, as together they present the Lord's message of wisdom.

2. The context of Job

The book of Job in a sense takes up where Proverbs leaves off as it supplements practical wisdom. In the prologue, Job is presented as the paragon of practical wisdom when he is introduced in Job 1:1: *In the land of Uz there lived a man whose name was Job. This man was blameless and upright; he feared God and shunned evil.* This impeccably good man was incredibly blessed by the Lord with a large family, extensive holdings of livestock and many servants, so that *He was the greatest man among all the people of the East* (1:3). Here is a man who fully exemplifies the practical wisdom maxim in Proverbs 10:22:

> The blessing of the Lord brings wealth,
>> without painful toil for it.

As the prologue continues to narrate in Job 1 – 2, Job then suffers a horrific calamity, which he and three friends will try to explain within the parameters of practical wisdom. As we read the book, the narrator gives us information of which Job was unaware, as he describes a set of conversations between the Lord and Satan. The text of Job actually speaks of 'the satan', which means literally the adversary or the accuser,[3] rather than being the personal name of Satan, who is described elsewhere in the Bible as the arch-enemy of the Lord (cf. Rev. 20:2, 7). Whether this is speaking specifically of Satan or of another angelic being, this individual in Job 1 – 2 is an implacable adversary to both the Lord and Job. On the one hand, the Lord twice commends Job to the adversary in glowing terms: *Have you considered my servant Job? There is no one on earth like him;*

---

[3] P. L. Day, *An Adversary in Heaven: śāṭān in the Hebrew Bible*, Harvard Semitic Monographs 43 (Atlanta: Scholars, 1988), p. 147.

he is blameless and upright, a man who fears God and shuns evil (1:8; 2:3). On the other hand, the adversary argues that Job only reveres the Lord because of the blessings he gets from him, and that if the Lord were to withhold his blessing, then Job would curse him to his face (1:9–11). The Lord gives the adversary permission to afflict Job, which he does immediately and with ferocious force. In a single day, Job loses all of his possessions, and even his ten children are killed by a mighty wind that collapses the house in which they are feasting. To top it off, the adversary afflicts Job with painful sores that cover his whole body, reducing Job to a pitiable state. By the end of the prologue, Job is scraping himself with a shard of pottery as he sits among the ashes in great agony and abject humiliation. As three friends, likely notable sages like Job, come from their respective homes to comfort Job, they are struck by the enormity of his suffering (2:11–13). The prologue discloses to us, the readers, that the Lord and the adversary have acted in ways that affect Job's experience, but neither Job nor his friends have any idea of these crucial factors as they endeavour to make sense of what has happened to him.

3. The controversy in Job

Most of the book of Job consists of three rounds of alternating speeches by Job and his three friends (Eliphaz, Bildad and Zophar), and these are then followed by three long monologues by Job, by a young man named Elihu and at last by the Lord. When Job speaks in chapter 3, he is stunned as he absorbs the full measure of his calamity. In his deep pain, he tries to make sense of what he is experiencing within the retribution formula, but he is not conscious of any sin in his life that could have prompted his profound adversity. In his subsequent speeches, Job increasingly argues that the rigid connection between acts and consequences presumed by retribution does not hold up under scrutiny, pointing out, for example in Job 12:6,

> The tents of marauders are undisturbed,
>   and those who provoke God are secure.

By the time the dialogue proceeds to Job 26:14, Job realizes that the things that can be observed of God

are but the outer fringe of his works;
  how faint the whisper we hear of him!

Job wants to receive a fair trial from the Lord, and he is not willing to offer contrived repentance for sin he has not committed just to be able to get back onto the path of divine blessing, as his friends have urged him to do. In his final oath of innocence in Job 31, Job employs the ancient legal strategy of a negative confession, by which he invites the Lord either to punish him to the full extent of the law if he is guilty, or else by not punishing him to indicate tacitly that Job is innocent.

The three friends are Job's intellectual peers as wisdom teachers, and they all try to make sense of what Job is experiencing. This, then, is the best effort of the wisdom tradition to explain Job's experience that challenges retribution theology. All of the friends argue from effect to cause, that the calamity Job has received is proof positive that he must have committed personal sin that has prompted his downfall. Eliphaz begins in Job 4 – 5 in a compassionate tone, but he quickly becomes insensitive and then hostile to Job. As a wisdom teacher, he naturally argues from what he observes in the world, but we readers realize that he does not know the facts that have been disclosed in the prologue, so we are aware that he is ignorant of some vital information. Eliphaz supposes that retribution theology is a perfectly satisfactory explanation for Job's predicament, but he fails to understand the larger dimension of Job's situation, and therefore he misconstrues what has happened to him. In his second speech in Job 15, Eliphaz assumes the role of a prosecutor as he employs a barrage of questions to humiliate and intimidate Job. He concludes that Job is vainly venting his rage against God (15:13), because in God's world the wicked man

will not escape the darkness;
  a flame will wither his shoots,
  and the breath of God's mouth will carry him away.
  (15:30)

In his third and final speech, Eliphaz has a hostile tone of confrontation, as he protects his own belief system by attacking Job's integrity. He hurls at Job unsupported accusations of grievous evils, and then urges Job,

> *Submit to God and be at peace with him;*
> *in this way prosperity will come to you.*
> (22:21)

In effect, Eliphaz says to Job, 'You are a great sinner who has received just what you deserve, so you need to repent!'

The second wisdom teacher is Bildad, and he speaks for the first time in chapter 8. Bildad doubles down on the retribution formula by insisting on a rigid dualistic theology in which the blameless are always blessed by the Lord and the wicked are always punished by him. To Bildad, retribution is more than a general pattern; it is a fixed formula. He adamantly refuses to consider evidence that would contradict or qualify what he holds to be the law of retribution. When Bildad speaks for the second time in Job 18, he simply repeats his theological dogma, only with more decibels. He views Job's suffering in cold, academic terms that allow for no compassion for Job. To him, Job is a theological case study rather than a friend wracked by pain. Bildad's final speech in Job 25 consists of just five verses, apparently because he has run out of things to say to Job. His closing words are particularly telling, as he regards human beings before the transcendent God as just maggots and worms (25:6), and therefore too insignificant to call God into question, as Job has done.

Job's third friend is Zophar, who speaks first in chapter 11. Zophar evaluates Job's situation through the lens of deductive logic as he pushes retribution theology to its logical conclusion. He reasons that the effect of punishment necessarily proves the cause of prior personal sin. In Job's case, Zophar contends that *God has even forgotten some of your sin* (11:6), so actually Job is getting better treatment from God than he deserves. In Job 20, Zophar coldly retreats into theory and fails to feel Job's pain. Because he considers Job as beyond hope, he does not even call upon him to repent as Eliphaz did. When the time comes for Zophar to speak in the third cycle of speeches, he does not, which prompts Job to continue his discourse in 27:1.

When read against what the narrator has revealed in the prologue, where the Lord clearly affirms that Job is blameless and upright (1:8; 2:3), it is evident that all three friends miss the mark as they assess Job's situation. None of them has a convincing explanation of Job's predicament, and with the third round of speeches their conversation falls apart.

After Job utters his oath of innocence in Job 31, the reader expects that the Lord will finally speak and resolve the controversy. However, instead of that, a young man named Elihu bursts on the scene in Job 32. In the wisdom tradition, youths are the students (cf. Prov. 1:4; Eccl. 12:1), not the teachers. Elihu has observed Job and the three sages as they have discussed what has happened to Job, and he regards them all as failures. Determining to teach them, Elihu seeks to assume the role of the young man who saves the day when all the recognized authorities have failed, as Joseph and Daniel did at other times (cf. Gen. 41; Dan. 2). The narrator is careful to describe Elihu four times as *angry* in Job 32:2–5,[4] which in the wisdom tradition is a mark of folly and not of wisdom.

Elihu is convinced that both Job and his friends are wrong. According to Elihu, Job is wrong because he thinks that he is more righteous than God. He says that Job has said in effect,

> *I am pure, I have done no wrong;*
> *I am clean and free from sin.*
> *Yet God has found fault with me;*
> *he considers me his enemy.*
> (33:9–10)

Elihu also says that the sages have failed to refute Job, arguing,

> *I gave you my full attention.*
> *But not one of you has proved Job wrong;*
> *none of you has answered his argument.*
> (32:12)

Elihu himself reasons that because God is transcendent, his ways must not be questioned. In saying this, he comes very close to arguing that whatever is, is right, which is the claim of classical deism. In Job 36 – 37, Elihu turns from asking what *caused* Job's suffering to consider what his suffering *produces*, as he suggests that God uses suffering for the discipline and development of his people. Elihu says,

> *He makes them listen to correction*
> *and commands them to repent of their evil.*

---

4 The NIV uses the terms 'angry' and 'anger' three times in this passage, once each in vv. 2, 3, 5. The Hebrew text uses the term *'ap* ('anger') twice in v. 2, as well as once each in vv. 3, 5.

If they obey and serve him,
they will spend the rest of their days in prosperity
and their years in contentment.
(36:10–11)

Although Elihu does not provide the final answer as he thinks he does, in the structure of the book he summarizes the human appraisals of Job's situation, and he clears the stage for the long-awaited appearance of the Lord.

Although the Lord speaks *to* Job in chapters 38 – 41, it is important to notice that he has already spoken *about* Job in the prologue. It is clear from his description of Job in 1:8 and 2:3 that the Lord is completely confident in Job's righteousness as he speaks with the adversary about him. Likewise, in the epilogue in Job 42:7–8 the Lord says twice to Eliphaz, *you have not spoken the truth about me, as my servant Job has.*

The Lord's appearance is also anticipated in the interlude by the narrator in Job 28.[5] In this chapter, God is viewed as the source of wisdom, because

[God] understands the way to it
and he alone knows where it dwells.
(23)

When God said to human beings,

The fear of the Lord – that is wisdom,
and to shun evil is understanding,
(28)

he was reaffirming the core of wisdom in Proverbs 9:10.

After all of the human speakers have given up their efforts to explain what has happened to Job, the Lord finally appears in Job 38 – 41. In the structure of the book, the Lord is the final speaker who alone knows the final answer. When he speaks, the Lord does not indict Job for sin, as the friends had predicted he would, so their charges against Job are not

---

[5] For a detailed discussion of this important chapter in Job, see D. J. Estes, 'Job 28 in Its Literary Context', *JESOT* 2 (2013), pp. 151–164.

substantiated. Neither does the Lord enter into a legal debate with Job, as Job wanted him to do. Rather, as a master teacher the Lord poses to Job more than seventy questions that Job cannot answer. The Lord points to various features in his world and asks Job to explain them, but Job cannot.

The cumulative effect of the barrage of divine questions makes it evident that although Job is innocent of the charges of sin levelled against him by the friends, he is also ignorant of the ways of the Lord. Just as there are many things in the Lord's created world that lie beyond human understanding, so there are many aspects of the Lord's ways that transcend what Job, or any human being, can comprehend and explain. Practical wisdom is rooted in observation that leads to lessons for life (cf. Prov. 6:6–11), but because human observation is limited in its scope, practical wisdom is necessarily limited in its conclusions. The retribution principle may well summarize the general pattern by which the Lord orders his world, but the sovereign Lord is not captive to a rigid formula like retribution. He is free to do what appears mysterious to finite humans, and because finite humans like Job cannot understand the workings of the creation, they are not in a position to call into question the infinite Creator.

Although it is not stated explicitly, the divine questions and Job's subsequent response to them indicate that the Lord has changed the focus of the discussion. Job and his friends have been arguing about *why* Job is suffering. As the Lord speaks, the prominent question becomes 'Who is the Lord, and can he be trusted in his governance of the world?' In other words, in a world in which there is so much that human beings cannot know, can they know that they can trust the Lord?

4. The conclusion of Job

As the Lord poses dozens of questions that Job cannot answer, he leads Job into an enlarged perspective of the wisdom of the Lord and to a greater humility before him. What Job comes to realize is expressed in his reply to the Lord in Job 42:2–3:

> *I know that you can do all things;*
>   *no purpose of yours can be thwarted.*
> *You asked, 'Who is this that obscures my plans without knowledge?'*
>   *Surely I spoke of things I did not understand,*
>   *things too wonderful for me to know.*

Job does not confess his sin, as his friends had urged him to do, but instead he demonstrates humility before the transcendent and omniscient Lord. He acknowledges that he has spoken beyond what he truly understood, and now he has come to realize how much more the Lord knows than human beings like Job do. As a result, Job declares,

> My ears had heard of you
>> but now my eyes have seen you.
> Therefore I despise myself
>> and repent in dust and ashes.
> (5–6)

Many readers have taken *repent* here as Job's confession of sin, but that would contradict the Lord's assessment of him in Job 1:8 and 2:3 as blameless and upright, as well as the Lord's statement to Eliphaz that Job has spoken the truth about him (42:7–8). Instead of repenting of sin, Job retracts his insistence that the Lord clear him (cf. Job 31). He accepts that he is ignorant before the incomprehensible God, as he comes to the realization that what he now knows is that he does not know everything, but that the Lord does, and that is sufficient for him.

Job comes to understand that the Lord's ways are inscrutable to him. As a created human being, Job is too finite to comprehend all that the Lord does in his world. He cannot answer the Lord's questions about the physical creation, and neither can he fathom the Lord's moral governance of his creation, including how the Lord has worked in his own experience. Job's conclusion has been anticipated in the book of Proverbs in the wisdom saying in 20:24:

> A person's steps are directed by the LORD.
>> How then can anyone understand their own way?

Job's experience demonstrates that the Lord's rule of his world cannot be reduced to the tidy formula of rigid retribution theology, as Job's friends confidently but inaccurately maintained, and as also Job himself had supposed. What the book of Job demonstrates is that although the retribution principle of practical wisdom is reliable as a general pattern, it must not be extrapolated into the sum total of all divine wisdom. It is true that in the book of Job the prologue (Job 1 – 2) and the epilogue (42:7–17) provide a framework in which the righteous Job is blessed by the Lord, just as retribution would predict. Nevertheless, within the overall framework of retribution there is divine mystery in the details. The book of Job, then, supplements the typical pattern taught in practical wisdom, in which wisdom leads to life and folly leads to death. In Job, the Lord is revealed as free to work in ways that to the finite human mind may appear to conflict with the principle of retribution.

5. Concluding comment

In order to understand the message of wisdom in the Bible, and to be true to the *whole* counsel of God, we must read together both the practical wisdom of Proverbs and the speculative wisdom of Job. In Proverbs the prominent emphasis is on retribution, how the Lord rewards wisdom and righteousness and how he punishes folly and wickedness. However, that is not the complete story, because there are hints in Proverbs that are fleshed out in Job that retribution has its limits. The infinite wisdom of the Lord includes aspects that are mysterious to our finite human minds. The book of Job challenges us to trust the Lord who knows all, rather than leaning on our own understanding, which is finite and fallible. Like Job, the wise person trusts the character of the Lord even without comprehending all of his ways, as one commentator well summarizes the message of this book:

> Man can trust God even when explanations are missing. Man must
> live with mystery. He must recognize that his questions may remain
> unanswered, that God may choose to respond in silence to his inquiries
> about the reason for undeserved suffering, that God may remain silent to
> his probing about the problem of unmerited tragedy. The Christian must
> learn to remain content with problems he cannot understand, realizing
> that man's finitude keeps him from having eternity's perspective, which
> only God possesses.[6]

For Christians living in the twenty-first century, the message of wisdom in the book of Job speaks with great relevance. Like Job, we too face experiences, sometimes very painful experiences, when life does not seem to be keeping

---

[6] R. B. Zuck, *Job*, Everyman's Bible Commentary (Chicago: Moody, 1978), p. 190.

the rules. We too may hear ourselves asking if God is good and just and in control. In times like this, as we walk along the difficult path trod earlier by Job, we too need to remember that although we will not understand all that the Lord does or comprehend all that the Lord knows, we can trust his perfect character, and in him find the faith we need to persevere as Job did (cf. Jas 5:10–11).

Ecclesiastes 9:7–10

15. Enjoy God's portion as his gift

One of the least read and rarely studied books of the Bible is Ecclesiastes, which along with Job is an example of speculative wisdom. Many people have written off Ecclesiastes as hopelessly pessimistic, and they even wonder why and how a book like this found a place in the canon of Scripture when it sounds so much like twentieth-century existential writing by Albert Camus, Franz Kafka or Jean-Paul Sartre. When read carefully, however, Ecclesiastes contributes greatly to our understanding of the message of wisdom from God's perspective.[1] This chapter will present a brief introduction to the book as a whole, and then look in detail at the important passage in Ecclesiastes 9:7–10 that draws together some of the key teachings of the book. In particular, Ecclesiastes teaches us that even though our lives contain many things that we cannot understand or control, we still can and should enjoy the blessings God has given to us.

1. Context of Ecclesiastes

Ecclesiastes begins with a prologue in 1:1–11, and it concludes with an epilogue in 12:9–14. In between is the main body of the book, in which there are four rounds of observations of various aspects of life. The thesis for the book is stated in 1:2–3, which begins like a fanfare in an overture that introduces the leading motif of the composition. Verse 2 along with

---

[1] This chapter draws from my exposition of the book of Ecclesiastes in D. J. Estes, *Handbook on the Wisdom Books and Psalms* (Grand Rapids: Baker Academic, 2005), pp. 271–392.

12:8 frames the central portion of the book, as the Teacher, the speaker in the book, exclaims that all is *hăbēl hăbālîm*. This phrase, which is a superlative construction in Hebrew, is rendered by the NIV as 'utterly meaningless'. The meaning of its root term *hebel*, however, is debated by scholars. This word is found thirty-eight times in Ecclesiastes, so it is clearly a crucial term for the writer, and we must be careful to interpret it accurately. In some cases in Ecclesiastes, *hebel* has the sense of 'unsubstantial' or 'transitory' as it does in Psalm 144:3–4:

> LORD, what are human beings that you care for them,
>> mere mortals that you think of them?
> They are like a breath [*hebel*];
>> their days are like a fleeting shadow.

Other times, it has a negative nuance, which is reflected in renderings such as 'absurd' or the NIV 'meaningless'. It may well be that a good single gloss for *hebel* is 'enigmatic' or 'puzzling'. As Ecclesiastes views life, sometimes life's brevity raises questions, and other times it does not seem to make sense, both of which cause humans to find life a puzzle or an enigma that they cannot figure out.

It may be significant that Adam and Eve called one of their sons Abel (Gen. 4:2), which is also the Hebrew word *hebel* that is found so frequently in Ecclesiastes. This term has the literal sense of 'breath', and as such it speaks of the present human condition after the human fall into sin in Genesis 3. Paul alludes to the fall and its consequences in Romans 8:20–21 when he says,

> For the creation was subjected to frustration, not by its own choice, but by the will of the one who subjected it, in hope that the creation itself will be liberated . . . into the freedom and glory of the children of God.

Assessing humanity's condition after the fall, Ecclesiastes demonstrates that the life we experience now is not how God originally designed it, nor is it what it will be when he has liberated it from the curse due to sin; rather, today it is full of puzzles and enigmas that make our lives difficult and unpredictable. This book truly speaks of life as it actually is, and not how we might wish to idealize it. For this reason, Ecclesiastes presents us with an honest and realistic view of life.

Ecclesiastes 1:3 poses the question that will be asked and answered in the book:

> What do people gain from all their labours
> at which they toil under the sun?

Everything in the book will tie back to this initial programmatic question. The investigation in Ecclesiastes analyses a subject that pertains to all human beings, not just to some of us. In the traditional wisdom of Proverbs, diligent work brings reward, in contrast to slothfulness that leads to poverty (see chapter 9). Ecclesiastes, however, challenges that retribution principle, as it points out that life has many variables that make it hard to predict or control what we gain from our labours.

The investigation in Ecclesiastes is limited to human toil under the sun. The term translated 'toil' is the Hebrew word *'āmāl*, which echoes the painful toil that Adam will have to exert after the fall into sin (Gen. 3:17–19; cf. Ps. 90:10), as he works by the sweat of his brow and has to contend with thorns and thistles. By 'under the sun' the sage indicates that he will exclude from his consideration God, who is above the sun, as well as anything that comes after death and is therefore beyond the sun. This book, then, is a thought experiment that endeavours to look at life in the here and now, without reference either to God or to a future reward after death. In effect, the sage speaks to secular audiences by assuming for the sake of the argument their premises that God is irrelevant and that all that matters is the present we can see, and not some unknown and unseen future. Although this book was written in ancient times, it is clearly speaking in language that most men and women in the twenty-first century relate to well.

As the wise man goes through four cycles of observation of life in chapters 1–2; 3–5; 6–8; and 9–12, he finds in each case that when human activity is considered under the sun alone, what it produces is puzzling and enigmatic; it is *hebel*. That is why when Ecclesiastes 12:8 concludes the observation section of the book, it gives as its verdict, '*hăbēl hăbālîm* . . . Everything is *hābel*.' This is not to say that there are no worthwhile human activities, but the question posed in Ecclesiastes 1:3 is whether human labours under the sun can produce genuine gain. The term translated 'gain' is the Hebrew term *yitrôn*, which is an accounting term that refers to the net profit that is realized after the benefits are considered and the costs have been paid. If the expenses are greater than the benefits, then the investment is considered a loss and not a profit, and that is what is seen again and again throughout the book of Ecclesiastes. What this wisdom teaching demonstrates is that a secularist world view collapses into a venture without a profit, and that is truly an enigma and a profound disappointment for human beings whose focus is on living for the here and now.

At the same time, each section of the book hints that even though human beings cannot achieve genuine profit under the sun, there is joy within life that they can and should grasp. These hints point ahead to the epilogue in Ecclesiastes 12:9–14, which provides a corrective to the thought experiment in the body of the book. In the final verses of Ecclesiastes, the sage re-evaluates the programmatic question, only now including God, who is above the sun, and his future judgment, which comes after death, as he says,

> Now all has been heard;
>   here is the conclusion of the matter:
> fear God and keep his commandments,
>   for this is the duty of all mankind.
> For God will bring every deed into judgment,
>   including every hidden thing,
>   whether it is good or evil.

As in the book of Job, the key for understanding Ecclesiastes hangs at the back door in the final verses. In Ecclesiastes, the retribution principle does hold true at the end, but it cannot always be applied to all of the details of life, in which many things remain an enigma to finite humans, who must place their faith in the Lord. For this reason, when Ecclesiastes is read as a whole, it is not a pessimistic book, as many regard it, but rather it is profoundly realistic as it points us away from the many ways in which human beings seek but fail to find profit in their labours, and instead directs us to God, who gives us his good gifts today and who will evaluate all that we do in our lives.

2. Exhortations to enjoy life as God's good gift (9:7–10)

This paragraph is located in the fourth and final round of observation. Because it is towards the end of the thought experiment in Ecclesiastes, it brings together most of the key points in the book, enabling us as readers to grasp the essentials of what this wisdom book is teaching.

In the midst of his argument that shows how one activity after another in life is *hebel*, a puzzle or an enigma, and that no human activity is profitable, the sage gives a strong positive exhortation in verse 7: *Go, eat your food with gladness, and drink your wine with a joyful heart, for God has already approved what you do.* This is not merely a 'feel good' message, but rather a firm charge to accept joyfully what God has given, as it repeats his earlier similar exhortations in 2:24–25; 3:13; 5:18; and 8:15. The eating envisioned is not what is necessary for nutrition, but rather refers to feasting and celebration. Because, as Ecclesiastes states repeatedly, a sense of *hebel* pervades much of life, God has provided his antidote of joy:

> Enjoying what God provides and allows is integral to a life that is not dominated by *hebel*, vanity. While vanity demarcates the limits of human ability to understand and change the way life works, joy offers relief in the midst of life's frustrations.[2]

When human beings cannot understand or control the factors that affect their lives, they may well be tempted to surrender to grief, but the sage urges them instead to celebrate the joys God has given them. Thus, Ecclesiastes challenges us to change our perspective; 'The tendency to brood and to mope about has to be resisted in the lives of those who fear God, take life as a gift from His hand, and receive God's plan and enablement to enjoy that life.'[3] Feasting is often done for the wrong reasons, as the sage indicates in his failed effort in Ecclesiastes 2:3: 'I tried cheering myself with wine.' However, eating and drinking can and should be done for the right reasons, as this verse encourages. Food and wine are gifts from the generous God, who delights in the joy of his people,[4] so the sage counsels them to accept joy where it can legitimately be found. God has created life to be enjoyed, not just endured, so wise people even while aware of life's griefs will choose to focus on life's joys. This exhortation applies what the sage has affirmed in Ecclesiastes 8:15:

---

[2] M. A. Grisanti, *NIDOTTE* 3:1253–1254.

[3] W. C. Kaiser, *Ecclesiastes: Total Life*, Everyman's Bible Commentary (Chicago: Moody, 1979), p. 98.

[4] Ps. 104:14–15 praises the Lord by saying, 'He makes grass grow for the cattle, and plants for people to cultivate – bringing forth food from the earth: wine that gladdens human hearts, oil to make their faces shine, and bread that sustains their hearts.'

> So I commend the enjoyment of life, because there is nothing better for a person under the sun than to eat and drink and be glad. Then joy will accompany them in their toil all the days of the life God has given them under the sun.

It is true that life has its pains, some of them excruciating indeed. At the same time, life also has its pleasures, and verse 8 emphasizes the importance of grasping them. In the ancient world, sackcloth and ashes were used for mourning. By contrast, *white* clothes and anointing *oil* were features of festive and celebratory occasions. Anointing with oil was a mark of hospitality, as is seen in Psalms 23:5 and 104:15; and it is indicative of joy in Isaiah 61:3. In the arid conditions of ancient Israel, white clothes and oil provided additional practical benefits, because white clothes reflect rather than absorb the heat and oil protects against dry skin.[5]

In our modern world, white clothes are often reserved for special occasions such as weddings and christenings, and that was likely the case in the ancient world, especially since walking on dusty paths would quickly soil white clothing. However, the sage urges that they *always* be clothed in white, because 'No matter what the circumstances, the daily necessities of life can provide some cause for thanksgiving.'[6] What verse 8 emphasizes is the importance of making celebration a prominent tone in life. Rather than reserving celebration for Christmas, birthdays and anniversaries alone, we must nurture an appreciation for the festive side of life. Jesus said in John 10:10, 'I have come that they may have life, and have it to the full.' This abundant life does not have to be deferred until the future after we die, but should begin in the present. Even though life's puzzles and enigmas could easily sour us towards life, wise people celebrate life today as God's good gift to be enjoyed, and they are alert to ways in which to do that. This does not mean being *less* serious about the pains of life, but it is being *more* celebratory about the pleasures that God gives to us in life.

Continuing in the same line of thought, the first part of verse 9 exhorts, *Enjoy life with your wife, whom you love, all the days of this meaningless [hebel = puzzling] life that God has given you under the sun – all your meaningless [hebel = puzzling] days.* When the Lord formed Adam and Eve

---

[5] T. Longman, *The Book of Ecclesiastes*, NICOT (Grand Rapids: Eerdmans, 1998), p. 230.

[6] J. Bollhagen, *Ecclesiastes*, Concordia (St. Louis: Concordia, 2011), p. 331.

in the beginning, he designed them to be united in one flesh (Gen. 2:24–25). In the wisdom literature, the enjoyment of their sexual union is encouraged in Proverbs 5:15–19, and the same language is featured in the Song of Songs, especially in 4:12 – 5:1. Love within marriage is one of God's pleasures that sustains human beings through the toil of their lives. During their life in the here and now *under the sun*, humans will experience many things that are *hebel*, an enigma or puzzle. At the same time, one of the great joys that God gives in life is the marriage relationship. Because the wisdom literature of the Old Testament typically has in view a young man, as indicated by the frequent address in Proverbs 'Hear, my son', the sage here speaks in terms of enjoying life with one's *wife*, but this is easily applied to a woman as well, who is to enjoy life with her husband.

The final part of verse 9 states, *For this is your lot in life and in your toilsome labour under the sun.* The term translated *lot* is the Hebrew word *ḥēleq*, which means a portion or share. It is the term used frequently in the book of Joshua to refer to the territories allotted to the tribes of Israel. In the teaching of Ecclesiastes, humans are not able to achieve a profit (*yitrôn*) by their toil under the sun, but God does give to them the ability to enjoy the portions (*ḥēleq*) that he has given to them. What several passages in Ecclesiastes teach is that God has given to us the capacity for enjoyment in the here and now, and it is both our opportunity and our obligation to accept this gift and to enjoy it. For example, the sage says in Ecclesiastes 3:12–13,

> I know that there is nothing better for people than to be happy and to
> do good while they live. That each of them may eat and drink, and find
> satisfaction in all their toil – this is the gift [*ḥēleq*] of God.

It is important that we accept gratefully God's portions, rather than refusing to rejoice as he intends. One commentator has warned wisely,

> Believers are to be rebuked for rejecting God's worldly gifts and refusing
> to use them in a proper way. Out of a distorted view of worldliness, wherein
> every pleasure ordained by God for man's enjoyment is either denied or
> begrudgingly used, many have developed a superpious, unhappy, and
> even miserable existence. This text proclaims liberation to them.[7]

---

[7] Kaiser, *Ecclesiastes*, p. 101.

God wants his people to rejoice in his gifts, such as food, drink, celebrations and family, and by them to enjoy his sustaining blessing in the midst of the many puzzles and heavy burdens that so often afflict our lives. This is the *ḥēleq* the Lord has given to us and which we should accept gratefully from him.

This section concludes in verse 10 with a final exhortation: *Whatever your hand finds to do, do it with all your might.* With these words, the sage urges his student to grasp life forcefully, or as we might say today, 'Go for it!'[8] This is a challenge to grasp every portion God has given and to use to the fullest every opportunity he provides. Instead of allowing the puzzles of life to deter us from productive activity, God's people need to ask what they can do, and then do it with all of their might.

This paragraph, Ecclesiastes 9:7–10, gives three reasons why we should live joyfully and energetically. First, God has approved activities such as times of feasting and celebration (7–8). Second, God gives portions in life that should be accepted joyfully as a relief from the toilsome labour that we endure during our time in this life (9). Third, life is short and fleeting, so its unique opportunities must not be missed but grasped (10). As will be developed later in Ecclesiastes 11:1–6, we must not let the puzzles of life paralyse us from productive action, but we must be willing to take reasonable risks, even when we cannot control the outcomes. This is a call to activity, in contrast to a pessimistic giving up on life, as so many people in the contemporary world find themselves doing. We must remember, 'There is work to be done. The strength that we have is to be used, and where opportunity of putting it to use presents itself, such an opportunity is to be utilized.'[9]

The sage also warns that *in the realm of the dead, where you are going, there is neither working nor planning nor knowledge nor wisdom.* Death is approaching, as is pictured in the memorable extended image in Ecclesiastes 12:1–7, so it is vital that the present opportunities do not slip by. The time to grasp life is *now*, and God has given us knowledge and wisdom so that we can work and plan in life *today*. It is crucial not to postpone to eternity what can only be done today during the here and now. The New Testament reveals that the people of God do indeed have a glorious future

---

[8] C.-L. Seow, *Ecclesiastes*, AB 18C (New York: Doubleday, 1997), p. 302, points out that in other Old Testament passages, such as Lev. 12:8; 25:28; Judg. 9:33; 1 Sam. 10:7; 25:8; Isa. 10:10, 'this saying has to do with ability, rather than the luck of the draw'.

[9] H. C. Leupold, *Expositions of Ecclesiastes* (Grand Rapids: Baker, 1952), p. 217.

that he has prepared for them (cf. 1 Pet. 1:4), but that does not mean that life today is unimportant. From God's perspective, the life he gives today is his gift to us, and we must live it and enjoy it as he intends. To do less is to refuse to accept his gracious gift, and in effect to hold the Lord in contempt. This, however, is not at all permission for hedonism, in which we do just as we please, but it is an invitation to enjoy life in the ways that please and honour God.

3. Concluding comment

In our contemporary world, it is all too common to see people who are living only for the moment, with no concern about eternal matters, and this is typified by the slogan, 'You only go around once in life, so grab for all the gusto you can get.' Like the sage in Ecclesiastes, they seek to find their significance in their achievements, their pleasures and their experiences, only to come to the sad realization that all their accomplishments still leave their lives as a puzzle without an answer. For them, the book of Ecclesiastes is a sober wake-up call telling them that their path will lead nowhere good. In that sense, Ecclesiastes has a negative message, in that it warns human beings how *not* to live. They must not live under the sun, as though God does not exist and today is all the life there is. The careless and cynical cry 'Eat, drink and be merry, for tomorrow we die' falls far short of what God designed for human life.

However, there is more to the book of Ecclesiastes than just a negative message of how *not* to live. It also contains a positive message that we must learn and live. Throughout the book, we are exhorted to enjoy life to the fullest by accepting it as God's gift. What we read in Ecclesiastes 9:7–10, as well as in several other places in the book, are not mere suggestions or words of advice, but imperatives, and this indicates a great sense of urgency. In the life we live today, we cannot find profit (*yitrôn*) under the sun by leaving God and the eternal out of consideration, but God has provided for us portions (*ḥēleq*) that we can enjoy now. Ecclesiastes, then, urges us to live joyfully for what pleases God and to make full use of his gift of life today.

People who suppose that the ancient texts of the Bible are irrelevant to those who live in the twenty-first century have not grasped the important message of this wisdom book. Ecclesiastes is anything but out of date. Rather, it speaks with great relevance to every generation, including our own today, as it deconstructs our vain attempts to secure our lives apart from God, and instead shows us how life can be truly enjoyed as we accept the gracious portion God has given to us. When read in the context of the rest of the Bible, 'Ecclesiastes anticipates dimly what emerges in full light after the death and resurrection of Christ',[10] because when Jesus was crucified and then rose from the grave, he demonstrated that 'for believers death is not the end of all meaning, but the entrance into the very presence of God'.[11] In its unique way, Ecclesiastes points us to God, who is the source of all wisdom and the fount of all life.

---

[10] Estes, *Handbook*, p. 284.

[11] Longman, *Ecclesiastes*, p. 40.

Part 5
The culmination of wisdom

Matthew 7:13–29

16. Jesus, the teacher of wisdom

In moving from the Old Testament message of wisdom into the New Testament, wisdom is now clearly focused on Jesus Christ.[1] As the incarnate Son of God (cf. John 1:14; Heb. 1:1–3), in his earthly ministry Jesus echoed the themes and language of wisdom made familiar in the Old Testament, and he also demonstrated his skill as a wisdom teacher by using wisdom sayings, riddles and parables (Matt. 13:10–13). Both in *what* he taught and in *how* he taught, Jesus was the master teacher of wisdom.[2] His extraordinary wisdom was recognized by those who heard him (Mark 1:22), and Jesus himself stated in Matthew 12:42 that his wisdom exceeded that of Solomon. His mastery of wisdom is evidenced in his Sermon on the Mount found in Matthew 5 – 7, which is a distillation of Jesus' teaching throughout his three-year earthly ministry. This sermon as it represents Jesus' prevalent themes frequently recalls what we have seen already in Old Testament wisdom – for example, in his Beatitudes in Matthew 5:3–12 (see Pss 1:1; 112:1; Prov. 3:13; 8:32, 34), his emphasis on righteousness in Matthew 5:20; 6:1–7, 33 (see the discussion of wisdom as righteousness in chapter 12), his call to purity in Matthew 5:27–30 (see Prov. 5:15–20) and

---

[1] For a lucid discussion of several key New Testament passages in which wisdom is related to Christ, see D. J. Ebert, *Wisdom Christology: How Jesus Becomes God's Wisdom for Us*, Explorations in Biblical Theology (Phillipsburg: P&R, 2011).

[2] R. Riesner, 'Jesus as Preacher and Teacher', in H. Wansbrough (ed.), *Jesus and the Oral Gospel Tradition*, JSNTSup 64 (Sheffield: Sheffield Academic Press, 1991), p. 204, observes, 'Jesus condensed the main points of his theological and ethical teaching in summaries, the aphoristic meshalim [proverbs]. These were uttered, not spontaneously, but consciously pre-formulated. If Jesus created a deliberate formulation and a poetical form of a teaching, then it was done not to make his hearers forget but to make them memorize. This would have been possible through the highly poetic form of most of the sayings.'

his clear differentiation between the way of wisdom and the way of folly in Matthew 7:13–14 (see Prov. 9:1–6, 13–18).

This chapter examines the final portion of the Sermon on the Mount, Matthew 7:13–29, as Jesus brought his teaching to a rhetorically powerful conclusion and the crowd who heard him responded to it. What he taught on that day in the first century was timeless truth that speaks with equal relevance to us today in the twenty-first century.

1. Two roads (7:13–14)

In these two verses, Jesus echoes the language of Old Testament wisdom and of the book of Deuteronomy as he contrasts the two alternative paths that human beings can choose to take in their lives. This portrayal of the ultimate life choice was frequently used not only in the biblical texts, but also in the Second Temple Jewish literature and by some of the earliest extant Christian teachings.[3] Jesus says that there are only two ways (cf. Deut. 30:19; Ps. 1), and those who are not on one way are necessarily on the other. The imperative *Enter* indicates the intentional choice that each person must make. On the one hand, there is the wide gate that leads to a broad road. This broad way wrongly supposes that there is plenty of room for all sorts of divergent beliefs and behaviours, for it is the way of tolerance, or in Old Testament terms the path of folly. Although many people choose this apparently delectable way, in reality it leads to eternal destruction.[4] This teaching of Jesus contrasted profoundly with what others were propounding, because

> The false prophets and religious opposition offer the people what is on the surface a more appealing invitation, for theirs is the easier way to fit into conventional wisdom. But those who choose to enter the gate to popular opinion by rejecting Jesus' invitation will find it opens onto a road that leads to eternal destruction.[5]

Jesus, however, calls his disciples to enter through a narrow gate that leads to a narrow road. This is not the path that is popular or ordinarily taken.

---

[3] D. A. Hagner, *Matthew 1 – 13*, WBC 33A (Dallas: Word, 1993), p. 178.

[4] The Greek term *apōleia* that is translated as *destruction* is also used in John 17:12; Rom. 9:22; Phil. 1:28; 2 Thess. 2:3; 2 Pet. 2:1; and Rev. 17:8, 11 to refer to eternal destruction by God.

[5] M. J. Wilkins, *Matthew*, NIVAC (Grand Rapids: Zondervan, 2004), p. 322.

One who goes on Jesus' narrow road does not go with the flow of the crowd, because to follow Jesus is to choose to be in the minority. The way that leads to life is restricted, not roomy. By these words, Jesus indicates that his path of discipleship is not easy, but it is worth the effort, for it leads to life, as he makes clear in Mark 8:34–35:

> Whoever wants to be my disciple must deny themselves and take up their cross and follow me. For whoever wants to save their life will lose it, but whoever loses their life for me and for the gospel will save it.

In contrast to the broad road that leads to destruction, which many traverse, the narrow road that leads to life is found by only a few. That is the road we must find and follow, even when most people around us choose as their route for life the road that to them seems more enjoyable and less restrictive.

2. Two trees (7:15–20)

Even on the narrow road there are great dangers that threaten Jesus' disciples, so Jesus warns them in verse 15, *Watch out for false prophets. They come to you in sheep's clothing, but inwardly they are ferocious wolves.* Throughout the Old Testament, false prophets were a danger to the people of Israel, and they continued to be a threat to the early Christians.[6] The false prophets offer 'an easier alternative to the narrow way of Christian discipleship'.[7] They present themselves as though they are harmless sheep, but in reality they are ravenous wolves that devour (Gen. 49:27), tear (Ezek. 22:27) and ravage (Jer. 5:6) their prey. In the face of this lethal threat, the disciples of Jesus will need to be discerning and not gullible.

Jesus tells his disciples how they can discern who the false prophets are. Changing his metaphor in verse 16, Jesus says that they will know the false prophets by their fruit, not by their foliage. Anyone knows where to find the good and nourishing fruit of grapes and figs. They are not found

---

[6] D. A. Carson, 'Matthew', *EBC*, vol. 8, rev. edn (Grand Rapids: Zondervan, 2010), p. 227, notes, '[Matthew] was doubtless steeped in the OT reports of earlier false prophets (Jer 6:13–15; 8:8–12; Eze 13; 22:27; Zep 3:4). Certainly the first Christians faced the false prophets Jesus had predicted (Ac 20:29; 2 Co 11:11–15; 2 Pe 2:1–3, 17–22; cf. 1 Jn 2:18, 22; 4:1–6).'

[7] R. T. France, *The Gospel according to Matthew*, TNTC (Downers Grove: InterVarsity Press, 1988), p. 147.

on thorns or thistles, but instead on the proper vines and trees. The way Jesus teaches here is reminiscent of passages such as Proverbs 6:6–11, where the observation of features in nature is the procedure of the wisdom teacher, as their observations produce patterns, and the patterns yield lessons for life. By this means, Jesus cautions his disciples to look at the lives of those who purport to be prophets and not to be deceived by their words. As they view the quality of their lives, they will be able to discern whether what the 'prophets' say is true or not.

Continuing his teaching into verse 17, Jesus says, *every good tree bears good fruit, but a bad tree bears bad fruit.* By these words, Jesus warns his disciples that they must not be deceived by appearances, but rather they must discern the reality in those who present themselves as prophets, or spokesmen, for God. As Proverbs 1:31 indicates, foolish people produce fruit of poor quality in their lives, in contrast to the wise woman in Proverbs 31:31, whose righteous life is evidenced by the good quality of her fruit ('Honour her for all that her hands have done, and let her works bring her praise at the city gate'). By encouraging his disciples to careful observation as they scrutinize fruit in order to discern the character of the person who produced it, Jesus demonstrates the skilful approach of the wisdom teacher. He evidences wisdom in *what* he teaches as well as in *how* he teaches.

In verse 18, Jesus clarifies that *what* a person manifests in his or her conduct reveals *who* that person is in his or her character. One commentator notes well the significance of Jesus' teaching when he reasons,

> That which a man is ultimately in the depths is always going to reveal and manifest itself, and it does so in belief and life. The two things are indissolubly linked together. As a man thinks, so eventually he is. As a man thinks, so he does. In other words, we inevitably proclaim what we are and what we believe. It does not matter how careful we are, it is bound to come out.[8]

In words that echo the warning in Jeremiah 23 against false prophets, and that anticipate the language of James 3:12, Jesus emphasizes that a righteous person, like a good tree, is not able to produce bad fruit, and a sinful person, like a rotten tree, is not able to produce good fruit.

---

[8] D. M. Lloyd-Jones, *Studies in the Sermon on the Mount* (Grand Rapids: Eerdmans, 1971), p. 254.

It is standard practice in gardening for a tree that does not bear good fruit to be cut down, and if the tree is diseased it is burned, so that it does not infect other trees (19), because

> Such trees take up space, and besides cumbering the ground they may spread their corruption to perfectly sound trees. There is no reason for their continuing to exist and no reason why a competent orchardist should let them continue to grow.[9]

In the words of John the Baptist in Matthew 3:10 and of Jesus in John 15:6 ('If you do not remain in me, you are like a branch that is thrown away and withers; such branches are picked up, thrown into the fire and burned'), trees that are cut down and thrown into fire picture God's eschatological judgment.[10] Similarly, false prophets can and likely will adversely influence other people towards beliefs and behaviours that are condemned by the Lord. They are, then, a clear and present danger to Jesus' disciples.

With words that are equivalent to verse 16a, verse 20 concludes the paragraph of verses 15–20. By the fruit that can be observed in their lives, the false prophets (15) will be revealed for who they really are. In this context, their *fruit* likely refers generally to what they are in their character, although a secondary reference could be to their words, because what they teach leads others to destruction and it is antithetical to Jesus' exhortation to follow the narrow road that leads to life (13–14). This paragraph, then, teaches that

> One's spiritual identity is determined not by what one says but by what one does, because what one does inexorably reveals one's heart. The truism holds: actions speak louder than words. The latter are empty and hypocritical when the former are missing. What one does reveals who one is.[11]

3. Two claims (7:21–23)

These verses include a sobering and even troubling caution that although some people may think that they know the Lord, in reality they do not,

---

[9] L. Morris, *The Gospel according to Matthew*, Pillar (Grand Rapids: Eerdmans, 1992), p. 178.

[10] F. Lang, *TDNTA*, p. 978.

[11] D. L. Turner, *Matthew*, BECNT (Grand Rapids: Baker Academic, 2008), p. 219.

because Jesus says, *Not everyone who says to me, 'Lord, Lord,' will enter the kingdom of heaven* (21). Read with the preceding paragraph, the verses suggest that these people could be the false prophets referred to in verse 15, but it could also have a broader referent of those who are self-deceived about their relationship with God. Jesus here warns that

> it is not only false teachers who make the narrow way difficult to find and still harder to tread. A man may also be grievously self-deceived, and fondly imagine that he is walking along the right road when he is not. He may use the believer's vocabulary, repeat the believer's formulas, recite the believer's creed, and take part in the believer's activities without being a real believer himself.[12]

It is quite possible to call God *Lord* and yet not actually live under his authority and rule. Jesus, therefore, goes on to say that *only the one who does the will of my Father who is in heaven* will enter into his kingdom.

Jesus' stunning words continue into verse 22, when he reiterates his point: *Many will say to me on that day, 'Lord, Lord, did we not prophesy in your name and in your name drive out demons and in your name perform many miracles?'* They may have done impressive religious deeds, but they did not do the will of the Father. They claim to have acted in the Lord's name, as his commissioned representatives, even having done the acts of Jesus' disciples (cf. Matt. 10:1, 8). These miracles likely refer to miraculous healings, similar to what Jesus did in his ministry and to what was also done by his first disciples and then later by the apostles in the early church.[13] Although this might appear to be irrefutable evidence of their genuine relationship to God, it must also be noted that passages such as 2 Thessalonians 2:9–10 indicate that Satan can connive to 'use all sorts of displays of power through signs and wonders that serve the lie, and all the ways that wickedness deceives those who are perishing'. Therefore, 'It is clear from many biblical texts that supernatural phenomena must not be equated with genuine faith and divine endorsement.'[14] Although these individuals may have deceived others and themselves, the Lord knows the real story about them: that they are not on the narrow road that leads to

---

[12] R. V. G. Tasker, *The Gospel according to St Matthew*, TNTC 1 (Grand Rapids: Eerdmans, 1961), pp. 83–84.

[13] Hagner, *Matthew 1 – 13*, p. 188.

[14] Turner, *Matthew*, p. 219.

life. The tragedy is that this is not just an isolated and rare case, but *many* people will be surprised at the judgment. The weighty import of Jesus' warning is that

> It is possible for a man to preach correct doctrine, and in the name of Christ, and yet himself remain outside the kingdom of God. That is the statement, nothing less. If anyone other than the Lord Jesus Christ had said this we would not believe it. Moreover, we would feel that he was a censorious, narrow-minded person. But it is the Lord Himself who says it.[15]

On *that day* (22), which is the day of God's judgment,[16] Jesus himself (*I*) will exercise his divine prerogative[17] as he will utter a verdict of condemnation upon those who wrongly suppose that they are on God's path (23). Like students expecting a top grade but who in fact fail the examination, they will be stunned by Jesus' words: *I never knew you. Away from me, you evil-doers!* What is crucial is not the religious activities they have performed, but their personal relationship with Jesus. Because Jesus does not know them, they will not enter into life, but will be numbered among those who are on the broad road that leads to destruction (13).

4. Two builders (7:24–27)

Jesus concludes his Sermon on the Mount with a double comparison that is familiar to children who have grown up in church and which has become a familiar proverb in broader culture. Using the standard approach of a wisdom teacher, Jesus employs a concrete comparison from life to teach an abstract theological concept.[18] He compares everyone who hears and obeys his teaching to a wise man who builds a house on the rock (24).

---

[15] Lloyd-Jones, *Sermon on the Mount*, p. 267.

[16] G. Delling, *TDNTA*, p. 310, notes the similar uses of 'day' to refer to the time of divine judgment in Matt. 11:22; Rom. 2:5; 1 Cor. 3:13; 1 Thess. 5:5; Heb. 10:25; Jude 6; Rev. 6:17.

[17] Carson, 'Matthew', pp. 229–230, observes, 'Verse 23 presupposes an implicit Christology of the highest order. Jesus himself decides not only who enters the kingdom on the last day but also who will be banished from his presence. That he never knew these false claimants strikes a common biblical note, namely, how close to spiritual reality one may come, while knowing nothing of its fundamental reality (e.g., Balaam; Judas Iscariot; cf. Mk 9:38–39; 1 Co 13:2; Heb 3:14; 1 Jn 2:19).'

[18] *DBI*, pp. 449–450, states, 'It is easy to see Jesus in the role of a sage, a figure in the tradition of wise men such as Solomon. Like a wise man, he speaks in riddle-like sayings, aphorisms and parables that subvert the accepted wisdom of the day, and parables that speak of the wise and the foolish (Mt 7:24–27; 24:45–51; 25:1–13). He is skilled in the use of rhetorical devices such as paradox, hyperbole, contrast, irony and emphasis, all designed to take hold in the mind and germinate.'

The rock refers to obedience to the teaching of Jesus, not just knowledge of what Jesus says. A life of obedience to Jesus' words[19] is likened to a foundation that provides stability for one's life.

The image is continued into verse 25, as after the house is built a strong storm batters it with torrential rain, floods and wind, all terms that are used in the Old Testament for future judgment (cf. Ezek. 13:10–15). In this verse,

> Matthew describes typical storms in the hot, dry climate of the Near Eastern lands: blasting winds and torrential rains that produce sudden rivers where formerly there were dry wadis. It is not unusual in the OT for eschatological judgment to be portrayed with this sort of imagery.[20]

God's judgment reveals a person's actual character, just as a severe storm reveals whether a structure has a foundation or not. The rock upon which the house is built represents one's commitment to *doing* the words of Jesus – how a person *lives*, and not just what he or she knows or has heard.

Verses 26–27 form an antithesis to verses 24–25. In verse 26 Jesus compares those who hear his words but do not obey them to a foolish man who builds his house upon sand rather than upon the rock. The sand here likely refers to the alluvial soil around the Sea of Galilee, the area where Jesus preached this sermon, because

> The alluvial sand ringing the seashore was hard on the surface during the hot summer months. But a wise builder would not be fooled by surface conditions . . . When the winter rains came, causing the Jordan River pouring into the sea to overflow its banks, houses built on the alluvial sand surface would have an unstable foundation.[21]

Building on the sand was easier, more convenient and doubtless less expensive than digging down to bedrock to lay a solid foundation, but that

---

[19] C. S. Keener, *Matthew*, IVPNTC 1 (Downers Grove: InterVarsity Press, 1997), p. 167, reasons cogently, 'Jesus here refers to his own words the way other Jewish teachers referred to God's law. The language at least implies that Jesus is God's prophetic spokesperson (Ezek 33:32–33) but is more authoritative than is typical even for prophets; in this context (Mt 7:21–23; see also 18:20), the claim is far more radical. One cannot be content with calling Jesus a great teacher, for he taught that he was more than a mere teacher; one must either accept all his teachings, including those that demand we submit to his lordship, or reject him altogether. Jesus is not one way among many; he is the standard of judgment.'

[20] Hagner, *Matthew 1 – 13*, p. 191.

[21] Wilkins, *Matthew*, p. 327.

was the way of the fool. In the long tradition of wisdom teachers, Jesus contrasts the wise man and the foolish man, and the foolish man in contrast to the wise man hears the words of Jesus *but does not do them.*

In verse 27, it is evident that the two houses experience the same conditions, but with contrasting consequences. When the storm beats against the house built on sand, it collapses, but the house built on rock stands. It is the foundation that makes all the difference. In the same way, both the wise man and the foolish man hear the same teaching of Jesus, but they respond differently to him. It is obedience to Jesus' word that makes all the difference and is the line of demarcation between those who are on the narrow road leading to life and those on the broad road leading to destruction. As a skilled preacher concluding his sermon with a convincing final illustration, Jesus tells this parable in verses 24–27 to clinch the major point in his Sermon on the Mount, that obedience to his teaching is essential if a person is to enter God's narrow road to life.

5. The response to Jesus' teaching (7:28–29)

Jesus' sermon concludes with verse 27, and then Matthew records the response of the crowds to his teaching. Those who heard him were *amazed*, overwhelmed, by what Jesus had said. The Greek term *ekplēssō*, used as well in Matthew 13:58, indicates their astonishment at, but not necessarily their acceptance of, what Jesus had preached to them. In his instruction (the term *didachē* may echo wisdom teaching), Jesus exceeded their expectations and left them stunned.

The conjunction *because* that begins verse 29 signals why the crowds were amazed at Jesus' teaching. They no doubt had heard a lot of scribal teaching, but nothing they had heard was like this instruction from Jesus. It is evident that Jesus was a masterful teacher, and was easily the equal of the scribes of Israel. In one important factor, however, Jesus was starkly different from the teachers of the law they had heard. Earlier in the Sermon on the Mount, in Matthew 5:21–48, Jesus six times contrasted his own teaching with what 'you have heard', as he distinguished his teachings from the distortions of the Scriptures by the scribes. Rather than following the common practice of citing prior rabbis as his authority, Jesus spoke on his own authority, as he said repeatedly, 'I tell you . . .' It is evident that Jesus is not just another human teacher, but the divine King, who has 'all authority in heaven and on earth',[22] so 'What astonished them so much . . . was not his use of proverbs, parables, hyperboles or other standard pedagogic devices of his day; what astonished them was his claim to authority.'[23] The crowd would now have to decide what they would do with Jesus' words. Would they by their obedience be wise and accept his claims, or would they be foolish and reject his challenges by failing to put them into practice? They had *learned* what Jesus taught, but would they *live* it? The answer to that question would determine whether they were wise or foolish, and would lead them either towards life or towards destruction.

6. Concluding comment

In this passage, Jesus demonstrates that he is the master wisdom teacher, both in the content of his instruction and in his skilful techniques. Jesus, however, is much more than just an excellent wisdom teacher, because his pronouncement of judgment in verse 23 indicates that he is God, who alone has that prerogative. As God, Jesus does not just teach wisdom; he is the source of all wisdom. He does not just offer another opinion for us to consider, but he teaches divine truth that demands our obedience.

Just as Jesus called the first-century crowds who heard his teaching to consider their response to his words, so we today must evaluate what kind of students we are in Jesus' school of wisdom. Every time we read the Bible or hear it proclaimed, we must decide what we will do with what we have read or heard. Are we faithful in hearing *and obeying* the teaching of Jesus? Are we building our lives upon the solid rock of obedience, or on the shifting sand of disobedience to what Jesus has said? Does the Lord know us to be on his narrow road that leads to life, or are we in fact on the broad road that leads to destruction?

There are many people in the twenty-first-century church who are cultural Christians. They may have grown up in the church, perhaps received a Christian education, participated in various ministries and maybe even been in positions of leadership in Christian organizations. Nevertheless, there is a world of difference between being a cultural Christian and truly having a relationship with God. Jesus asks a probing question of all who profess to be Christians: 'Do I know you?' The only way

---

[22] Matt. 28:18.

[23] Keener, *Matthew*, p. 167.

to be known by Jesus is to be born again by personal faith in God's gracious saving work accomplished by Jesus' substitutionary death for us (cf. Eph. 2:8–9). That is the essential and most crucial factor in life, and nothing else can substitute for it.

1 Corinthians 1:18–25

17. Christ, the wisdom of God

In several of his epistles, Paul speaks of God's wisdom and connects it to Christ, but in 1 Corinthians this is one of his prominent themes, particularly in chapters 1–3. The Corinthian church had a number of significant problems that Paul addressed as he wrote to them. Paul begins this letter by raising an issue that has come to his attention. In the Corinthian church there were divisions and quarrels, with various parties all considering themselves the followers of prominent Christian leaders such as Paul, Apollos and Cephas (Peter), likely because they valued the wisdom of that particular person.[1] Speaking from the heart, he pleads,

> I appeal to you, brothers and sisters, in the name of our Lord Jesus Christ, that all of you agree with one another in what you say and that there be no divisions among you, but that you be perfectly united in mind and thought.[2]

Paul goes on to say in verse 17, 'Christ did not send me to baptise, but to preach the gospel – not with wisdom and eloquence, lest the cross of Christ be emptied of its power.' His mention of 'cross' and 'power' in contrast to merely human wisdom sets the stage for what he explains in detail in 1:18–25. This section explains 'how genuine, full-orbed Christianity stands opposed to the fundamental values of a fallen, sinful world but provides the

---

[1] P. Lampe, 'Theological Wisdom and the "Word about the Cross": The Rhetorical Scheme of 1 Corinthians 1 – 4', *Int* 44 (1990), p. 118. He reasons that 'I belong to Christ' in v. 12 'hardly represents a Corinthian slogan but a rhetorical formulation by Paul himself, exposing the absurdity of the party slogans' (p. 117).

[2] 1 Cor. 1:10.

necessary antidote to the self-centered factionalism of the Corinthians'.[3] In this passage, Paul makes it clear that Christ is the wisdom of God, in contrast to the foolishness of what human beings purport to be their wisdom. What he says to correct the Corinthians in the first century speaks with great relevance to Christians in the twenty-first century, who too often are more divided into their partisan groups than united with other Christians in their shared commitment to Christ.

1. The message of the cross is the power of God (1:18)

Verse 18 functions as the thesis statement for 1:18–25, as Paul here introduces three themes that are restated and elaborated through the paragraph: '(1) The proclamation of the cross, (2) the two basic human responses to the gospel message, and (3) the decisive triumph of God's wisdom over the wisdom of the world'.[4] In this context, *message* (*logos*) likely has the sense of the message preached by Paul and other Christians. The term *cross* (*stauros*) is a metonymy in which the cross represents the whole work of Christ that he accomplished through his death on the cross. Paul continues to assert that this message that he and others preach about what Christ has brought to pass through his death is not comprehended by *those who are perishing*. In other words, those who are on the path of folly (cf. Proverbs) or on the broad road (cf. Matt. 7:13) are on the way to death, and to complicate the problem they do not understand what Christ has done for their benefit. One commentator notes, 'No mere human, in their right mind or otherwise, would ever have dreamed up God's scheme for redemption – through a crucified Messiah. It is too preposterous, too humiliating, for a deity.'[5] This was particularly the case in the first-century Roman world, in which the cross was not a cherished symbol featured on jewellery, as it is today, but rather represented an especially shameful mode of execution. In the world of Paul and the Corinthians, 'the cross was repugnant to ancient sensibilities and assailed the world's self-centeredness and self-destructive ways'.[6]

By contrast, those who are *being saved* know Christ's death not as a shameful failure but as the *power of God* that has saved them. For this

[3] C. L. Blomberg, *1 Corinthians*, NIVAC (Grand Rapids: Zondervan, 1994), p. 52.

[4] M. Taylor, *1 Corinthians*, NAC 28 (Nashville: B&H, 2014), p. 62.

[5] G. Fee, *The First Epistle to the Corinthians*, NICNT, rev. edn (Grand Rapids: Eerdmans, 2014), p. 71.

[6] D. E. Garland, *1 Corinthians*, BECNT (Grand Rapids: Baker Academic, 2003), p. 61.

reason, Paul writes in Romans 1:16, 'I am not ashamed of the gospel, because it is the power of God that brings salvation to everyone who believes: first to the Jew, then to the Gentile.' The crucifixion of Christ was the lowest point in his humiliation as the Son of God became incarnate as a human being (cf. John 1:14). In the words of Philippians 2:7–8, Christ

> made himself nothing
> > by taking the very nature of a servant,
> > being made in human likeness.
> And being found in appearance as a man,
> > he humbled himself
> > by becoming obedient to death –
> > > even death on a cross!

Later in this chapter, Paul will explain that God chose what the world considers foolish to shame those who consider themselves wise, and what the world considers weak to shame those who consider themselves strong (1:27). The Lord is not limited to the procedures and priorities of human beings as he accomplishes his plan, for his wisdom and power transcend all that human beings know and seek to control. The cross in the Roman world was a symbol of the dominant authority of the empire, which had the power to condemn people to death by means of this humiliating form of execution. By contrast, in God's reckoning the cross represents his great mercy by which he manifested his love to unworthy people and provided for them his gracious gift of life. The message proclaimed through Christ's crucifixion made no sense to human beings, who regarded it as total foolishness, but in the economy of God it was his great wisdom, by which he could 'be just and the one who justifies those who have faith in Jesus'.[7]

2. Through the cross the wisdom of God has made foolish the wisdom of the world (1:19–21)

To support his point in verse 18 that the message of the cross is foolishness to those who are perishing, Paul in verse 19 cites Isaiah 29:14, where the Lord through his prophet says to the unfaithful people of Judah,

---

[7] Rom. 3:26.

the wisdom of the wise will perish,
the intelligence of the intelligent will vanish.

The original sense of the divine word for the eighth century BC, when Isaiah prophesied, can be summarized in this way:

Yahweh declares through the mouth of the prophet that he will himself save Jerusalem from the Assyrians, apart from all political calculations and alliances. He will therefore dumbfound those who have a reputation for wisdom, that is, for political sagacity, by again doing 'marvellous things with this people, wonderful and marvelous'.[8]

As Paul cites the Old Testament verse in Greek, he uses the term *apolō* (*destroy*), which links with 'perishing' (*apollymenon*) in verse 18. His term *frustrate* is the Greek term *atheteō*, which has the nuance of nullify, thwart, declare invalid or confound.[9]

In Isaiah 29:14 the Judeans are warned against trying to match their wits with the all-wise God (cf. also Isa. 40:12–14), because to attempt that is completely foolish. In fact, 'it is the folly of our human machinations that we think we can outwit God, or that lets us think that God ought to be at least as smart as we are'.[10] When Paul uses terms such as *wisdom*, *wise*, *intelligence* and *intelligent* in verse 19, he employs them ironically, because in fact what human beings suppose is wise and intelligent is in reality foolish when compared with the Lord, and what they consider wisdom and intelligence is in truth folly when measured against what the Lord knows. All of the purported wisdom and intelligence of humans will be destroyed and frustrated by the Lord, and that is especially the case when the message of the cross of Christ is in view. The message of the cross is in reality divine wisdom, and when human beings reject it as though it is folly, it is actually their rejection of salvation through the crucifixion of Christ that is the height of folly. Paul could not be clearer in stating that the Lord's true wisdom vastly surpasses the supposed wisdom of human beings. This was true in Paul's time in the first century, and it is equally true today when so many people reject the gospel of Christ as unworthy of their serious consideration.

---

[8] N. Watson, *The First Epistle to the Corinthians*, Epworth, 2nd edn (London: Epworth, 2005), p. 14.

[9] *BAG*, p. 20.

[10] Fee, *First Epistle to the Corinthians*, p. 73.

In verse 20 Paul builds his argument on four rhetorical questions. The implied answer to the first three questions is 'nowhere', and the final question anticipates the answer 'yes, he has'. With these questions Paul alludes to several Old Testament texts. The first question, *Where is the wise person?*, links with Isaiah 19:12, where the wise counsellors of the Egyptian pharaoh claim to be wise, but the divine prophecy asks them,

> Where are your wise men now?
> Let them show you and make known
> what the LORD Almighty
> has planned against Egypt.

Paul's second question enquires, *Where is the teacher of the law?* The term Paul uses is *grammateus*, which in first-century Jewish culture referred to scribes, or scholars of the Mosaic law, but in Greek and Roman culture it indicated a clerk in one of the official guilds. One scholar has concluded,

> if we allow for a blend of Graeco-Roman and Jewish nuances, we might translate person of letters, to preserve the connection with the word history, or perhaps less controversially, expert. Today we might well use some such term as 'the professional'.[11]

Paul faintly echoes the language of Isaiah 33:18, as that divine word prophesied how the people of Judah would recall the ineffectual experts in whom they had placed their confidence:

> Where is that chief officer?
> Where is the one who took the revenue?
> Where is the officer in charge of the towers?

The final question may well be drawn from Isaiah 44:25, where the Lord describes himself as the one

> who foils the signs of false prophets
> and makes fools of diviners,

---

[11] A. C. Thiselton, *The First Epistle to the Corinthians: A Commentary on the Greek Text*, NIGTC (Grand Rapids: Eerdmans, 2000), p. 164.

who overthrows the learning of the wise
and turns it into nonsense.

It is evident both in Paul's rhetorical questions and in the Old Testament passages to which they point[12] that the Lord unmasks people who falsely suppose they are wise, along with their purported wisdom. Measured against the Lord's genuine wisdom, what these human beings declare is not worthy to be called wisdom. In the context of verse 18, Paul contends that in the message of the cross God has provided salvation through what Christ accomplished through his substitutionary atonement in his crucifixion, and by this divine action the Lord has silenced all so-called experts who consider the message of the cross as mere foolishness. The rhetorical eloquence that was highly prized in the first-century world has been effectively countered by the Lord, because 'their talk has already been swept away by God's shocking and amazing act of reversal: the cross'.[13] However, Paul dismisses their purported expertise as mere *wisdom of the world*, because

> The experts of 1:20 are those whose intellect operates solely at the human level and whose values, influence, and admiration are tied to this world . . . Paul does not denigrate wisdom or human reason as such (see 2:6) but rather wisdom that is wedded to the value system and the motivations of this present world order.[14]

Verse 21 begins with *For*, which indicates that Paul now provides an explanation for what he has asserted through his rhetorical questions in verse 20. This verse also gives the backstory for his statement in verse 18, as well as for his argument in the entire paragraph. The first part of verse 21 summarizes Paul's more complete argument in Romans 1:18–32,

---

[12] The third question, *Where is the philosopher of this age?*, does not allude to a specific Old Testament text, as do the other three questions in v. 20, but it is consistent with their general meanings. Paul may have added this question as a rhetorical flourish to augment his argument that the wisdom of God has made foolish what philosophers of this age erroneously claim to be wisdom.

[13] R. B. Hays, *First Corinthians*, Interpretation (Louisville: John Knox, 1997), p. 30. Hays notes, 'In the ancient Greco-Roman world, rhetorical eloquence was highly prized. Powerful orators received the same sort of acclaim and public adulation that is today lavished on movie stars and sports heroes. But Paul now regards all this acclaim as utterly negated by God.' For a detailed discussion of Paul's response to the emphasis upon rhetorical excellence in his day, see A. D. Litfin, *Paul's Theology of Preaching: The Apostle's Challenge to the Art of Persuasion in Ancient Corinth* (Downers Grove: IVP Academic, 2015).

[14] Taylor, *1 Corinthians*, p. 68.

in which he traces how all human beings have suppressed the truth God has made known about his eternal power and divine nature through the created world. Paul states in Romans 1:21–23,

> For although they knew God, they neither glorified him as God nor gave thanks to him, but their thinking became futile and their foolish hearts were darkened. Although they claimed to be wise, they became fools and exchanged the glory of the immortal God for images made to look like a mortal human being and birds and animals and reptiles.

Human beings by their deficient 'wisdom' did not know God, so God in his genuine wisdom chose a means that the world regarded as foolish in order to save those who would believe in him. In language flavoured with irony, Paul states, *God was pleased through the foolishness of what was preached to save those who believe.* What God resolved to do through the preaching of the crucifixion of Christ is foolishness to human thinking, because 'How can the ignominious death of Jesus on a cross be the event of salvation for the world? One would have to be a fool to believe *that.* Yet that is precisely what the gospel declares.'[15] Nevertheless, even though the gospel does not make sense to human minds, it is, as Paul asserts in Romans 1:16, God's power for the salvation of those who believe in Christ.

Just as the message of the cross was regarded as foolishness by most people in the first century, so it continues to seem foolish to most people in the twenty-first century. God's good news of the gospel is dismissed as fake news by those who think that they can reason or work their way to God on their own. It does not make sense to them that the death of Jesus on the cross two thousand years ago is God's means of saving those who believe in him today. And yet, in the wisdom of God, it is.

3. Christ crucified is the wisdom and power of God in contrast to human expectations (1:22–24)

Paul makes it clear that the message of the cross flies in the face of human expectations, because God did not craft his proclamation of salvation through the crucifixion of Christ to suit what people wanted to hear. In the Gospels, the *Jews* repeatedly asked for divine *signs* by which Jesus

---

15 Hays, *First Corinthians*, p. 30.

could prove to them who he was by his powerful deeds (Matt. 12:38–42), similar to how Moses had performed signs to persuade Pharaoh to obey the word of the Lord. The Gospel of John is built upon several miraculous signs that Jesus performed, and John concludes,

> Jesus performed many other signs in the presence of his disciples, which are not recorded in this book. But these are written that you may believe that Jesus is the Messiah, the Son of God, and that by believing you may have life in his name.[16]

Nevertheless, John also narrates how the Jews did not respond positively to the signs performed by Jesus; instead they rejected him and called for Jesus to be crucified.

The *Greeks* of the first century were renowned for seeking *wisdom* through philosophical inquiry, as Luke indicates as he describes Paul's address to the Athenians in Acts 17:16–32. To the Greeks, the crucifixion was a shameful act, so Christ's death on the cross made no sense to them. Their insistence on their human wisdom blinded them to the wisdom of God in the message of the crucifixion.

What human beings expected and what God actually did in Christ are two very different things (23). In striking contrast both to the Jews who demanded spectacular signs and to the Greeks who sought what seemed wise to their thinking, Paul preaches the surprising message of *Christ crucified*. It seems as though God went out of his way to reject what human beings sought, because in order to accept the message of Christ they had to set aside their own faulty expectations. For the Jews, the crucifixion was a *skandalon*, a *stumbling-block* or offence, and not the sign of divine power that they had anticipated. In Romans 9:33, Paul cites Isaiah 28:16 as he explains that the Jews wrongly pursued the law as the way to right-eousness, because they stumbled over the stumbling stone laid by the Lord in the crucifixion of Christ:

> See, I lay in Zion a stone that causes people to stumble
>   and a rock that makes them fall,
>   and the one who believes in him will never be put to shame.[17]

---

[16] John 20:30–31.

[17] Similarly, 1 Pet. 2:4–8 explains in detail the reference to Christ in Isa. 28:16, together with citations of the same image of the rejected stone or the stone that causes stumbling in Ps. 118:22 and Isa. 8:14.

Because Deuteronomy 21:23 says that a person hanged on a tree is cursed by God, 'from a Jewish standpoint, a crucified Messiah was an oxymoron, which became a major stumbling block'.[18] For the Gentiles represented by the Greeks, the crucifixion as the epitome of shame could not be envisioned as anything positive, so they regarded the crucifixion of Christ as total foolishness.

Verses 22–23 explain Paul's initial statement in verse 21 that the world through its wisdom did not know God, and now verse 24 elucidates the final clause of verse 21, 'God was pleased through the foolishness of what was preached to save those who believe.' The unsaved person 'does not accept the things that come from the Spirit of God but considers them foolishness',[19] but for those who are called to salvation by God, Christ is the power and wisdom of God.[20] In this paragraph, Paul equates the *called* in verse 24 with those who 'believe' in verse 21 and with 'us who are being saved' in verse 18. When viewed through the eyes of faith, the crucified Christ is the power of God that the Jews sought as they demanded a sign, and he is the wisdom of God that the Greeks looked for. However, because they were not saved, the Jews and the Greeks could not see God's signs or grasp his wisdom in Christ, because, as Paul explains in 2 Corinthians 4:4, 'The god of this age has blinded the minds of unbelievers, so that they cannot see the light of the gospel that displays the glory of Christ, who is the image of God.' That spiritual blindness continues today, and for that reason so many people in our contemporary culture cannot see or grasp the message of salvation through Christ. As the power and the wisdom of God, the crucified Christ surpasses all that human beings apart from him can do or understand. This message of the cross is addressed to all people, because 'it is the power of God that brings salvation to everyone who believes: first to the Jew; then to the Gentile'.[21]

---

[18] Garland, *1 Corinthians*, p. 70.

[19] 1 Cor. 2:14.

[20] E. J. Schnabel, *NDBT*, pp. 847–848, notes, 'An emphasis unique to the NT is the conviction that God's wisdom is now embodied in a climactic and final way in Jesus the Messiah, Son of Man and Son of God. Referring to OT passages in which wisdom, God's communication with his creation was personified, the early Christians asserted that God in his wisdom became incarnate in Jesus Christ, who is the source of life.'

[21] Rom. 1:16.

4. In the cross God surpasses human wisdom and power (1:25)

Paul brings this paragraph to a close in verse 25 with a concluding statement that gives the reason for his assertion in verse 24 that 'Christ [is] the power of God and the wisdom of God.' Human wisdom decries the message of the cross as foolishness, but in fact it is the wisdom of God. Human beings dismiss as weakness one who is crucified, but in fact the crucifixion of Christ is the power of God, because the crucifixion was followed by the resurrection, when God

> raised Christ from the dead and seated him at his right hand in the heavenly realms, far above all rule and authority, power and dominion, and every name that is invoked, not only in the present age but also in the one to come.[22]

Human beings suppose that they are wise, but compared to God they have no clue. The *foolishness of God*, that is, the message of the crucifixion of Christ, is wiser than any plan that human beings can devise to bring salvation. Human beings value power, but compared to God they have no clout. The *weakness of God*, that is, the death of Christ in the most humiliating fashion known in the Roman culture, accomplished salvation that exceeded anything that human beings could achieve by their own efforts. The surprising truth of the gospel is that 'In the cross God "outsmarted" his human creatures and thereby nullified their wisdom. In the same cross God also "overpowered" his enemies, with lavish grace and forgiveness, and thereby divested them of their strength.'[23]

5. Concluding comment

Paul will go on in verses 26–31 to apply what he has discussed in verses 18–25 to the situation in the church at Corinth. The Corinthians have become distracted from the foundational message of the cross. They are boasting in their human leaders rather than in the Lord. They have forgotten that when the Lord saved them, not many of them were wise,

---

[22] Eph. 1:20–21.
[23] Fee, *First Epistle to the Corinthians*, p. 81.

influential or of noble birth (26). Instead, the Lord chose to display his wisdom by working in those whom the world regarded as foolish, and he revealed his power by working in those who were viewed as weak. In God's economy, the last will become the first, it is through death that life is gained and it is the weak who are made strong. The message of the cross, which seems so foolish to those who are without Christ and are therefore perishing, is God's power for his people, and they always need to remember that crucial fact.

Throughout its history, the church has been in greatest spiritual danger when it has sought to wield power and to gain acceptance and approval in the world. Although such efforts may begin with the good intention of influencing the culture for Christ, in so many cases the world has got more into the church than the church has got into the world, and that seems particularly the case at the present time.

If Paul were speaking today, he would remind us that the power of God is not political clout, a legislative agenda, economic leverage or cultural dominance, but it is the message of the cross. The church best influences its culture not from the top down, but from the ground up, as individual lives are transformed by the gospel so that they live out the values of Christ in their jobs, families and communities. In the same way, the wisdom of God is not measured in degrees earned, books published and universities founded, all achievements that are valued by our contemporary culture, but it is found in Christ. We must be careful to keep Christ our central focus in what we proclaim and how we live, rather than letting our attention be diverted to other endeavours that only appear to be wise to our world.

Colossians 2:1–7

18. Knowing Christ, the source of wisdom

The message of wisdom, which is rooted in the Old Testament, finds its biblical culmination in Jesus, the incarnate Son of God. This is evidenced in the teaching of Jesus in the Gospels (see chapter 16), and then is explained in several of the New Testament epistles. This chapter discusses how Paul develops the theme of knowing Christ, who is the source of wisdom, in Colossians 2:1–7. He teaches this truth to a church for which he has great concern, because they are in danger of departing from God's wisdom in Christ into the error propounded by false teachers. Although Paul spoke to a specific situation in the first century, what he says has great relevance for Christians today in the twenty-first century. We all know people who have slipped away from Christ, or who are in danger of doing so. This may be due to deep disappointment they have experienced in their lives, or because they have become distracted by other commitments that seem more compelling to them, or perhaps they have been deceived by false teaching that leads them away from God's truth. At every time in history, Christians need to remember that the ultimate source of true wisdom is Christ, so he must be the one from whom they learn and in whom they trust. What Paul wrote to the Colossians, then, is crucial as well for our spiritual well-being.

1. Paul's concern for the Colossians (2:1–3)

Paul declares in verse 1, *I want you to know how hard I am contending for you and for those at Laodicea, and for all who have not met me personally.* It is evident that Paul has deep feelings for the Christians in Colossae, as well as those in the nearby city of Laodicea. The New Testament does not explain how Paul came to be involved with these churches; they may well have been planted by Paul's co-workers, people such as Timothy and Titus whom he mentored. For example, Paul left Titus in Crete with the responsibility of organizing the churches there and appointing elders in every town (Titus 1:5), so it would be reasonable to think of Paul sending one of his protégés to minister in a location where he himself had not been. If that was the case, then Paul would in effect be the spiritual grandfather of the Colossians. It could also be that because Paul was called by the Lord to be an apostle to the Gentiles (Acts 9:15; Rom. 11:13) he felt a general sense of responsibility for the Gentile Christians in Colossae and elsewhere, because

> Paul's self-understanding as apostle to the Gentiles, and hence as an integral part of God's plan to disclose the mystery of Christ among the Gentiles, emboldened him not to limit his work only to those churches that he had actually founded.[1]

Whatever may have prompted Paul's deep concern for the Colossians, he clearly evidences the heart of a pastor as he cares deeply even for these Christians whom he had not personally met. The term *contending* translates the Greek word *agōn*, which has the nuance of a struggle or fight in Philippians 1:30; 1 Thessalonians 2:2; and 1 Timothy 6:12, but here likely refers to Paul's deep care or concern for the Colossians.[2] This intense yearning is what drives Paul's ministry in general, as he explains in Colossians 1:28–29: '[Christ] is the one we proclaim, admonishing and teaching everyone with all wisdom, so that we may present everyone fully mature in Christ. To this end I strenuously contend with all the energy Christ so powerfully works in me.' Paul has this fervent compassion even for the Colossians, the Laodiceans and other Christians he did not personally know.

Several commentators have considered Paul's *agōn* (*contending*) in verse 1 to be his wrestling in prayer for the Colossians, as Epaphras always wrestled in prayer for them (Col. 4:12). Vaughan supports this view with his reconstruction of Paul's setting in confinement:

---

[1] M. Meye Thompson, *Colossians and Philemon*, THNTC (Grand Rapids: Eerdmans, 2005), p. 47.

[2] *BAG*, p. 14.

At the time he wrote these words he could not move beyond the walls of his 'rented house' (Acts 28:20), being continuously held by the chain linking him to a Roman soldier. But even under these circumstances he could engage in the combat of prayer and so exert himself strenuously in behalf of his readers.[3]

This background is possible, but Witherington may be on more solid ground as he describes Paul's *agōn* as his effort in writing this letter to encourage the Colossians to stand true for Christ. He reasons,

Perhaps Paul is referring to his general labor for the gospel or to the work he is putting into this letter as part of his struggle on their behalf, since he will be dealing with the false philosophy. V. 2 gives substance to this last suggestion since Paul says he has been struggling in order to encourage their hearts, or better said, to give their hearts courage, and in this verse he is surely referring to this letter.[4]

Paul wants the Colossians to be *encouraged in heart* (2), which refers to their whole person, and not just to the emotional aspect of their lives, as *heart* is often used in English. He also wants them to be *united in love*, which speaks of their unity both with Christ, who is the head of the church (cf. Eph. 4:16), and with one another (cf. Eph. 4:3; Phil. 2:2–5). The goal of this encouragement and unity is *that they may have the full riches of complete understanding, in order that they may know the mystery of God, namely Christ.* Lurking about the Colossian church are false teachers with error that discourages and divides God's people, in place of Christ, who encourages and unites them. Later in this chapter, Paul warns the Colossians about those who 'have lost connection with the head [Christ], from whom the whole body, supported and held together by its ligaments and sinews, grows as God causes it to grow'.[5] The language Paul uses in verses 2–3, terms like *understanding, wisdom* and *knowledge*, echoes the wisdom vocabulary in the book of Proverbs. What Paul emphasizes here is that the deepest truth of God, the full riches of complete understanding,

---

[3] C. Vaughan, 'Colossians', *EBC*, vol. 11 (Grand Rapids: Zondervan, 1978), p. 194.

[4] B. Witherington, *The Letters to Philemon, the Colossians, and the Ephesians: A Socio-Rhetorical Commentary on the Captivity Epistles* (Grand Rapids: Eerdmans, 2007), p. 148.

[5] Col. 2:19.

finds its source in Christ; 'The great truth taught is that all that is deepest in God is summed up in Christ.'[6]

The thought that Paul begins in verse 2 continues into verse 3, where he states that in Christ *are hidden all the treasures of wisdom and knowledge*. The key theme of the first chapter of Colossians is knowledge, and this sets the stage for the rest of the letter, in which Paul warns the Colossians against erroneous teaching and challenges them to live in accordance with the truth.[7] In Proverbs 8:10–11, personified Wisdom exhorts,

> Choose my instruction instead of silver,
>> knowledge rather than choice gold,
> for wisdom is more precious than rubies,
>> and nothing you desire can compare with her.

Paul, too, affirms that wisdom is a treasure to be valued, and not neglected or scorned. All of the treasures of wisdom and knowledge find their source in Christ, who is the fullness of God, as Paul will go on to say in Colossians 2:9: 'For in Christ all the fullness of the Deity lives in bodily form.' These treasures are *hidden*, that is, stored up, because many of wisdom's treasures are known only to God, who makes them known to human beings by his Spirit (cf. 1 Cor. 2:6–11).

It is evident that 'Paul is . . . portraying Christ as the embodiment of wisdom, and through him alone can one understand the divine will and plan'.[8] Specifically, wisdom and knowledge in this first-century context refer to spiritual understanding that enables one to live a life worthy of the Lord (Col. 1:9–10), because Paul will go on in the rest of chapter 2 (cf. vv. 4, 8, 16–23) to contrast the true wisdom sourced in Christ with the false teaching that the Colossians have been hearing. Notably, he warns in Colossians 2:8, 'See to it that no one takes you captive through hollow and deceptive philosophy, which depends on human tradition and the elemental spiritual forces of this world rather than on Christ.' In order for

---

[6] Vaughan, 'Colossians', p. 195.

[7] *DBI*, p. 159, summarizes well: 'The key motif of Colossians is knowledge. Paul fights the fire of gnostic thinking with a fiery Christian *gnosis*. Indeed, the initial mention of knowledge comes in his introductory prayer as he asks God to fill the Colossians with "the knowledge of his will through all spiritual wisdom and understanding" (Col 1:9 NIV [1984]). Significantly, the word he uses for knowledge is *epignōsis*, "full knowledge." His prayer was for a full decisive knowledge that would instill a spiritual wisdom.'

[8] D. W. Pao, *Colossians and Philemon*, ZECNT (Grand Rapids: Zondervan, 2012), p. 139.

the Colossians to live rightly, they must learn and live God's truth in Christ, because 'to seek further or deeper knowledge of God apart from Christ or in other directions leads not to further hidden treasure, but to a dead end'.[9] What was true for the Colossians is equally valid for Christians today, because all of the treasures of divine wisdom and knowledge continue to find their source in Christ for the contemporary church, just as they did for the early church.

2. Paul's caution for the Colossians (2:4–5)

Paul has a clear purpose in writing this letter to the Colossians, which he discloses in verse 4: *I tell you this so that no one may deceive you by fine-sounding arguments.* The Colossians are being targeted by false teachers who seek to delude them. This is a contest for the minds and hearts of the Colossian Christians, whom Paul has not met and yet for whom he has a deep concern. To counter the deceptive errors that have infiltrated Colossae, Paul reaffirms the truth about Christ. The false teachers use arguments that sound persuasive to the Colossian Christians, but in reality their smooth talking is not truthful. What they say is likely rhetorically sophisticated and emotionally compelling, but its content is false, and therefore they are dangerous. In the Greek rhetorical literature, the term for *fine-sounding arguments* (*pithanologia*) is the antithesis of *apodeixis*, logical demonstration that leads to a valid conclusion. One scholar explains,

> As this chapter proceeds, the nature of the false teaching becomes clearer. Someone is teaching what Paul calls a *philosophia* (v. 8) that apparently includes logical or rhetorical arguments to convince others, and a few have indeed been convinced already.[10]

Whether in the first century or in the twenty-first century, Christians have always been in peril of being led astray by clever communicators who seek to cause them to question and to abandon the truth that is in Christ, so Paul's caution to the Colossians should also be read as a caution for Christians today. What looks fine on the surface may actually be fatal in

---

[9] Meye Thompson, *Colossians and Philemon*, p. 50.
[10] Witherington, *Letters*, pp. 149–150.

its effect. What sounds reasonable may in reality be a rejection of God's truth. We must always be like the Christians in Berea, who 'examined the Scriptures every day to see if what Paul said was true' (Acts 17:11). Only by following their commendable example will we be able to discern and discard what is deceptive and to cultivate godly convictions centred in God's truth.

Although Paul is physically *absent* from Colossae when he writes this letter, he is spiritually *present* with the Christians there (5). He is confident that they are staying firm for Christ, and that they have not succumbed to the attractive delusions communicated to them by the false teachers. Paul uses two military terms to describe how the Colossians are disciplined like a military division drawn up in ranks (*taxis*), and how they are *firm* (*stereōma*) like a castle or bulwark.[11] He commends them because their response to the threat of false teaching has been well ordered and they have remained firmly committed to faith in Christ. They have not panicked and got out of line, but have stayed the course in this spiritual battle. They have resisted the attack of error by holding fast to the truth of Christ. Paul 'sees the situation of the Colossians as being like that of an army under attack and affirms that their lines were unbroken, their discipline intact, and their . . . reliance on Christ unshaken'.[12]

With these affirming words, Paul seeks to fulfil in part his goal in verse 2 to encourage the Colossians in their hearts. The force of the assault against them could easily have dislodged the church in Colossae from its firm footing in Christ, but it has not. The subtlety of the error could have deceived them away from the truth, but it has not. They have indeed been in very great spiritual and theological danger, but up to this point they have endured, and this has deeply delighted Paul. Nevertheless, the Colossians must not falsely presume that they are out of danger, because the threats are still lurking, so they must remain on their guard.

The threat facing the Colossians was not unique to them, because in every generation false teaching is a danger for God's people. As Paul exhorted Timothy to preach the word, he warned him,

---

[11] D. J. Moo, *The Letters to the Colossians and to Philemon*, Pillar (Grand Rapids: Eerdmans, 2008), p. 174, rightly qualifies the military nuance of these terms: 'Both terms do, indeed, occur as technical military terms, but they also occur much more widely in the general sense simply of "order" and "firmness".'

[12] Vaughan, 'Colossians', p. 195.

For the time will come when people will not put up with sound doctrine. Instead, to suit their own desires, they will gather round them a great number of teachers to say what their itching ears want to hear. They will turn their ears away from the truth and turn aside to myths.[13]

What was the case for Christians in the first century is equally apparent today in the twenty-first century. We too must be vigilant in discerning error and diligent in holding fast to God's truth, so that our faith in Christ will stand firm.

3. Paul's challenge to the Colossians (2:6–7)

The words *So then* that introduce verse 6 indicate that this section is the logical conclusion of what Paul has said to the Colossians in verses 1–5. This is what their present response should be. Paul has no doubt about the genuineness of the salvation of the Colossians, because in the past they *received Christ Jesus as Lord*, and receiving Christ 'is not only a matter of believing in his person; it also involves a commitment to the apostolic teaching about Christ and his significance'.[14] Now, Paul says, they need to *continue to live . . . in him*. To communicate his point, Paul uses the Greek term *peripateō*, which in its literal sense means 'to walk'. This image is familiar in the Old Testament wisdom literature, and throughout both the Old Testament and New Testament texts. Walking suggests routine, consistent faithfulness to Christ over the long haul, and in this sense it described the lives of Enoch (Gen. 5:22, 24), Noah (Gen. 6:9) and Abraham (Gen. 17:1). Paul frequently uses this image to speak of the Christian life. For example, he says in Romans 6:4, 'We were therefore buried with [Christ] through baptism into death in order that, just as Christ was raised from the dead through the glory of the Father, we too may live [literally, "walk"] a new life.' In Galatians 5:16, he urges, 'So I say, walk [or "live", NIV] by the Spirit, and you will not gratify the desires of the flesh.' Paul exhorts the Ephesian Christians to walk worthy of their calling (4:1), in the newness of their minds (4:17–24), in love (5:2), as children of light (5:8) and in wisdom (5:15).

In Colossians 1:10, Paul prays that the Colossians might 'live [*peripateō*] a life worthy of the Lord and please him in every way', and this would come

---

[13] 2 Tim. 4:3–4.
[14] Moo, *Letters*, p. 177.

about by God filling them with the knowledge of his will through all the wisdom and understanding that the Spirit gives. He now indicates that a life worthy of the Lord is a life that continues in Christ. Paul's goal in ministry is not just to convert people to Christ, because he says in Colossians 1:28, '[Christ] is the one we proclaim, admonishing and teaching everyone with all wisdom, so that we may present everyone fully mature in Christ.' The Colossians, though they have been truly converted to Christ, are in danger of following the false teaching that Paul counters in this letter. If they succumb to that temptation, they will not continue in Christ and attain the spiritual maturity that Paul and the Lord desire for them.

There are many factors that can cause Christians to fail to continue in Christ. In his parable of the soils, Jesus describes seed that falls on rocky ground as a picture of Christians with shallow spiritual roots that are unable to sustain them when trouble or persecution comes (Matt. 13:20–21). He also cautions about the seed that falls into thorns, a picture of Christians in whom 'the worries of this life and the deceitfulness of wealth choke the word, making it unfruitful'.[15] Paul sadly comments, 'Demas, because he loved this world, has deserted me.'[16] We must not think that we are not subject to these temptations that can deter us from becoming all God wants us to become, for, as Paul warned the Corinthians, 'if you think you are standing firm, be careful that you don't fall!'[17] We too must be consistently faithful each day as we continue to live our lives in Christ.

Verse 7 elaborates on the previous verse, with Paul combining several metaphors as he pictures how the Colossians have received Christ and are now living in him. In contrast to his profound concerns about the Galatians, to whom he exclaimed with exasperation, 'You foolish Galatians! Who has bewitched you? Before your very eyes Jesus Christ was clearly portrayed as crucified',[18] and the Corinthians, who had numerous significant spiritual problems (cf. 1 Cor. 1:11; 3:1–4; 4:18–21; 5:1; 6:1–7; 11:17–22), Paul is confident of the spiritual condition of the Colossians. They have responded positively to the truth they have been taught. God has worked powerfully in their lives, so that they are *rooted* in Christ, a word picture that Paul also uses when he prays for the Ephesians:

---

[15] Matt. 13:22.

[16] 2 Tim. 4:10.

[17] 1 Cor. 10:12.

[18] Gal. 3:1.

And I pray that you, being rooted and established in love, may have power, together with all the Lord's holy people, to grasp how wide and long and high and deep is the love of Christ, and to know this love that surpasses knowledge – that you may be filled to the measure of all the fullness of God.[19]

They have also been *built up* in Christ, a metaphor Paul develops more fully in Ephesians 2:20–22, as he explains that they are

built on the foundation of the apostles and prophets, with Christ Jesus himself as the chief cornerstone. In him the whole building is joined together and rises to become a holy temple in the Lord. And in him you too are being built together to become a dwelling in which God lives by his Spirit.

As a result they are established or *strengthened* in the Christian faith (cf. 1 Cor. 1:8). In this context, *faith* has an objective sense of the content of Christian truth that they have been taught and on which they stand, as it does in Jude 3 when Jude states, 'I felt compelled to write and urge you to contend for the faith that was once for all entrusted to God's holy people.' In their response to what God has done in their lives, the Colossians manifest a spirit that overflows with abundant *thankfulness* for the work of God in them. Their joyful appreciation of what God has done in them will fortify them against the false teaching that seeks to undermine their commitment to Christ (8, 16–23). The Colossians have had an excellent start in their spiritual lives, and now Paul exhorts them to continue to live faithfully for Christ in the face of the threats challenging them.

4. Concluding comment

Paul's key message to the Christians in Colossae in this passage is that when error threatens to deceive them away from Christ, they must stand firm in the Christian faith. The content of the Christian faith is rooted in Christ, in whom are hidden all the treasures of wisdom and knowledge. What has been anticipated in the Old Testament, particularly in the wisdom books but also throughout the entire Old Testament, finds its culmination in Christ, the Son of God. It is the truth sourced in Christ that

---

[19] Eph. 3:17–19.

will provide them with spiritual roots and with stability to stand firm in the face of the error that confronts them.

As it was for the Colossians in the first century, so it is for Christians today in the twenty-first century. We too face many voices of error that seek to undermine and to weaken our commitment to God's truth in Christ. Like the Colossians, we must continue to live in Christ, who is the source of God's true wisdom. Anything else will be folly that seeks to deceive and delude us.

We live in a culture that emphasizes the individual, and there is certainly clear biblical teaching that 'each one should carry their own load'.[20] When we come to Christ, however, we are also placed into the family of God, the church, in which we have mutual responsibility with and for one another. For this reason, Paul urges in Galatians 6:1–2,

> Brothers and sisters, if someone is caught in a sin, you who live by the Spirit should restore that person gently. But watch yourselves, or you also may be tempted. Carry each other's burdens, and in this way you will fulfil the law of Christ.

A crucial part of our responsibility for each other as Christians is to minister to those who are endangered by the threats of personal sin and false teaching that attack us from within and from outside. As Paul writes to the Colossians, he models encouragement to those who are living faithfully for Christ, along with a challenge to keep at it. As Paul writes to the Corinthians, he has to name their sins and reprove them as he seeks to restore them to God's way when they have begun to depart from it. To the Galatians, Paul speaks with stern rebuke as he tries to bring them to their senses as they stand on the precipice of dangerous error.

When we reach out to help those who are facing spiritual challenges, we must be careful lest we too slip into sin. Jude provides pastoral counsel for us when he urges, 'Be merciful to those who doubt; save others by snatching them from the fire; to others show mercy, mixed with fear – hating even the clothing stained by corrupted flesh.'[21] In the family of God, we are our brothers' and sisters' keeper, but we must exercise great care if we are to help them without harming ourselves in the process.

---

[20] Gal. 6:5.
[21] Jude 22–23.

James 3:13–18

19. Living by wisdom from above

The book of James in its content and form contains numerous unmistakable references to wisdom. In fact, of all of the New Testament books, it is the one most similar to the book of Proverbs. In his opening paragraph, James writes, 'If any of you lacks wisdom, you should ask God, who gives generously to all without finding fault, and it will be given to you.'[1] With these words, James echoes the theme of Proverbs 2:1–11 (see chapter 2), where the sage describes how the son should seek wisdom and find it. Later, in James 3:13–18, the apostle contrasts earthly wisdom with wisdom from above, two conflicting approaches to life that parallel well the antithesis between wisdom and folly that pervades Proverbs.

In several places, James draws specifically upon specific texts in the Old Testament wisdom books. For example, he quotes Proverbs 3:34 in James 4:6:

But he gives us more grace. That is why Scripture says:

> 'God opposes the proud
>   but shows favour to the humble.'

James also alludes to verses in Proverbs as he uses some of the same language in James 4:13–14 (cf. Prov. 27:1),

Now listen, you who say, 'Today or tomorrow we will go to this or that city, spend a year there, carry on business and make money.' Why, you

---

[1] Jas 1:5.

do not even know what will happen tomorrow. What is your life?
You are a mist that appears for a little while and then vanishes.

In addition, in saying, 'whoever turns a sinner from the error of their way
will save them from death and cover over a multitude of sins' in 5:20, James
alludes to Proverbs 10:12,

Hatred stirs up conflict,
but love covers over all wrongs.

More indirectly, James 5:11 recalls the perseverance of Job, and there
are echoes of Ecclesiastes 7:9 in James 1:19 and of the frequent theme in
Ecclesiastes of life as a vapour (*hebel*) in James 4:14, when James asks,
'What is your life? You are a mist that appears for a little while and then
vanishes.'

In its form, the book of James often includes brief memorable proverbs,
rhetorical questions and striking analogies from life, just as are found in
the Old Testament wisdom books. Consequently, when people from a
Jewish background in the first century heard or read this letter from
James, they immediately recognized it as closely related to Old Testament
wisdom. Both in its content and in its style the book of James bears the
distinctive marks of wisdom teaching. As we read this letter, once again
we learn the message of wisdom as the Bible speaks to us today.

1. James through the lens of wisdom

If we are to understand what James has written, we must read this book
through the lens of wisdom as it has been developed especially in the Old
Testament wisdom books. As in passages such as Proverbs 2:1–5, James
takes the tone of a teacher, and he expects us as his readers to accept the
stance of the learner. In Proverbs, wisdom is skill in living according to
the Lord's way, and the image of life as a way occurs as well in James 5:20.
James frequently employs contrasts that point to the difference between
the goal of wisdom, which is the crown of life (1:12), and sin, which leads
to death (1:13–15; see also 1:22–25; 3:9–12; and 4:4). James also indicates
in 1:4; 1:25; and 3:2 that growth into maturity is where all wisdom is
leading, reflecting the heart of Old Testament wisdom teaching, which is
the development of responsible character.

Proverbs 9:10 says that the fear of the Lord, or reverence for the Lord, is the essence of wisdom, so that all of life is grounded in our relationship to the Lord. In keeping with that wisdom emphasis, James urges his readers to humble themselves before the Lord (4:7–10) as they keep his law (4:11). In Proverbs, reverence for the Lord affects every area of life, and in James speech is particularly a mirror of what is in one's heart (cf. Jas 1:26; 3:1–12; 4:11–17), just as it frequently is in Proverbs (cf. Prov. 12:18; 15:2; 17:27–28; see chapter 10). Also, both books make it clear that godly wisdom is better than the riches typically sought and treasured by humans (Prov. 3:13–15; 8:11; 16:16, cf. Jas 4:13–17; 5:1–6).

Old Testament wisdom highlights the many cases in which the retribution principle that God blesses wise and righteous behaviour and punishes foolish and wicked behaviour holds true (see chapter 13). However, wisdom also includes the book of Job, in which adversity fits within God's plan, and James too speaks of the role of adversity when he says,

> Consider it pure joy, my brothers and sisters, whenever you face trials of many kinds, because you know that the testing of your faith produces perseverance. Let perseverance finish its work so that you may be mature and complete, not lacking anything.[2]

James clearly has the wisdom literature of the Old Testament in mind as he writes this letter. What James does is to restate the Old Testament wisdom emphases in terms of the Christian life, in effect equating the wise life with the life that is mature in Christ. The passage that will be examined in detail in the rest of this chapter contrasts wisdom from below (that is, folly) with wisdom from above (Jas 3:13–18), which is the genuine wisdom described in Proverbs and then embodied and taught by Jesus, as James challenges us to become the wise people God wants us to be.

2. A challenge to wisdom (3:13)

As he begins this paragraph, James in the classic style of a wisdom teacher asks a question, which he then answers: *Who is wise and understanding among you? Let them show it by their good life, by deeds done in the humility that comes from wisdom* (13). Most people want to think of

---

[2] Jas 1:2–4.

themselves as wise and understanding, but not all people actually are. *Understanding* refers to having the knowledge of an expert,[3] that is, the knowledge of how to live wisely and skilfully in God's world. Earlier in this chapter, James has warned, 'Not many of you should become teachers, my fellow believers, because you know that we who teach will be judged more strictly.'[4] Apparently some of the people who had taken it upon themselves to be teachers in the church were speaking in sinful ways (3:2–12), so James calls out those who claim to be wise and understanding so that he can examine whether this is in fact the case. As one commentator notes,

> James assesses these people's claim to wisdom not in theological terms – how much doctrine do they know, how many Greek verbs can they parse – but in practical terms: Let him show it by his good life, by deeds done in the humility that comes from wisdom.[5]

A comparison with the other New Testament epistles indicates that this was a common problem in the early church, as it is today as well. Having knowledge is not the same as being wise. Being gifted is not the same as having understanding.

Those who present themselves as wise and understanding teachers, James declares, are obligated to manifest a demonstration of the veracity of their claims. If they are truly wise, then they will evidence lives that are characterized by what is beautiful and good, because wisdom is a matter of how one behaves and not just of what one knows. Therefore, 'James's description will not permit the teacher to think of his or her mastery of theology or exegesis as sufficient to pass muster. What passes muster for James is behavior shaped by humble wisdom.'[6] In other words, true wisdom is evidenced in the observable proof of good deeds and good attitudes. In particular, James speaks of the *humility that comes from wisdom*, and he uses the term *praütēs*, which is translated 'gentleness' in the list of the fruit of the Spirit in Galatians 5:23. In Greek culture, a society that valued power, *praütēs* was scorned as unworthy servility,[7] but Christianity turned this value system upside down. Jesus embodied

---

[3] *BAG*, p. 300.

[4] Jas 3:1.

[5] D. J. Moo, *The Letter of James*, Pillar (Grand Rapids: Eerdmans, 2000), p. 169.

[6] S. McKnight, *The Letter of James*, NICNT (Grand Rapids: Eerdmans, 2011), p. 299.

[7] D. G. McCartney, *James*, BECNT (Grand Rapids: Baker Academic, 2009), p. 199.

praütēs when he said to his disciples, 'Take my yoke upon you and learn from me, for I am gentle [*praüs*] and humble in heart, and you will find rest for your souls';[8] and he also extolled it in the Beatitudes, when he exclaimed,

> Blessed are the meek [*praeis*],
>> for they will inherit the earth.[9]

In agreement with Proverbs 11:2, James indicates that true wisdom is not proud and demanding, but humble and gentle. The wise life, then, is in reality the godly life that follows the example of Christ.

3. Wisdom from below (3:14–16)

In verse 14 the introductory conjunction *But* signals a contrast with the true wisdom James has extolled in verse 13, and the pronoun *you* likely links back to 'you' in verse 1, referring to the teachers who threatened the spiritual welfare of James's readers. These teachers harboured *bitter envy and selfish ambition in [their] hearts*, the opposite of the humility or gentleness that comes from wisdom (13). Because those who are motivated by envy and ambition reject the wisdom of Christ, they in effect deny God's truth.

The Greek term translated *selfish ambition* is *eritheia*, which was used by Aristotle of electioneering for office, and more generally refers to egotistical self-promotion and partisanship. As James uses the term, he calls out those who endanger his readers, because 'Some who pride themselves on their wisdom and understanding are displaying a jealous, bitter partisanship that is the antithesis of the humility produced by true wisdom.'[10] This unchristian attitude, which emanated from their sinful hearts (cf. Prov. 4:23, in which the sage admonishes, 'Above all else, guard your heart, for everything you do flows from it'), should have caused them to be ashamed of their bitter envy and selfish ambition, but instead they boast about what God calls shameful. In place of the humility of wisdom (13), their ambition for themselves causes them to distort the truth rather than declaring the truth, as teachers should do. What James makes clear

---

8 Matt. 11:29.

9 Matt. 5:5.

10 Moo, *James*, p. 171.

is that 'The truth denied is that wisdom is accompanied by meekness. In other words, those who are boasting of wisdom are not of God, because their lives are not characterized by humility.'[11] Their ambition is the opposite of the servant attitude of Jesus (cf. Mark 10:42–45), and it is a rejection of God's truth, which is the basis for regeneration, because '[God] chose to give us birth through the word of truth'.[12]

When James speaks of *Such 'wisdom'* in verse 15, he is referring back to verse 14 and the bitter envy and selfish ambition of the teachers who by their attitudes and actions deny God's truth. Even though envy and ambition may be the way that many people promote themselves in order to achieve worldly success, they are not the values of godly wisdom, but in fact manifest the opposite of wisdom. In distinguishing between these two alternative approaches, James echoes the two paths developed in Old Testament wisdom. The wisdom from the earth that he describes in verses 14–16 is what Proverbs calls folly, the path characterized by wickedness and leading to death; and the wisdom from above in verses 17–18 correlates with the wisdom taught in Proverbs, the path characterized by righteousness and leading to life. This teaching of the two ways also recalls Jesus' teaching in Matthew 7:13–14, when he contrasts the broad road that leads to death and the narrow road that leads to life (see chapter 16).

James says that the false wisdom of the teachers *does not come down from heaven*. The Greek term *anōthen* means literally 'from above', but the NIV rendering *from heaven* rightly catches the sense that true wisdom derives from God, in contrast to the false wisdom of the teachers that comes from the human realm and not from God. What James discloses is that 'True wisdom comes not (or, at least, not only) through intellectual effort or study; it is the gift of God (cf. Prov. 2:6).'[13]

In contrast to genuine wisdom that comes from God, the wisdom from below grows from ungodly roots. It is *earthly*, that is, produced by earthbound motives and thinking. Paul uses similar language to describe those who are opposed to Christianity when he says in Philippians 3:18–19,

> For, as I have often told you before and now tell you again even with tears, many live as enemies of the cross of Christ. Their destiny is destruction,

---

[11] R. P. Martin, *James*, WBC 48 (Waco: Word, 1988), p. 131.

[12] Jas 1:18.

[13] Moo, *James*, pp. 172–173.

their god is their stomach, and their glory is in their shame. Their mind is set on earthly things.

Even when they teach about God they reflect earthly values (cf. 1 Tim. 4:1). Their counterfeit wisdom is also *unspiritual* (*psychikē*), a term used in 1 Corinthians 2:14 to describe people who have not been regenerated and who are therefore governed by their human soul rather than by the Spirit of God (cf. Jude 19). Wisdom from below produces the deeds of the flesh (Gal. 5:19–21), and similar attitudes such as *envy* and *ambition* (16), rather than the fruit of the Spirit (Gal. 5:22–23), such as humility (13) and peace (18). Human wisdom is also *demonic* in its rebellion against God, following the devil's lead rather than fleeing his corrupting influences, as James details in his description of their evil speech in 3:6: 'The tongue also is a fire, a world of evil among the parts of the body. It corrupts the whole body, sets the whole course of one's life on fire, and is itself set on fire by hell.' There is no place in the life of a Christian for behaviours like this, because the wisdom from below is opposed to the Lord and to all that he values. In fact, it is anything but real wisdom.

James continues his line of thought as in verse 16 he gives the reason for his assessment of human wisdom in verse 15. Envy and selfish ambition are evidences of wisdom from below because they are sinful attitudes that produce sinful actions. Even among those who present themselves as teachers (cf. 1), self-interest can become the justification for all sorts of evil deeds. The disorderliness and evil practices that result from their attitudes are devastating in the church, undermining its credibility before the watching world and opening it up to destructive attacks by the devil.[14] The term rendered as *disorder* (*akatastasia*) is used in Luke 21:9 with the sense of political anarchy, and it has much the same sense here. Wisdom from below brings the negative effects of disorder, disaster, confusion and calamity. This is antithetical to what Paul urges in Ephesians 4:3 when he exhorts Christians to 'keep the unity of the Spirit through the bond of peace'.

4. Wisdom from above (3:17–18)

In keeping with the longstanding approach of wisdom teaching seen frequently in the book of Proverbs, James contrasts the folly and wickedness

---

[14] C. L. Blomberg and M. J. Kamell, *James*, ZECNT (Grand Rapids: Zondervan, 2008), pp. 174–175.

of the wisdom from below (14–16) with the wisdom and righteousness of the wisdom from above (17–18). In verse 15 he said briefly that the wisdom from below does not come down from heaven, and now he fills in the details of what the *wisdom from above* is like. This wisdom is one of God's good and perfect gifts which comes from above (1:17), that is, from God in heaven. Therefore, it is not surprising that there is a striking similarly between the features of this wisdom and the fruit of the Spirit in Galatians 5:22–23, because both lists speak of what God produces in his people when they are devoted to him.

James says that the wisdom from above is *first of all pure*. In this context, *pure* speaks of what is morally blameless because it is completely devoted to God. Because it is pure, wisdom from above provides many blessings that are life-enhancing, as godly wisdom leads to life in all its dimensions. These blessings are antithetical to the evil effects produced by the envy and selfish ambition that mark the wisdom from below (16). True wisdom is *peace-loving*, because it promotes peace among people, in contrast to the *disorder* that results from the wisdom from below (16). It is also *considerate*, fair in its demands on others, not insisting on what it considers its rights but rather deferring to others.[15] Wisdom from above is also *submissive*, responsive to reasonable requests from others. It reaches out to minster to those in need, because it is *full of mercy and good fruit*. In contrast to the instability produced by earthly wisdom (16), true wisdom is *impartial*, resolute in doing what is right. Finally, it is *sincere*, genuine and real, not phoney or manipulative.

James concludes his description of the wisdom from above in verse 18 with a maxim that sounds much like a wisdom saying in Proverbs: *Peacemakers who sow in peace reap a harvest of righteousness*. Echoing the Beatitude of Jesus,

Blessed are the peacemakers,
    for they will be called children of God,[16]

James indicates that a commitment to peacemaking is tangible evidence that one is committed to the wisdom that comes from above. Using the

---

[15] Moo, *James*, p. 177, states of the Greek term *eupeithēs*, which is used only here in the New Testament: 'What is meant is not a weak, credulous gullibility, but a willing deference to others when unalterable theological or moral principles are not involved.'

[16] Matt. 5:9.

familiar metaphor of sowing and reaping that pervades biblical wisdom literature (Prov. 22:8; cf. Gal. 6:7), James says that wisdom from above is the environment that nurtures the fruit of righteous attitudes and actions. In contrast to the foolish attitude of anger, which 'does not produce the righteousness that God desires',[17] godly wisdom bears a harvest of righteousness.

Righteousness here must be read not through the lens of Paul's soteriological emphasis of the righteousness of Christ imputed to those who believe in him, but rather through the lens of Old Testament wisdom, with its emphasis on righteousness as living according to God's moral norms (see chapter 12). Wise living is good and godly living that does what God regards as right, and therefore bears fruit, which is righteousness, or right living. By contrast, wisdom from below (14–16) produces the weeds of sinful attitudes and actions that choke out the fruit of righteousness. The peacemaking of those committed to godly wisdom is the opposite of the disorder produced by human wisdom, and the harvest of righteousness that results from the wisdom from above is antithetical to the evil practices that are the yield of the wisdom from below.

5. Concluding comment

The book of James contains many broad principles of wisdom for our lives today. It particularly emphasizes how wisdom transforms life, rather than merely being an additive to life. When children are born into a family, their parents expect and desire to see them grow into adulthood. When children do not progress in their development, it is cause for great concern. What human parents want for their children God also wants for us, because the purpose of being born is to grow into maturity. Paul reflects this when he says in Colossians 1:28 that his goal in ministry is to 'present everyone fully mature in Christ'. This is so much more than just accepting Jesus as Saviour and then going to heaven when we die. The wisdom teaching in James is an essential component in our development as Christians from the point of our conversion towards becoming complete, mature in Christ, as we are conformed to the image of God's Son (Rom. 8:29) and are transformed by the renewing of our minds rather than being conformed to the pattern of this world (Rom. 12:2).

---

[17] Jas 1:20.

Wisdom throughout the Bible generally, and in the book of James specifically, focuses on the journey of life. The beginning of the trip is essential, and the destination is critical, but wisdom describes God's itinerary for life today: how God wants his people to live on their way to heaven. In keeping with the wisdom concept that the fear of the Lord is the essence of wisdom, James delineates how the Christian life should look 24/7. It should be a life characterized by integrity and evidenced by godly character as measured by the fruit of the Spirit.

It is also clear in James that godly wisdom must be taught and learned. Growing in wisdom does not just happen automatically, but we must be intentional about cultivating godly wisdom in our own lives and in one another. Each person is responsible for heeding the instructions of the wisdom from above, not just knowing it but also doing it as a good learner in God's school of wisdom. In addition, we are responsible for helping our Christian brothers and sisters to learn and to live God's Word. Growth in wisdom will not automatically come with years of being a Christian unless the seed of truth is nurtured into the harvest of righteous living. This requires a process of cultivation, by which we receive regularly the nutrients of God's truth through our own personal Bible study and through the teaching of God's Word in the community of believers. It also necessitates weeding out the sins and bad habits that can so easily curtail our growth in godliness.

Finally, God's wisdom from above must replace human wisdom from below in our lives. Many people in the contemporary world say, 'I like Jesus, but Christians offend me.' Sadly, there have been too many times when the lies, pride, greed, ambition and lust of Christians have become celebrated headline stories, and no doubt there are many more cases that are less widely known. If that is how people in our culture see Christians behaving, it is no wonder that they are repelled by it. However, that is not genuine Christianity as God intended it to be lived, and it certainly is not what is produced by the wisdom from above. Godly wisdom is not just a garnish of Jesus on the side of a life that is otherwise unchanged. Rather, when the world watches Christians as they live, work and play, they should see the attitudes and values of Christ reflected in their actions, speech and decisions. The book of James, in keeping with wisdom throughout the Bible, shows us how that looks in practice, and it challenges us to live in a truly countercultural way, the way of righteousness that conforms to God's moral norms in a world that routinely rejects them. When people see that kind of authentic Christianity lived out before them, they cannot help but notice, for, as Jesus exhorted, 'let your light shine before others, that they may see your good deeds and glorify your Father in heaven'.[18]

---

[18] Matt. 5:16.

Ephesians 5:15–21

20. Walking in godly wisdom

This survey of the message of wisdom in the Bible began in the book of Proverbs, where the concept of wisdom is clearly taught (chapters 1–4). Wisdom invites youths to search for her and to find her, as she represents the Lord's righteous path, in contrast to the wicked way of Folly. Although wisdom is especially centred in Proverbs, we have seen that its themes and language reverberate throughout the whole Old Testament, including the law, the historical narratives, the oracles of the prophets and the Psalms (chapters 5–8).

How wisdom works out in life is demonstrated by the many topics we have viewed in Proverbs. By synthesizing the various individual sayings that relate to a topic, the teaching of wisdom can be discovered for practical areas of life, such as work, speech, decisions and living righteously (chapters 9–12). The predominant teaching of Proverbs is that wise living leads to life, while foolish living leads to all sorts of problems, but that general pattern of retribution is qualified even in the book of Proverbs, and especially in the books of Job and Ecclesiastes (chapters 13–15). Wisdom, then, accounts both for the general pattern and for the observable exceptions, all of which are subsumed under biblical wisdom.

Although what the Old Testament teaches about wisdom has often been considered, it is also important to see that wisdom finds its culmination in the New Testament, where Jesus is presented as the ultimate teacher of wisdom (chapter 16), and in fact he himself is the source of all wisdom (chapters 17–18). In responsive obedience to Christ, therefore, it is crucial for Christians to live (chapter 19) and to walk in godly wisdom, and that is the emphasis of Ephesians 5:15–21, the final stop in our journey. In this passage, Paul challenges the Ephesians to live in the light of the wisdom they have been taught, as his practical exhortations in Ephesians 4 – 6 build upon his theological explanations in Ephesians 1 – 3. Using the familiar biblical metaphor of life as a walk, Paul in this passage exhorts the Ephesian Christians to walk in wisdom (5:15–17), explains how the Spirit of God controls Christians who walk in wisdom (5:18) and describes some of the expected consequences of walking in wisdom (5:19–21). What Paul teaches his first-century readers is equally relevant to Christians today in the twenty-first century, as we too need to learn to live wisely as the Lord intends.

1. Command to walk in wisdom (5:15–17)

The conjunction *then* links this paragraph with the previous section, in which Paul exhorted the Ephesians to 'Live [literally, "walk"] as children of light' (8). In this context, Paul's great concern for them is evident, because 'His readers must walk through a mental minefield of ideas that, if they are not careful, will lead them to despair, shame, and the wrath of God (4:19; 5:6, 12). Therefore they should carefully watch their step.'[1] Verse 15 functions as the topic sentence for the paragraph, as it gives a general statement that is then spelled out in the particular details in verses 16–21. This is also the final of five occurrences of the verb *peripateō*, which has the literal sense of 'walk' but is used by Paul to speak of living in a way that is worthy of the calling they have received from the Lord (cf. 4:1). This paragraph also has clear links back to the doctrinal first half of Ephesians, particularly 1:8–9, 17–19; and 3:10, which all speak of the wisdom that 'has been given by God for insight into the true nature of God's plan'.[2]

The Ephesians must *Be very careful* (literally, 'see') because they live in evil days (cf. 16). With this language, Paul echoes the cautions Jesus gave to his disciples in his Olivet Discourse in Matthew 24; Mark 13; and Luke 21. As Jesus prepared his disciples for his imminent crucifixion and the challenges ahead of them, he repeatedly urged them to watch out as he readied them 'for a life of discipleship in the context of the difficulties of the last days',[3] and Paul is keenly aware that the Ephesians too are living

---

[1] F. Thielman, *Ephesians*, BECNT (Grand Rapids: Baker Academic, 2010), p. 356.

[2] H. W. Hoehner, *Ephesians: An Exegetical Commentary* (Grand Rapids: Baker Academic, 2002), p. 391.

[3] C. E. Arnold, *Ephesians*, ZECNT 10 (Grand Rapids: Zondervan, 2010), p. 345.

in challenging times that require vigilance. Living in wisdom will not happen naturally, but requires intentional effort, so Paul warns them to take great care. The term he uses is *akribōs*, which has the nuance of 'something done accurately, precisely, or given close attention'.[4] However, if they are careless, they run the great risk of falling into folly, with all its attendant dangers and difficulties.

Paul's use of the metaphor of walking, rendered by NIV as *live*, and the language of wisdom in this paragraph clearly allude to the rhetoric of Old Testament wisdom. In particular, the contrast between *unwise* and *wise* corresponds to the antithetical ways of folly and wisdom that occur frequently in the book of Proverbs. Also, just as for the Israelites whom Moses exhorted in Deuteronomy 30:15–20, so the Ephesians need to choose life by choosing wisdom. The wise life to which Paul exhorts the Ephesians is the opposite of merely human wisdom, because it is the 'manifold wisdom of God'.[5]

In verse 16, Paul shifts his figure of speech as he urges the Ephesians as they live carefully as wise people to be *making the most of every opportunity*. The verb *exagorazō* is a commercial term, which here and in Colossians 4:5 means to 'buy up' the opportunities one has, which is 'a metaphorical way to speak of using time well'.[6] They need to buy up the *kairos*, the suitable time at hand, which means grasping the opportunities they have at the moment. Waiting for another day or for a more promising situation may well result in missed opportunities. They must not presume that there will always be another opportunity to do what they can do now, so they must grasp the chance they have. This is what the psalmist meant when he prayed,

Teach us to number our days,
    that we may gain a heart of wisdom,[7]

and it also echoes the language of Proverbs 4:5, 7 about buying wisdom:

Get wisdom, get understanding;
    do not forget my words or turn away from them . . .

---

[4] K. Snodgrass, *Ephesians*, NIVAC (Grand Rapids: Zondervan, 1996), p. 288.

[5] Eph. 3:10.

[6] Snodgrass, *Ephesians*, p. 288.

[7] Ps. 90:12.

> The beginning of wisdom is this: get wisdom.
> Though it cost all you have, get understanding.

Wise living requires vision to see the opportunity and then courage to grasp it.

Paul says that it is crucial to make the most of every opportunity, *because the days are evil*. The Ephesians live in a world under the control of the evil one, so they must resist him (cf. 2:2; 6:10–17). Similarly, Christians today, as in every era of history, live in a world filled with dangerous and destructive threats. What was true about the Ephesians in the first century applies equally to God's people in the twenty-first century: 'In a world of such exterior and interior evil forces, it was especially critical to know the Lord's will and to make wise decisions about what it involved in one's day-to-day existence.'[8] Because we too live in an age in which evil is a clear and present danger, it is incumbent on us to make good use of the time and opportunities we have been granted to do what is wise and righteous before the Lord.

In verse 17, the introductory *Therefore* connects back to what Paul has said in verses 15–16, and particularly to the fact that the days are evil. As in verse 15, and in wisdom teaching throughout the Bible, Paul uses a contrast when he exhorts the Ephesians, *do not be foolish, but understand what the Lord's will is*. The antidote to living in a foolish way is understanding how the Lord wants them to live. This is more than just an intellectual knowledge of what God's way is; Paul's main concern 'is on wise living, on an understanding of God sufficient to produce insight into life and obedience', because 'wisdom involves considering all information in light of one's relation to God and acting on what one knows'.[9]

There is always the danger for Christians that they might slide into an unthinking, unwise life, but the Lord does not want us to drift unthinkingly in the current of our culture or of our personal preferences. That is *foolish* (*aphrōn*), because it fails to discern how we should live as God intends. Nevertheless, the sad reality is that 'the uncareful believer can easily be enticed by the god of this age to become foolish in the practical application of knowledge'.[10]

---

[8] Thielman, *Ephesians*, p. 357.

[9] Snodgrass, *Ephesians*, p. 300.

[10] Hoehner, *Ephesians*, p. 696. He goes on to explain: 'This perception or understanding is more than just the understanding of facts; it is an intelligent grasp of knowledge that has resulting consequences. As in the

The verb *understand* (*syniēmi*) and its related noun form *synesis* are often used in the Old Testament wisdom writings in the Septuagint, the Greek translation of the Hebrew Bible, and in particular in Proverbs 2:1–9. Throughout the Bible, the heart of wisdom is understanding the will of the Lord, which involves both learning it and living it. For example, Paul says in Colossians 1:9–10,

> For this reason, since the day we heard about you, we have not stopped praying for you. We continually ask God to fill you with the knowledge of his will through all the wisdom and understanding that the Spirit gives, so that you may live a life worthy of the Lord and please him in every way: bearing fruit in every good work, growing in the knowledge of God.

Rather than viewing life in terms of what we want or what we think is good, we need to look at life through the lens of what the Lord desires, and make that what we desire, because 'Part of what it means to live wisely is to discern how God would want believers to think and live in every unique situation that confronts them and in every opportunity that presents itself.'[11]

2. Control for walking in wisdom (5:18)

After commanding the Ephesians to walk in wisdom in verses 15–17, Paul reminds them in verse 18 of God's control that will enable them to do that. Once again Paul uses a set of contrasts that distinguish between the foolish and the wise ways of living. It is important to note that both *Do not get drunk* and *be filled with the Spirit* are commands to obey, not merely suggestions to consider. For the Ephesians and for us today, walking in wisdom requires an intentional decision to do as the Lord has directed.

Getting drunk is an example of being foolish (cf. 17), and it is presented as unwise behaviour in Proverbs 20:1, which declares,

> Wine is a mocker and beer a brawler;
>> whoever is led astray by them is not wise.[12]

(note 10 *cont.*) OT, the NT also teaches that the lack of understanding is not just a simple lack of knowledge but results from human beings' rejection of God' (p. 698).

[11] Arnold, *Ephesians*, p. 347.

[12] Cf. also the striking portrait of the drunkard in Prov. 23:29–34.

In the New Testament, drunkenness is a key indication of spiritual darkness, as Paul indicates in Romans 13:12–13:

> The night is nearly over; the day is almost here. So let us put aside the deeds of darkness and put on the armour of light. Let us behave decently, as in the daytime, not in carousing and drunkenness, not in sexual immorality and debauchery, not in dissension and jealousy.

Similarly, he says in 1 Thessalonians 5:5–7,

> You are all children of the light and children of the day. We do not belong to the night or to the darkness. So then, let us not be like others, who are asleep, but let us be awake and sober. For those who sleep, sleep at night, and those who get drunk, get drunk at night.

In the ancient world, as at the present time, drunkenness was a perennial problem that was decried in non-biblical texts in the Hellenistic world.[13] The evil days confronting the Ephesians in the first century as well as Christians today require spiritual clarity and control, but drunkenness by contrast leads to *asōtia*, which refers to dissipation, debauchery and disorderliness, as its uses in Luke 15:13; Titus 1:6; and 1 Peter 4:4 indicate. This term 'refers to people who waste their resources to gratify their own sensual desires',[14] and their lack of discipline leads to their ruin.

In contrast to the foolish behaviour of getting drunk, being *filled with the Spirit* is an example of wisdom that understands the will of the Lord (17). The Spirit of God controls the wise person in the same way that wine controls the foolish person who is under its influence. Rather than producing a life that is *out of* control, as drunkenness does, the Spirit produces a life that is *under* control. Being filled with the Spirit, then, is the same as what Paul pictures as walking by the Spirit in Galatians 5:16, when he urges, 'Live [or "walk"] by the Spirit, and you will not gratify the desires of the flesh.' This positive influence of the indwelling Holy Spirit is crucial for Christian living that is in accord with the will of the Lord. It is evident that 'Paul calls believers to yield their lives completely to the

---

[13] Snodgrass, *Ephesians*, p. 300.

[14] Hoehner, *Ephesians*, p. 701.

Spirit's influence and to resist coming under the pull of other mind-altering and numbing substances'.[15]

3. Consequences of walking in wisdom (5:19–21)

Being filled with the Spirit (18) leads Christians to both wisdom (15–17) and worship (19–21). In the Greek text, the command 'be filled with the Spirit' is modified by a series of participles that detail the resulting behaviours of those who are under the Spirit's control. Paul indicates first in verse 19 that when the Spirit is in control, singing is the expected consequence. This is not just music, however, but worship, because the singing envisioned by Paul is the verbal overflow of what the Spirit is producing in the hearts of believers who are living wisely.

The early Christians often used the ancient songs in the book of Psalms in their worship, but the New Testament also includes new songs, particularly about Christ, such as the lyrics presented in Philippians 2:6–11; 1 Timothy 3:16; and Revelation 4:11; 5:9–10; 7:12; 19:6–8. The *psalms*, *hymns* and *songs* Paul mentions here and in Colossians 3:16 are probably overlapping terms rather than clearly differentiated categories of music in praise to the Lord,[16] because Paul lists 'the three most important terms of the LXX (and thus also of the Hellenistic-Jewish and Christian worship service) for the religious song'.[17] It should be noted that this singing is done *to one another*. These songs, then, emerge from the heart, they are directed towards the Lord in adoration of him and they also serve to edify the community of believers. In sum, 'It is in and through singing and making music, by which other members of the body are instructed and edified, that praise is offered to the Lord Jesus. The same singing has a twofold function and purpose.'[18]

Continuing the thought of verse 19 into verse 20, Paul indicates that those who are filled with the Spirit are *always giving thanks to God the Father for everything, in the name of our Lord Jesus Christ*. When the

---

[15] Arnold, *Ephesians*, p. 348.

[16] A. T. Lincoln, *Ephesians*, WBC 42 (Dallas: Word, 1990), p. 345. Alternatively, B. Witherington, *The Letters to Philemon, the Colossians, and the Ephesians: A Socio-Rhetorical Commentary on the Captivity Epistles* (Grand Rapids: Eerdmans, 2007), p. 312, suggests the possibility that the three terms refer respectively to praise songs with accompaniment, to a cappella liturgical pieces and to more spontaneous songs, but he also grants, 'This could just be another example of Asianism, with the love for piling up near synonyms.'

[17] M. Hengel, *Studies in Early Christianity* (London: T&T Clark, 2004), p. 273.

[18] P. T. O'Brien, *Ephesians*, Pillar (Grand Rapids: Eerdmans, 1999), p. 387.

Spirit of God controls a life, he produces in it thanksgiving to God. This thanksgiving is not merely an occasional event, but it should be given all the time and for everything, because every day the Lord provides ample reasons for thanking him. For this reason, in 1 Thessalonians 5:18 Paul exhorts, 'give thanks in all circumstances; for this is God's will for you in Christ Jesus'. It is God's desire that his people give thanks to him across the full range of their experiences in life, and in the book of Psalms the declarative praise psalms give us patterns for doing that.[19] Thanksgiving, then, is not optional but obligatory for Christians; 'Constant gratitude to the Father for all that he has done for his people in and through the Lord Jesus Christ should be a defining characteristic of the lives of all believers.'[20]

This passage refers to all three persons of the Trinity, with God the Father and the Lord Jesus Christ in verse 20 and the Spirit in verse 18. The attitude of thanksgiving that should pervade the lives of Christians is grounded in the fact that they know that the Triune God is sovereignly governing all that comes into their experience, and that he provides amply for their needs. Therefore,

> thanksgiving to God should encompass all things that come into life's path, and when believers are filled by the Spirit this will be their response in lieu of dissatisfaction and complaints. In difficult circumstances an attitude of thanksgiving is easier to achieve with the knowledge that God is always in control.[21]

Although the NIV begins verse 21 with the imperative *Submit*, it actually is the final participle in the chain of five participles in verses 19–21 that modify 'be filled with the Spirit' in verse 18. This verse, then, brings the paragraph of Ephesians 5:15–21 to a conclusion, but it also leads into the section 5:22 – 6:9, in which submitting to one another is detailed in various interpersonal relationships in language similar to ancient household codes. Paul adapts the conventional form 'to Christian use as instructions are given for the proper behaviour of husbands and wives, parents and

---

[19] For a brief description of the declarative praise psalms, along with an exposition of an example in Ps. 138, see D. J. Estes, *Handbook on the Wisdom Books and Psalms* (Grand Rapids: Baker Academic, 2005), pp. 162–165.

[20] Arnold, *Ephesians*, p. 355.

[21] Hoehner, *Ephesians*, p. 714.

children, slaves and masters in family households newly constituted under the Lordship of Christ'.[22]

When the Spirit of God controls a life, he prompts the person to submit to others out of reverence for Christ. A Spirit-filled life is humble, and is not demanding of others. In fact, submitting to others is countercultural for people who prize individualism and independence, so it is a considerable challenge for Christians living in the contemporary world. By submitting to one another we choose to value others, because

> Such a submission is a strong and free act of the will based on real love of the other person. In the end, submission is nothing more than a decision about the relative worth of another person, a manner of dying and rising with Christ, and a way to respect and love other people.[23]

This is one of many New Testament passages that feature the phrase *one another* (*allēlōn*). By using this expression, Paul is describing how the community of Christians should function. Here, the Ephesians are to submit to one another out of *reverence for Christ*. The term *reverence* is *phobos* ('fear'), which clearly alludes to the fear of the Lord in Old Testament wisdom (cf. Prov. 1:7; 9:10). In this context, the reverence for Christ 'is an attitude that looks to Christ in awe at his overwhelming love and at his power and that also lives in the light of his sovereign claim and righteous judgment',[24] and this shared attitude becomes the foundation for the various interpersonal relationships that Christians maintain. Jesus demonstrated this spirit of submission when he washed his disciples' feet (John 13:4–5). What Paul indicates in this verse is that we cannot at the same time truly revere Christ and also run over other people. Christians who are filled with the Spirit live for the glory of God and for the good of others, and not merely to advance and exalt themselves at the expense of others.

Most commentators take *allēlōn* in a reciprocal sense ('one another'), as it is rendered by NIV. Read in this way, Paul calls Christians to mutual submission to one another, and that attitude should animate the relationships between wives and husbands (5:22–33), children and fathers (6:1–4) and slaves and masters (6:5–9), even though in each case there are also

---

[22] *DBI*, p. 240.

[23] Snodgrass, *Ephesians*, pp. 292–293.

[24] Lincoln, *Ephesians*, p. 367.

differing roles.[25] Alternatively, some have argued rather for a reflexive sense ('among yourselves'), but that does not seem to be Paul's emphasis in his other uses of the term in Ephesians, so it is not likely his intended nuance in this passage.

4. Concluding comment

We have arrived at the final destination of our journey as we have surveyed the message of wisdom throughout the Bible. There are, of course, many other passages we could have considered, but we have viewed most of the highlights pertaining to this important biblical theme. We have come to the end of our trip, but in reality we have only just begun, because from its earliest words of invitation in Proverbs to its latest words of instruction in the New Testament epistles, wisdom calls us to respond by our obedience. In other words, *learning* what wisdom teaches requires that we *live* in the wise way that we have learned.

Wise living does not come naturally to us, because we are born with a sin nature that distracts us away from God and his teaching of wisdom. In addition, we continually hear voices all around us that seek to influence us towards ways that are not pleasing to the Lord, enticing us to take the path of folly instead of God's path of wisdom. Consequently, all too often we make choices that are foolish and not according to God's righteous norm, and which therefore lead us away from the life that God intends us to enjoy as we walk in his way. We need to become disciplined to live carefully by making the most of every opportunity we have to pursue righteousness. As we strive with diligence to work out in our lives the salvation God has graciously given to us in Christ, we do so empowered by God, who works in us to give us both the desire and the ability to do what pleases him (cf. Phil. 2:12–13).

So we find ourselves in the same place as the youths in Proverbs 9. Both Wisdom and Folly are calling to us today, 'Let all who are simple come to my house', and we must choose which invitation we will accept. The choice we make will make all the difference, so we must choose wisely.

---

[25] Thielman, *Ephesians*, p. 373, reasons, 'Paul's use of the notion of reciprocity so far in Ephesians leads the letter's readers to understand the pronoun here in a fully reciprocal sense. The letter has just spoken of bearing with "each other" (4:2), being members of "one another" (4:25), and being kind to "one another" (4:32), using [*allēlōn*] in each case to refer to expectations of all believers. To hear now of "submitting to one another" might seem slightly strange, but it does hint that there is a sense in which everyone is involved in serving others.'

Study Guide

HOW TO USE THIS STUDY GUIDE

The aim of this study guide is to help you get to the heart of what Daniel Estes has written and challenge you to apply what you learn to your own life. The questions have been designed for use by individuals or by small groups of Christians meeting, perhaps for an hour or two each week, to study, discuss and pray together. When used by a group with limited time, the leader should decide beforehand which questions are most appropriate for the group to discuss during the meeting and which should perhaps be left for group members to work through by themselves or in smaller groups during the week.

PREVIEW. Use the guide, along with the contents pages, chapter and section headings, as a map to become familiar with what you are about to read, your 'journey' through the book.

READ. Look up the Bible passages as well as the text.

ANSWER. As you read, look for the answers to the questions in the guide.

DISCUSS. Even if you are studying on your own, try to find another person to share your thoughts with.

REVIEW. Use the guide as a tool to remind you of what you have learned. The best way of retaining what you learn is to write it down in a notebook or journal.

APPLY. Translate what you have learned into your attitudes and actions, considering your relationship with God, your personal life, your family life, your working life, your church life, your role as a citizen and your world view.

ⓠ Introduction (pp. 1–3)

1 Why are Proverbs, Job and Ecclesiastes significant for the study of wisdom, and why is a wider perspective necessary (pp. 1–2)?

2 How do the five parts of this book explore the theme of wisdom (pp. 2–3)?

PART 1: THE CONCEPT OF WISDOM

ⓠ Proverbs 1:1–7
1. An invitation to wisdom (pp. 7–18)

1 Which kind of teaching can we expect to read in the book of Proverbs (pp. 7–8)?

2 Why is King Solomon's name associated with wisdom, and is it significant that no particular recipient is named (p. 8)?

3 What are the three general outcomes in verses 2–3, and how do the Hebrew words *ḥokmâ*, *mûsār*, *bîn*, *ṣedeq*, *mišpāṭ* and *mēšārîm* contribute to the meaning of those outcomes (pp. 8–10)?

4 Who are the 'simple' who constitute the primary intended audience of Proverbs, and what specific outcomes are envisaged for them (pp. 10–12)?

5 How do the Hebrew words *pĕtāʾîm*, *ʿormâ*, *mĕzimmâ*, *qānâ*, *māšāl*, *mĕlîṣâ* and *ḥîdâ* contribute to the specific details of the general outcomes (pp. 10–12)?

6 What is meant by 'the fear of the LORD' (pp. 12–13)?

....

'Advancing in God's school of wisdom requires more than intellectual prowess, accumulation of knowledge and expert ability. It demands an attitude of humility before the Lord that pervades the entire scope of one's education' (p. 13).

....

7 What is, and is not, the meaning of *ʾĕwîl* (p. 13)?

8 'Yahweh . . . is the creator of the entire universe.' What implications does this have for us and our world view (pp. 13–14)?

9 What is the significance of the term *derek*, and how is it developed in Proverbs (pp. 14–16)?

10 The concluding comment invites us to consider invitations, choices and consequences. What is your personal response (pp. 16–18)?

ⓠ Proverbs 2:1–11
2. Searching for wisdom (pp. 19–29)

1 Which conditions in the search for wisdom are presented by the 'if' clause in verses 1–2 (pp. 19–20)?
2 'Many people today urge us to follow our hearts.' What warning does God's word give us and what is the alternative (pp. 20–21)?
3 How does the 'if' clause in verse 3 demonstrate the need for two-way communication (p. 21)?
4 Which analogies are presented in the third 'if' clause in verse 4 (pp. 21–22)?
5 What is 'the essence of wisdom, and therefore . . . the goal of the search for wisdom' (pp. 22–23)?
6 What are the two images used and developed in verses 7–8 (p. 24)?
7 How does verse 9 echo verse 5? See also verses 2, 3, 6 and 11 (pp. 24–25)?
8 How should a superficial approach to the book of Proverbs be avoided (pp. 25–26)?

....

'In addition to receiving wisdom, the learner must respond to wisdom, by joining living to listening' (p. 26).

....

9 Which four responsibilities does the student of wisdom need to accept, and how are they worked out in practice (pp. 26–29)?

ⓠ Proverbs 9
3. The contrasting paths of wisdom and folly (pp. 30–39)

1 In which way does Proverbs 9 present the contrast between wisdom and folly (pp. 30–31)?
2 What do Wisdom's preparations indicate about her and the invitation she issues (pp. 31–32)?
3 What do we know about those who are invited to Wisdom's house (pp. 32–33)?
4 Which character is introduced in verse 7, and how should caution be exercised (pp. 33–34)?
5 Which contrast is provided by the wise, and with whom are they paralleled (p. 34)?

6 What is meant by the 'beginning' of wisdom, and what are its rewards (pp. 34–35)?

7 How is Woman Folly contrasted with Woman Wisdom (pp. 35–37)?

8 What is the key concept of the book of Proverbs, and how does it differ from the Greek concept of *hubris* (pp. 37–38)?

9 Which response is required of those who choose the way of wisdom (pp. 38–39)?

ⓠ Proverbs 8
4. The personification of wisdom (pp. 40–50)

1 Which features underline the importance of Wisdom's message (pp. 40–42)?

....

'People typically choose to pursue what they most value, and that choice inevitably shapes their lives. Wisdom is so much more valuable than the lesser values to which many people devote their lives. To seek wisdom is to seek the best that the Lord has for one's life; anything else is bound to disappoint' (p. 43).

....

2 What are the characteristics of Wisdom's words, and how do they contrast with our contemporary world's values (pp. 42–43)?

3 How are the benefits of wisdom expressed (a) positively and (b) negatively (pp. 43–44)?

4 How is the reference to power developed in verses 14–16 (p. 44)?

5 'I love those who love me.' In which ways is that love expressed and reciprocated (pp. 44–45)?

6 What is the relationship between the Lord and Wisdom, and is there a case for a messianic theme (pp. 45–46)?

7 What does the link with creation tell us about Wisdom and her relationship with God (pp. 46–47)?

8 Why does *'āmôn* present a difficult textual problem, and which solutions have been offered (pp. 47–48)?

9 Which tone does Wisdom adopt in verses 32–36, and which stark contrast is laid out (pp. 48–49)?

10 In which way does Wisdom's speech resemble, and in which ways does it differ from, the great speeches of history and literature (pp. 49–50)?

PART 2: THE CONTEXT OF WISDOM

ⓠ Deuteronomy 30:15–20
5. Choose life (pp. 53–63)

1 Where does Deuteronomy fit in the history of Israel, and how do verses 1–14 of chapter 30 prepare for the culminating section, verses 15–20 (pp. 53–55)?

2 In which ways does Moses make 'a strong rhetorical appeal to the nation' (pp. 55–56)?

3 Which alternatives does Moses lay before the people, and how are the commands and promises reminiscent of the way of wisdom in Proverbs (pp. 56–57)?

4 To what alternative does Moses turn in verse 17, and how is it reiterated by Paul in 1 Corinthians (pp. 57–58)?

....

'If even a man as wise as Solomon was in danger of defecting from the Lord, how at risk was the entire nation of Israel, and how vigilant must we all also be against the allurements and encroachments of sin in our lives?' (pp. 58–59)

....

5 Where does the problem of disobedience begin, and where does it inevitably lead (pp. 58–59)?

6 How does Moses' picture of a courtroom scene differ from the language of other Ancient Near Eastern treaties (pp. 59–60)?

7 What is involved in choosing life, and is there an option not to choose (p. 60)?

8 Which aspects of commitment are included in choosing life (pp. 60–61)?

9 What does subsequent Old Testament narrative reveal about Israel's response to the challenge of Moses and which issues are at stake for readers today (pp. 61–63)?

ⓠ 1 Kings 3:5–15; 4:29–34
6. Solomon, the prototype of wisdom and folly (pp. 64–74)

1 What is the biblical evidence for Solomon as a prototype of wisdom, and why does he also function as a prototype of folly (pp. 64–65)?

2 How do verses 3–5 set the scene for the following narrative about Solomon (p. 65)?

3 In which way did Solomon respond to the Lord's approach (pp. 65 66)?

4 How did Solomon describe himself in verses 7–9, and what request did he make (pp. 66–67)?

5 What was the Lord's response to Solomon's answer in verses 10–12 (pp. 67–68)?

6 What did *Moreover* signal in verse 13, and what was the 'big *if*' in verses 14–15 (pp. 68–69)?

7 How does the focus of 1 Kings chapter 4 differ from that of chapter 3, and what evidence is there for Solomon's superior wisdom (pp. 69–71)?

8 In which ways did Solomon act foolishly, and which standards did he fail to live up to (pp. 71–72)?

9 Why is Solomon's folly 'a cautionary tale for all of us', and how should we respond (pp. 73–74)?

ⓆJeremiah 8:8–10; 9:23–24
7. The distortion of wisdom (pp. 75–84)

1 How does the Old Testament prophets' teaching on wisdom differ from that in Proverbs and elsewhere, and which lesson does this teach us (pp. 75–76)?

2 What did Jeremiah mean by *the lying pen of the scribes* (pp. 76–77)?

3 Who were the scribes, and why was their influence so dangerous (pp. 77–78)?

4 What was the essence of the Lord's indictment, and how is it relevant to the church in the twenty-first century (pp. 78–79)?

5 How is the general prophecy in verse 9 spelled out in verse 10 (pp. 79–80)?

....

'The wise men of Judah may have supposed that they had the freedom to do with the word of the Lord whatever they pleased, but in reality their sense of liberation would actually ensnare them. Their folly would cause them to be dismayed emotionally and trapped experientially, hardly the future they had conceived for themselves. That is how it always is with sin' (p. 80).

....

6 What was the sequel to the prophecies of Hosea in the north and Jeremiah in the south (pp. 80–81)?

7 What indicates that verses 23–24 of Jeremiah 9 are 'a strong divine word of warning', to whom are they addressed and what connects them to the narrative in 1 Kings (p. 81)?

8 How is the verb *hll* used in this context, and in which way does it pervert the praise that should properly be directed to the Lord (pp. 81–82)?

9 What is the 'profound contrast' in verse 24, and what does it say about values (pp. 82–83)?

10 Which pressures does the Christian face in implementing God's message through Jeremiah (p. 84)?

(Q) Psalm 112
8. The blessings of fearing the Lord (pp. 85–95)

1 Which features of Psalm 112 identify it as one of the 'wisdom psalms', and what is meant by describing it as 'kaleidoscopic' (pp. 85–86)?

2 What is the relationship between Psalm 112 and Psalm 111 (pp. 86–87)?

3 Which behaviours characterize a person who fears the Lord, according to verses 1–5, 9 (pp. 87–90)?

4 How does lending in the contemporary world differ from that in the Old Testament (p. 89)?

5 Which blessings will a person who fears the Lord gain, according to verses 1–9 (pp. 90–93)?

6 In which way do Psalms 49 and 73 provide a balance to Psalm 112's wisdom teaching (p. 91)?

7 What is the key teaching that emerges when the acrostic Psalm 112 is viewed as a unity (pp. 93–94)?

8 What is meant by 'Their goodness is godliness' (pp. 94–95)?

....

'Wise people who fear the Lord act righteously, because the Lord is righteous and they choose to follow his example. They delight in his Word, because they value it as the word of the Lord they respect and love. They are compassionate to those in need, because they are following the Lord's generous example' (p. 95).

....

PART 3: THE CONDUCT OF WISDOM

Ⓠ Proverbs 6:6–11
9. Wisdom in work (pp. 99–109)

1 Why does 'work' not equate simply to paid employment, and how is Paul's warning in 2 Corinthians 5:10 relevant (pp. 99–100)?

2 Which approach to wisdom is reflected in 1 Kings 4:29–34 and Matthew 6:28–30 (pp. 100–101)?

3 Which pattern of behaviour is observed in the ant both negatively and positively (pp. 101–102)?

4 Which aspects of diligence are illustrated in the terms *māhîr* (Proverbs 22:29), *šaḥar* (Proverbs 11:27) and *ḥārûṣ* (Proverbs 21:5; 10:4; 12:24; 12:27) (pp. 102–105)?

5 Which aspect of contemporary life is a distortion of true diligence (p. 105)?

6 Why is the sluggard rebuked in verses 6–8 (pp. 105–106)?

7 How is the sluggard's laziness depicted in Proverbs 19:24; 22:13; 24:30–34 (pp. 106–108)?

8 How does wisdom in work fit into the larger picture of the creation, the fall and redemption (pp. 108–109)?

10. Wisdom in speech (pp. 110–122)

1 How frequently is speech a subject in Proverbs and what does this indicate (pp. 110–111)?

2 How would you defend truthfulness against David Nyberg's arguments (pp. 111–112)?

....

'Because we live in a time when fake news, abuses of social media and general dishonesty are pervasive, what Proverbs teaches about truthfulness is particularly relevant to life today' (p. 111).

....

3 Which elements enumerated in Proverbs 6:16–19 are detestable to the Lord, and why (pp. 112–113)?

4 How do Proverbs 8:6–8; 23:16; 30:5–6 underline the positive aspects of truthfulness (pp. 113–114)?

5 How does twenty-first-century culture's view of truthfulness differ from that of the Lord (p. 114)?

6 How should truthfulness be evidenced in government and in the realm of business and commerce (pp. 115–116)?

7 Where does the major focus of truthfulness lie in the book of Proverbs, and which examples are cited to illustrate it (pp. 116–119)?

8 What are the benefits of truthfulness and the consequences of untruthfulness (pp. 119–121)?

9 In what ways can Christians default to our culture's pattern of falsehood, and why is it so hard to be truthful (pp. 121–122)?

11. Wisdom in decisions (pp. 123–134)

1 What general direction do we find in Proverbs 3:5–6 (p. 123)?

2 What does Proverbs teach about complacency (1:32), a cocky attitude towards the future (27:1) and taking hasty shortcuts (21:5) (pp. 123–125)?

3 What does Proverbs teach about neglecting to get advice (12:15), neglecting to take advice (14:16) and listening to bad advice (1:10) (pp. 125–128)?

4 Where are wise decisions ultimately derived from (p. 128)?

5 What does Proverbs teach about good character (4:23) and a pattern of wise behaviour (10:9) (pp. 128–130)?

....

'Wise people realize how much they do not know, so they ask someone who does know. They recognize that other people have wisdom that they need to hear and to heed (p. 130).

....

6 What does Proverbs teach about getting and following good advice (19:20), considering the facts (18:17) and making flexible plans (16:1) (pp. 130–132)?

7 When is 'humankind . . . functioning at its best' and how should it influence our plans (p. 132)?

8 What does Proverbs teach about anticipating future challenges and needs (22:3), focusing on the most crucial matters first (24:27) and recognizing the limitations of our human understanding (20:24) (pp. 132–134)?

12. Wisdom as righteousness (pp. 135–146)

1 What is relativism and what are its results (pp. 135–136)?
2 What logic is represented by the occurrences of *if* and *then* in Proverbs 2:1–9 (pp. 136–137)?
3 Which aspects of Proverbs 21:21 indicate the deep commitment required to find righteousness and its great benefits (pp. 137–138)?
4 What are the marks of righteousness according to Proverbs 8:8, 15, 20; 12:17 (pp. 138–139)?
5 Which standard contrasting pair of words occurs throughout the wisdom literature (pp. 139–140)?
6 In which ways do the rewards of righteousness pertain specifically to the individual according to Proverbs 11:5; 16:8; 10:2; 13:6; 16:13, 31; 15:9; 21:3 (pp. 140–144)?
7 In which ways does righteousness provide rewards for society according to Proverbs 14:34; 16:12; 25:4–5 (pp. 144–145)?
8 What is the meaning of the Hebrew words ṣĕdāqâ, 'ĕmûnâ, rāšā' and ṣaddîq, npl, ḥsd and ḥesed (pp. 138, 139, 140, 141, 144)?
9 What is the 'every day' choice we must make, and what will the outcome be (pp. 145–146)?

PART 4: THE COMPLEXITY OF WISDOM

13. Retribution and its limits (pp. 149–160)

1 What is the retribution principle, and which examples of it can be found in the Old Testament and the New Testament (pp. 149–151)?
2 Which side of the retribution principle is found in Proverbs 26:27 and Jeremiah 18:22, and which other Old Testament narratives illustrate it (p. 151)?
3 Which verses in Proverbs view both sides of the retribution principle, and which image is used to illustrate them (pp. 151–153)?
4 How do Klaus Koch and Patrick Miller explain the retribution principle and which Scriptures support Miller's approach (pp. 153–156)?

....

'In the book of Proverbs, observation reveals the general pattern of retribution, but also yields counter-examples' (p. 156).

....

5 Which counter-examples to the general pattern of retribution can be observed in Proverbs 11:16; 13:22; 20:17; 29:16 (pp. 156–159)?

6 Which Old Testament books 'extend the counter-examples to retribution in Proverbs into full-scale arguments' (p. 159)?

7 What was the error of Job and his friends, and how can we avoid it (pp. 159–160)?

8 What do the following Hebrew words mean: *klh, šlm, nāweh, hdp, mĕzimmâ, ge', 'ārîṣîm, rā'â bĕ* (pp. 152, 153, 154, 155, 157, 158)?

ⓠ Job
14. Wisdom resides in the all-knowing Lord (pp. 161–172)

1 Why does does this chapter take a different approach from other chapters in this book (p. 161)?

2 What is retribution theology, and why should it not be pressed too far (pp. 161–162)?

3 What is speculative wisdom, and how does it differ from practical wisdom (pp. 162–163)?

4 How is Job presented in the prologue? What is the role of 'the satan' and how does the prologue progress (pp. 163–164)?

5 What is the structure of the book following the prologue? How does Job respond to his suffering (pp. 164–165)?

6 How do Eliphaz and Bildad respond to Job's predicament (pp. 165–166)?

7 What do we learn about Elihu and how does he respond to Job's predicament (pp. 166–168)?

8 What is it important to notice in Job 1 – 2; 28; 42:7–8 (p. 168)?

9 What is God's approach in Job 38 – 41, and which lesson does it teach us (pp. 168–169)?

10 How should we interpret Job's 'I . . . repent' response (pp. 169–171)?

......

'As the Lord poses dozens of questions that Job cannot answer, he leads Job into an enlarged perspective of the wisdom of the Lord and to a greater humility before him' (p. 169).

......

11 Why is the message of wisdom in the book of Job relevant for Christians living in the twenty-first century (pp. 171–172)?

ⓠ Ecclesiastes 9:7–10
15. Enjoy God's portion as his gift (pp. 173–182)

1 How is Ecclesiastes structured, and what is the meaning of the key term *hăbēl hăbālîm* (pp. 173–174)?

2 What is the initial programmatic question in Ecclesiastes 1:3? What does the Hebrew word *'āmāl* mean, and how significant is the phrase 'under the sun' (p. 175)?

3 What does the Hebrew word *yitrôn* mean? Is Ecclesiastes saying that there are no worthwhile human activities (pp. 175–176)?

4 In which way does Ecclesiastes challenge us to change our perspective (pp. 176–178)?

5 What is the significance of wearing white clothes and anointing with oil (p. 178)?

6 How is sexual union viewed in the wisdom literature, and how is *hebel* distinct from *hēleq* (pp. 178–180)?

7 What are the three reasons why we should live joyfully and energetically (pp. 180–181)?

8 What negatives and positives in the message of Ecclesiastes are relevant to people living in the twenty-first century (pp. 181–182)?

PART 5: THE CULMINATION OF WISDOM

ⓠ Matthew 7:13–29
16. Jesus, the teacher of wisdom (pp. 185–195)

1 In which ways was Jesus the master teacher of wisdom (pp. 185–186)?

2 What is the choice that each person must consciously make, and which metaphor illustrates it (pp. 186–187)?

....

'In contrast to the broad road that leads to destruction, which many traverse, the narrow road that leads to life is found by only a few. That is the road we must find and follow, even when most people around us choose as their route for life the road that to them seems more enjoyable and less restrictive' (p. 187).

....

3 Which warning is issued in verse 15, and which metaphor is used to highlight it (p. 187)?

4 How does Jesus change the metaphor in verse 16, and where is it reflected elsewhere in Scripture (pp. 187–188)?

5   Which image pictures God's eschatological judgment (p. 189)?

6   Who is Jesus referring to in verse 21 (pp. 189–190)?

7   What is meant by 'that day', and why does verse 23 presuppose 'an implicit Christology of the highest order' (pp. 190–191)?

8   Which details of Jesus' double comparison would be familiar to his original hearers, and which lesson does he draw from it (pp. 191–193)?

9   What was the response of the crowds to Jesus' teaching? What made it different and which question did it pose (pp. 193–194)?

10 What is meant by being a cultural Christian, and why is that inadequate (pp. 194–195)?

ⓠ 1 Corinthians 1:18–25
17. Christ, the wisdom of God (pp. 196–206)

1   What is the background to 1 Corinthians 1:18–25 (pp. 196–197)?

2   What are the three themes introduced in Paul's 'thesis statement' (pp. 197–198)?

3   What is the sense of Isaiah 29:14 in its original context, and how does Paul apply it in this context (pp. 198–199)?

4   What is the background to Paul's four rhetorical questions in verse 20 (pp. 200–201)?

5   How does verse 21 fit into the progress of Paul's argument, and where in Romans is that argument developed (pp. 201–202)?

6   Why was the message of Christ crucified a stumbling-block to Jews and foolishness to Greeks (pp. 202–203)?

7   Why did God reject human expectations, and why did the wise people of the world reject his truth (pp. 203–204)?

8   What is 'the surprising truth of the gospel' (p. 205)?

9   How does Paul apply his discussion in verses 18–25 to the situation in Corinth in verses 26–31, and how should we apply it today (pp. 205–206)?

ⓠ Colossians 2:1–7
18. Knowing Christ, the source of wisdom (pp. 207–216)

1   Which connection did Paul have with the churches at Colossae and Laodicea (pp. 207–208)?

2   How should we understand Paul's *agōn* (pp. 208–209)?

3 In which way does Paul's aim contrast with the effects of false teaching (pp. 209–210)?

4 What is the key theme of the first chapter of Colossians, setting the stage for the rest of the letter, and how does it mirror the message of Proverbs (pp. 210–211)?

....

'What was true for the Colossians is equally valid for Christians today, because all of the treasures of divine wisdom and knowledge continue to find their source in Christ for the contemporary church, just as they did for the early church' (p. 211).

....

5 Why did the arguments of the false teachers sound so persuasive, and which danger did Paul see in them (pp. 211–212)?

6 Which metaphor does Paul use to commend the Colossians, and why is his caution still relevant (pp. 212–213)?

7 What does Paul mean by the Greek term *peripateō*? Where else is the image found in the Old Testament and New Testament other than Colossians (pp. 213–214)?

8 How does Paul's response illustrate the difference between the Colossians and the Galatians, and which further metaphors does he use (pp. 214–215)?

9 How does Paul encourage and challenge us to face spiritual threats (pp. 215–216)?

(Q) James 3:13–18
19. Living by wisdom from above (pp. 217–227)

1 What evidence is there that, both in its content and style, the book of James bears the distinctive marks of wisdom teaching (pp. 217–218)?

2 Where does the book of Proverbs provide a lens through which to read the teaching of James (pp. 218–219)?

3 Who is addressed by James in verse 13 and what criterion does he apply to them (pp. 219–220)?

4 How was the *praütēs* word group understood in Greek culture, and how is it understood in the New Testament (pp. 220–221)?

5 Who is being addressed in verse 14, and what is their problem (pp. 221–222)?

6 What are the characteristics of the wrong kind of 'wisdom', according to verse 15 (pp. 222–223)?

7 How does James continue his line of thought in verse 16 (p. 223)?

8 What are the characteristics of the wisdom from above, according to verse 17. Which of Paul's letters shows a striking similarity between these features of wisdom and the fruit of the Spirit (pp. 223–224)?

9 Should *righteousness* in verse 18 be read through the lens of Paul's soteriological emphasis (pp. 224–225)?

10 Which broad principles of wisdom in the book of James pertain to our lives today (pp. 225–227)?

(Q) Ephesians 5:15–21
20. Walking in godly wisdom (pp. 228–237)

1 How do the five parts of this survey explore the theme of wisdom (pp. 228–229)?

2 In which sense does verse 15 function as the topic sentence for the paragraph, and which echoes of the Olivet Discourse can be discerned in it (pp. 229–230)?

3 What figure of speech does Paul shift to in verse 16? Which Old Testament texts does it echo, and why is it crucial (pp. 230–231)?

4 How does Paul link verse 17 with verses 15–16 and which contrast does he use to exhort the Ephesians (pp. 231–232)?

5 What is 'important to note' in verse 18 (p. 232)?

6 Why is getting drunk an example of being foolish, and how does being filled with the Spirit contrast with it (pp. 232–234)?

7 Which ancient songs were used by early Christians? Are *psalms, hymns* and *songs* overlapping terms, and what was their function and purpose (p. 234)?

8 Which response is produced by a Spirit-filled life, and which truth is it grounded in (p. 235)?

9 How does verse 21 link what precedes with what follows it, and why is the imperative that begins the verse countercultural (pp. 235–236)?

10 What is the meaning of the Greek terms *peripateō, akribōs* and *exagorazō, aphrōn, syniēmi, asōtia, allēlōn* and *phobos* (pp. 229, 230, 231, 232, 233, 236)?

11 Why does wise living not come naturally to us, and what do we need to counteract that difficulty (p. 237)?

Listen to God's Word
speaking to the world today

The complete NIV text, with over 2,300 notes from the Bible Speaks Today series, in beautiful fine leather- and clothbound editions. Ideal for devotional reading, studying and teaching the Bible.

Leatherbound edition with slipcase
£50.00 • 978 1 78974 139 1

Clothbound edition
£34.99 • 978 1 78359 613 3

ivpbooks.com    /IVPbooks   @IVPbookcentre   @IVPbooks

The Bible Speaks Today:
Old Testament series

The Bible Speaks Today: New Testament series

The Message of Matthew
The kingdom of heaven
Michael Green

The Message of Mark
The mystery of faith
Donald English

The Message of Luke
The Saviour of the world
Michael Wilcock

The Message of John
Here is your King!
Bruce Milne

**The Message of the Sermon
on the Mount (Matthew 5 – 7)**
Christian counter-culture
John Stott

The Message of Acts
To the ends of the earth
John Stott

The Message of Romans
God's good news for the world
John Stott

The Message of 1 Corinthians
Life in the local church
David Prior

The Message of 2 Corinthians
Power in weakness
Paul Barnett

The Message of Galatians
Only one way
John Stott

The Message of Ephesians
God's new society
John Stott

The Message of Philippians
Jesus our Joy
Alec Motyer

**The Message of Colossians and
Philemon**
Fullness and freedom
Dick Lucas

The Message of Thessalonians
Preparing for the coming King
John Stott

The Message of 1 Timothy and Titus

The life of the local church

John Stott

The Message of 2 Timothy

Guard the gospel

John Stott

The Message of Hebrews

Christ above all

Raymond Brown

The Message of James

The tests of faith

Alec Motyer

The Message of 1 Peter

The way of the cross

Edmund Clowney

The Message of 2 Peter and Jude

The promise of his coming

Dick Lucas and Christopher Green

The Message of John's Letters

Living in the love of God

David Jackman

The Message of Revelation

I saw heaven opened

Michael Wilcock

The Bible Speaks Today: Bible Themes series

The Message of the Living God
His glory, his people, his world
Peter Lewis

The Message of the Resurrection
Christ is risen!
Paul Beasley-Murray

The Message of the Cross
Wisdom unsearchable, love indestructible
Derek Tidball

The Message of Salvation
By God's grace, for God's glory
Philip Graham Ryken

The Message of Creation
Encountering the Lord of the universe
David Wilkinson

The Message of Heaven and Hell
Grace and destiny
Bruce Milne

The Message of Mission
The glory of Christ in all time and space
Howard Peskett and Vinoth Ramachandra

The Message of Prayer
Approaching the throne of grace
Tim Chester

The Message of the Trinity
Life in God
Brian Edgar

The Message of Evil and Suffering
Light into darkness
Peter Hicks

The Message of the Holy Spirit
The Spirit of encounter
Keith Warrington

The Message of Holiness
Restoring God's masterpiece
Derek Tidball

The Message of Sonship
At home in God's household
Trevor Burke

The Message of the Word of God
The glory of God made known
Tim Meadowcroft

Printed and bound by CPI Group (UK) Ltd, Croydon, CR0 4YY

13/04/2025

14656475-0003